YOUR NI[illegible] ARE MY DOMAIN

Life of a paramedic on the streets

Dale Cropper NHSTA MEP0099
Former Merseyside Paramedic

CONTENTS

Title Page 1

PREFACE 5

INTRODUCTION 13

1 TREBLE NINE 999 CALLS 21

2 THE EARLY DAYS 36

3 AMBULANCE TRAINING 51

4 PARAMEDIC TRAINING 61

5 ROAD TRAFFIC ACCIDENTs 81

6 INDUSTRIAL ACCIDENTS 107

7 EVERY PARENTS NIGHTMARE 119

8 CHILD ABUSE 130

9 VIOLENCE AND THE PARAMEDIC 151

10 WEAPONS 167

11 THE THIN BLUE LINE 193

12 FIRE AND RESCUE 203

13 FIRE SERVICE STRIKE 1995 226

14 DOCTORS 239

15 ACCIDENT AND EMERGENCY 254

About The Author 263

PREFACE

These are my personal observations of people's lives at the point of injury and sudden illness, whilst I was working with the fastest ambulance service in U.K. namely Merseyside Ambulance Service now known as North West Ambulance Service.

This book is concerned almost entirely, with the real work of ambulance men and women (ambulance technicians and paramedics) within the U.K ambulance services. This 'fly on the wall' account is graphic in content without descending to the depths of gratuitous blood and guts detail.

Historically, my family has been part of the emergency services since the end of world war two. With my Uncle Bill joining the Birkenhead Fire service upon demob from The Chindits in 1945, and my Uncle Ernie joining Liverpool City Police when he was demobbed from the Royal Marines in 1945.

Most of my sisters (eight in all) have been in the nursing profession as too has one of my daughters. As I write I still have family and friends employed in all three services as well as nurses and now a Niece who is newly qualified doctor. How's that for family commitment?

Though written from a paramedical point of view, I hope this book will not be unintelligible to the wider public - those who stop and watch as we make our noisy progress through bustling streets toward (as yet) some unknown emergency. I hope you will find the book a 'good read' and one that gives some intelligent detail on what it is like to be a paramedic and what actually goes on in the back of an emergency ambulance.

In November 1977, after taking the advice of my uncle, I applied to join The Merseyside Ambulance Service.

He (my Uncle Bill) himself had served both as a fireman and ambulance attendant in The Birkenhead Borough Fire service and Ambulance Service.

He had joined the service after being de-mobbed from the Army after the Second World War. He had distinguished himself well whilst serving with 'The Chindits' (known as the 'Forgotten Army') in the Burmese jungle. He had been mentioned in dispatches twice for his bravery behind Japanese enemy lines. He and his comrades (many from Liverpool) had been dropped behind the enemy lines. Their job was deep penetration of the Burmese jungle to carry out sabotage of a ruthlessly cruel Japanese invader and their war machine.

Bill had been married to Doris (my Aunt) for just one week when he was suddenly sent on that mission; it would be another five years before she saw or heard of him or his group again. Little wonder that the Chindits were known as the Forgotten Army!

With the war over and once back in the relative quiet of post war civilian life, Bill needed something that could replace the excitement and intensity that his Army career had bred into him; so it was that he joined the fire service (now known as the Fire and Rescue Service).

Initially he served as a fireman but as time went by and he got older, he realised that the excitement of fighting wars and fires, had (for him) lost its appeal. He had long been harbouring a wish to transfer across into the ambulance service, where he could learn and practice first aid. He could have a 'hands on' approach to patient care and could have more frequent and closer contact with people who needed pre-hospital care. He felt (and many who knew him would agree) that he had a natural flare for dealing with and caring for sick and injured people. He was a genuine caring person with a really great sense of humour and a strong sense of pride in the service. In my opinion these are valuable assets in all ambulance staff, even today.

Bill never spoke much about his exploits in the Burmese jungle or his role in The Chindits; it was not until many years later when he died, that I learned that he had been mentioned in despatches twice during The Burma Campaign. Paradoxically he would speak at length about the ambulance service, recounting many a tale to those people who always seemed willing to listen. Even as a young boy I would sit and listen to him for hours on end as he sat telling me and his own children (my Cousins) Tommy, Mary and Joan all the details of the latest accidents and the fires that he had attended. Many of his tales were exciting but sometimes with a sad ending, sometimes funny too.

I remember one story where he had been called out to an emergency in the early hours of one summer morning. On arrival at the scene, Bill and his mate, Stan, were shown to the outside toilet at the bottom of a back-yard. There they found a very embarrassed young woman crying and complaining that she was stuck to the toilet seat. Apparently the previous night, the woman's father had waited until everyone had gone to bed before he had varnished the toilet seat. He assumed that by morning the varnish would be dry. He was right! Unfortunately his daughter had been 'caught short' in the night and had made her way quietly outside to the toilet and fell asleep whilst sitting there. To save the young woman any further embarrassment my Uncle (with a straight face) assured her that people getting stuck to lavatory seats was a common enough problem and that she indeed was the third that night!

On the day that I started work in the ambulance service I had to report for 'Induction' Training at the Ambulance H.Q. at Quarry Street (one hundred yards from ‘Strawberry Fields’) in Liverpool. Making my way to the training school I had to drive down (the now famous) ‘Penny Lane’ and there was indeed (as the song says) a fireman. In fact there were many of them and they weren't polishing the fire engine bell or keeping their machine clean. No! They were all standing outside the fire station, huddled around a fire, which they had set in an old oil drum, keeping warm in the morning cold... Some waving placards proclaiming their strike action. This was the first day of the first ever, Fire service Strike.

Little did I realise then that, many years later, there would be another such fireman's strike, whereupon events for me and my colleagues would be very different, as you will read about, later in the book.

Until recently, I was still at the 'sharp' end of the National Health Service, working for Merseyside Ambulance Service, the ambulance service that has worked hard to become and maintain its reputation as being the fastest ambulance service in the U.K.

During my twenty year career I have travelled thousands of miles at high speed through all types of traffic and in all sorts of weather condition; all without any great mishap.

However, in February 1996, whilst returning to base after attending an emergency with John my crewmate (a trainee paramedic) we pulled up in our ambulance behind a van which was stationary and waiting to turn right at a busy road junction. We were just twenty yards from our base and would soon be enjoying a welcome meal break...or so we thought. John was driving, and I was sitting forward in the passenger seat, head down and busy entering final details, onto an ERF (Emergency Report Form), of the call that we had just completed. Glancing across at the speedometer, I made a quick note of the ambulance mileage and almost finished the ERF. I did not see a bus turning (too fast) into our road, and losing control before careering towards us. Suddenly I was aware of an almighty bang and the sound of crunching metal and breaking glass. Our ambulance rocked and tilted over violently to the left before being shunted sideways. It seemed that we were about to overturn. Fortunately, a sturdy tree prevented a complete overturning of the ambulance. Even though I was wearing my seatbelt; such was the force of the side-impact, that my seat was knocked from underneath me and I was thrown from it and found myself lying with my body jammed and twisted between the passenger seat and that of the driver. My right arm, right hip and lumbar spine were suddenly hurting quite badly as I struggled to lift myself back into my seat. Looking around I could see that we had been hit side on, by the bus which was still embedded into the saloon part of the ambulance.

I looked at John, who was sitting quiet and looking pale, dazed and shocked. He was conscious but was a little incomprehensible maybe concussed. He complained that his head was hurting. I realised that I was unable to help him or anyone else who may be injured on the bus. Instinctively I reached for the radio hand-set and noticed that my hand was shaking violently, as was my right leg too. I called ambulance control, 'Priority message, over'. Immediately they replied. 'Last caller, pass your priority message'.

'Priority message' I replied, 'Vehicle 342 involved in RTA with double deck bus outside of our home station. Both crewmen are injured, so I am unable to make any survey of the scene. I am unable to give details of any other casualties on the bus. Over'.

Ambulance control acknowledged my call. Now sitting within the crashed ambulance, I listened as control began calling the nearest available ambulances to attend to our accident. Everything seemed surreal. I felt strangely emotional as I listened to the controller broadcasting to other ambulances. 'Vehicles 311- 341 and 322 please attend RTA involving a double deck bus and one of our emergency vehicles; both crew members are reported to be injured'.

Normally, whenever an accident happens there is confusion and people within the vicinity rush to help the victims. On this occasion that did not happen immediately. John and I seemed to be left alone for some time before anyone realised that we could not help ourselves. It was probably as much a shock to onlookers as it was to us to see an ambulance involved in a road accident. It seemed to us an eternity before the first ambulance arrived, but it was actually only a few minutes. Soon another two ambulances arrived on the scene along with the police and our own incident officer.

As we sat amidst the wreckage of the ambulance with our paramedic colleagues dealing with our injuries, I felt hopeless and totally inadequate. Suddenly I was no longer *in charge* at the accident. I was a patient! It was me who was being strapped into a neck collar and immobilised on a 'Scoop' stretcher before being carried into a waiting ambulance. I was aware of the crowds of onlookers and for the first time I realised just what it was like to be an accident victim.

After a prolonged period of sick leave I was called into Ambulance HQ to be told that I was to be released on medical grounds, I was truly 'gutted', although I had been told in a sympathetic and respectful manner that my career was over, I still felt terrible. The news was a 'bomb-shell'. I felt real distress. My paramedic career had been the pinnacle of my working life. I felt sorry for those people in the room with me, two of my bosses and my union representative. They seemed embarrassed by my obvious distress. I did not cry (just), but I was unable to converse any further and I left the room.

I have not been back since. Now I too, have experienced the same post-accident dilemmas and problems faced by many of those accident victims that I had previously dealt with.

Accidents have other consequences too and in my own case I have lost my ability to carry out my beloved hobbies of climbing and fell- walking, both of which were taken up to allow me to do outdoor photography. But even the loss of these and other hobbies is not as great as the loss of my career in the ambulance service.

Over the years many people have asked and continue to ask, both myself and my colleagues, questions relating to the job that the paramedic does. Usually the questions are of a general nature, but more often than not, they ask questions of a specific kind; relating maybe to a particular incident that they may have heard about through media channels, or by word of mouth; hoping to glean that extra piece of 'inside information' that only one who 'was there' could possibly know. One of the questions I am most often asked is, 'what is the worst thing that you have seen?' I'll get that one out of the way now; runny noses! The sight of snot makes my stomach turn.

For these reasons then I decided to write this book; not to titillate anyone's morbid curiosity, more to inform and/or educate the reader as to the true nature of the job and the complexities of today's modern paramedic. I hope that, through this book, I will answer many of the questions that you would wish to ask either me, or any one of the many hundreds of ambulance men and women from around the U.K. because this story, is theirs too.

Hopefully, you will find the stories within these pages interesting and informative. I owe it to good taste not to be as graphic in my description of some incidents, as, indeed, the full details actually were. For obvious reasons, names of people that I have worked and dealt with on a professional level, have had to be changed within this book, so too, have any precise details of times and places of incidents. Otherwise, all incidents referred to in this book did actually happen and are a true reflection of my experiences over the last nineteen years. Also, remember, I worked alongside other crew-members whose experience would be similar to mine.

Although I was based on the Wirral Peninsula, which is just across the River Mersey from Liverpool, my work took me to many different hospitals in and around Merseyside; therefore, the reader should not try to identify any particular location, treatment centre or hospital from the stories related within this book.

However it does go without saying, that we do see some incredibly horrendous sights and we are committed to dealing with them on a physical and practical level, as well as dealing with it psychologically on a personal level. Although ambulance staff cope with anything that comes their way, they may quite often feel deeply affected by certain events and, on rare occasions, can actually take the emotion of a particular job home with them. Not for us neither the luxury of post-traumatic stress syndrome, nor the financial gains that can be made from such claims; just the support of your colleagues along with the love and support of one's own family, to help me make it through this life.

I would like to pay special thanks to my wife, Margaret, for her patient cajoling and encouragement to me, to put pen to paper and to write this book. Also thanks to Catherine and

Elaine for their encouragement and patient proof reading of my literary efforts, for I am no great writer. I wish to thank too, all my colleagues throughout my years of service, special thanks to those who have allowed me to use their names. I hope that this book will be accepted by them as a true account; for no man can have a better judge than his peers.

Finally, I would like to dedicate this book, to my late Father: for I know he liked a 'good read' and he would have been one my first proof readers and also to the late Bill Matchett (Uncle Bill) who inspired me to join the ambulance service.

◆ ◆ ◆

INTRODUCTION

I had never expected to be looking down the barrel of a gun, nor did I ever realise what my reaction would be when faced with such a situation. I never expected to find myself fighting for my life, trying to prevent some madman from stabbing me. Being pelted with bricks and bottles during a riot or facing a tirade of vitriolic verbal abuse never registered high in my expectations either. I never expected to get punched and kicked or to have to stand and fight as par for the course, just to do my job. I never expected to enter a still smouldering building to bring out the victims with hideous injuries, or to scramble into petrol soaked, overturned vehicles only to be attacked inside the dangerous wreck by the drunken driver.

I never expected to have to wrestle a small baby from the hands of a deranged mother, too late to save the child's life, or to deal first- hand with a child injured by some Non-Accidental Injuries (NAIs). Nor to retrieve the broken body of a small child from under a vehicle, then half an hour later join in the fun at my own child's birthday party, as if nothing was wrong.

I never expected the nightmares that came from my experiences, and that even today, still pervade my sleep at night. I never expected any of the above. Why should I? I was only a paramedic.

Be them, victim, relative or witness, people directly involved in or around a serious incident, albeit an accident or sudden illness, may often recall the event as being 'like a nightmare'. In such nightmares it is the professionals such as the police, firefighters, paramedics, who will be called upon to enter that frightening and worrying domain. It will be for them to take control, even sometimes take risks, to care for those involved and to bring order to the mayhem and fear of that nightmare...hence the title of this book.

Your nightmare was, indeed, my domain.

This book is about one particular group of emergency professionals, namely, the paramedics. It is they who are the first link in the chain of emergency pre-hospital care. I write with authority because *I was* a paramedic, later becoming a Paramedic Trainee Assessor (PTA). As a PTA I was instrumental in the final training and qualification to a new paramedic; it is only then that they are allowed to work without supervision, to coin a phrase, fly solo, relying on their knowledge, skill, technical expertise and wit.

I worked for twenty years on front line emergency ambulances within the very busy area of Merseyside; in particular I was based at Wallasey ambulance station on the Wirral peninsula.

The work of the paramedic is nothing like that which is portrayed in sanitised and semi-fictional programmes often shown on television. The job is at times distressing, frightening and deeply emotional; sometimes it can even be amusing but not often. Whatever emotion we may be feeling personally at any particular time, our fundamental approach to every incident must be the same; calm, reassuring, caring and technically unimpeachable.

Based upon the lifespan of our own National Health Service, the paramedic is a relative newcomer and as such, much of paramedic's occupational activities are a mystery to the wider public. If you have ever watched an emergency ambulance speeding by (blue lights flashing and sirens blaring) and wondered what drama was unfolding behind those darkened windows, then this book is for you.

It is probably true to say that to the eye of the average citizen, a modern ambulance is nothing more than a noisy beast, barging its way along our busy roads. To most onlookers it drives fast and makes a lot of noise, dazzling everyone with its array of flashing lights, demanding and attaining the freedom of the highway with scant regard for the laws of speed restriction and red traffic signals.

During my ambulance career, Merseyside Ambulance Service was recognized nationally as having the fastest emergency ambulance response times in the United Kingdom.

These days ambulance services are prioritising emergency calls. This can and does lead to mistakes and poor response times to sick and injured victims. Recently whilst out driving in my car I happened upon a road accident. I stopped to deal with the victim, a little girl, who was lying injured by the roadside having been knocked from her bicycle. She was ten years old, very distressed, in pain and surrounded by strangers. It was raining and freezing cold on a dark winter evening. Initially I was told by a bystander (who seemed angry) that an ambulance had been called some twenty-five minute earlier. I attended to the injured child and waited for a further few minutes before (at my request) a second call was made to ambulance service. Again, we all waited for the emergency ambulance to arrive. Eventually, having accurately calculated that the child had lain injured on the roadside for 45 minutes, I personally made a third call to the ambulance service.

Having identified myself to the ambulance controller, as a former paramedic, I asked for an ETA (estimated time of arrival) of the ambulance. He refused point blank to give me any estimate of how long this child would wait for the arrival of an ambulance; he seemed unmoved even when I explained the details of her condition including the fact that she was becoming hypothermic. In my days in the service any such situation, involving an injured child, would have resulted in an immediate 'priority' response. On this occasion I waited a few minutes more and after a total 55 minutes I placed her on the rear seat of my car and took her to hospital myself. No ambulance ever arrived! This didn't happen in a third world country...but here in modern day Merseyside. I wondered what had happened to that ambulance service that had previously held the prestigious accolade of the fastest responding emergency ambulances in the UK.

Today's modern emergency ambulance is a very expensive machine. It is filled with a myriad of advanced life support equipment and drugs, as well as more basic items such as bandages, slings and splints. To the practitioner of pre-hospital care it is a sophisticated mobile medical treatment platform that is there to provide the all-important initial 'first response' treatment of the sick and injured...almost like bringing the hospital to the patient.

But what of the paramedic? What does their job really entail? How do they cope with the demands that the job brings, the sights that they see? How do they cope with such horrendous and frightening incidents, so calmly? How do they cope with the fear, threats and abuse issued against them from certain members of the public?

This book sets out to answer these questions and many more. It is an account of my own personal experiences, over a period of twenty years, whilst working at the sharp end of the National Health Service. I have written in anecdotal form, starting from the early days when the skills of ambulance-men/women were limited, through to the present day where paramedics now, routinely, carry out those advanced life support; procedures that previously only doctors would expect to perform. The modern paramedic is the next best thing to a doctor... at the scene of an emergency.

Paramedics are at the top of their profession having passed through all the various stages of training. They are uniquely trained and qualified to deal with absolutely *anything* that they are faced with, from a woman giving birth in a lift to someone lying seriously injured beneath a train, or even being first on scene at a bomb incident.

The paramedic's depth of medical knowledge and their well-defined skills in the pre-hospital treatment of emergency patients plays a unique part in the emergency care service. A paramedic should face the demands of the job with painstaking attention to detail, extreme care and reassurance in order to promote the wellbeing of those in their care. Demarcation lines should not exist in their world, for they go anywhere at any time and in any conditions; as ever, prepared to deal with people from all walks of life regardless of colour, creed, religion or social status.

The period which my story covers, was one of tremendous change, both within the NHS and within the ambulance service. It was also a period of great social change nationally. Mass unemployment, industrial strife, civil disorder (the 1981 Liverpool riots) and two wars (The Falklands and The Gulf) all had some impact upon the men and women in our service and the job that we were called upon to do.

This book covers a period *before* 'Health and Safety' replaced common sense. A time when (as someone once said) paramedics, police officers and firefighters *'would do what it takes to get the job done',* even if it meant an element of personal risk. It is my profound belief that people choosing to join these services should do so with pride, integrity, honesty and a certain amount of savvy. I am saddened today when I read of (some – a very few) paramedics failing the patient/victim because they have carried out a 'risk assessment' which precludes them from offering *immediate* aid to a victim; waiting until such time that they, themselves, feel safe and comfortable enough to proceed. In the meantime the patient is left lingering in distress, to suffer, or worse.

I am proud to say, that during the Liverpool riots, the Merseyside ambulance crews went where no police officer or firefighter could go. Ambulance crews were called in from our area to help back up the Liverpool staff. I recall speeding through the Mersey Tunnel within a convoy of police cars and fire engines who were also being drawn in from outlying areas.

Upon reaching the Toxteth area it was quickly realised that only the ambulance crews would be allowed into the area, this mandate being delivered by a local community leader. The Merseyside ambulance men and women had the tenacity, gall and savvy to enter the blazing riot strewn streets where they faced a frightening and ferocious mob throwing bricks, bottles and petrol bombs. Look at the old newsreel footage and you will see that we ambulance men and women entered the 'Toxteth Triangle', (as it is colloquially known) through the blazing barricades.

In typical Merseyside rectitude the ambulance crews cajoling, and sometimes negotiating with the rioters, still managed to go about the primary job of aiding sick and injured people. Guess what? We came out alive and unscathed! And our patients got to hospital too!

I recall driving over roads littered with bricks and broken glass from the thousands of empty milk bottles pillaged, by the rioters, from a local dairy which had been broken into and vandalised. Many of the milk floats had been stolen too, set on fire and somehow, with a piece of wood jammed against the accelerator, sent careering down the road into the lines of police officers. Every shop front window had been smashed and the contents looted; many buildings burned uncontrollably casting a frightening glow across the night sky. The fire service had been held back on police orders but we, the ambulance men and women seemed to be an acceptable intruder, by the rioters, into their domain.

On the Wirral peninsula (where I was based) each emergency ambulance was issued with a fifty foot length of rope as well as a device, which when thrown to a victim in distress in water, uncoiled a life-line. It was expected that the ambulance crew may use this in the event that someone needed rescuing from the local docks or water surrounding our area. Sometimes ambulance staff dived in to rescue drowning victims.

Two of my work mates responded to a serious 'in the water' emergency call; the controller gave the message as, 'A yacht sinking, with people in the water, at the Mersey Ferry landing stage'. At the time there was a high tide and a fast flowing river. On arriving at the scene the ambulance crew were further informed that the yacht was sinking after being in collision with a ferryboat. They didn't stand back pondering the issues, or assessing any health and safety issues; they could see the sinking yacht and people floundering in the water. Whilst one of the ambulance crew set about preparing the ambulance equipment to deal with any casualties the other crew member quickly stripped off his tunic and shoes before diving into the river. He dived in to make a successful rescue and recovery of the victims (well done 'H').

I read recently about all three emergency services (Police Fire and Ambulance) arriving at a scene where a man could clearly be seen struggling and distressed in a lake, estimated to be eighteen inches of water. Paramedics, police and firefighters all carried out a risk assessment of the poor victim's plight and together they concluded that it was reasonable for them to refuse to rescue him. It was sometime later that he was eventually recovered from the water...but dead!

A more recent health and safety type of case reported that a lone paramedic did not wish to enter a pub to deal with a heart attack victim, because the venue 'looked risky'. Eventually shamed, by a pub customer who had come outside to look for the ambulance, the paramedic reluctantly entered the pub but then refused to resuscitate the heart attack victim, claiming that she couldn't carry out CPR on her own! Was she kidding? My eight-year old grandsons can do 'one-man CPR'.

Over the years drugs, guns, knives and physical violence became part of a daily diet of violence, not just for the police but, as you will read, for the paramedic too. This was not the case when I first joined the service back in 1977.

It was within this period of time, that today's modern paramedic was born; the writer (me) playing a not insignificant part in that very important birth (more on my part in paramedic training later in the book).

Throughout the book, for ease of writing I have referred to paramedics in the masculine vernacular. I do, however, point out that paramedics can be either male or female, and I can assure the reader that female paramedics are equal to their male counterparts.

For obvious reasons too, the names of some of the people

that I have worked and dealt with on a professional level, have had to be changed, so too have certain details concerning times and places of incidents.

Finally, I would like to point out for the benefit of the reader and also to enhance understanding of the stories within this book, that when I first started in the service, the training and subsequent capabilities meant that, technically, the treatment offered to patients was not as excellent as it is today. Over the years the Ambulance Service has embraced many changes; training has become so technically enhanced, that today we can boast one of the finest emergency pre-hospital services in the world.

◆ ◆ ◆

1 TREBLE NINE 999 CALLS

There are millions emergency calls made through the treble nine system every year, but not all of these calls involve any threat to life and limb. The majority of 999 calls are received by the police, with the ambulance service receiving the next largest number. All other calls are directed to other emergency services such as the fire services, H.M. Coastguard and the lifeboat services. At the time of writing, the actual breakdown of emergency calls is:

Police receive 45% of all 999 calls but transfer 5% to the ambulance service. the ambulance Service receives 30% of all 999 plus 5% from police making a total of 35%. The remaining 20% go to the other emergency services.

Of those emergency calls made to the police, some may involve risk of injury to someone's life or wellbeing, therefore, they will request the attendance of an ambulance, hence the 5% of transferred calls.

It is true to say that of all the emergency calls made to the fire service, not all will be for assistance in saving someone's life. Unfortunately they do get a number of calls that will be false alarms, either well intentioned or malicious. Some false alarms are caused by automatic fire alarms (AFAs) because of a 'fault on system'. Many of the 999 calls made to the fire service, are to deal with such things as fires in derelict property, grass or rubbish fires, floods, or sometimes people locked out of their home, or trapped in lifts.

Sometimes the ambulance service will request the attendance of the fire service to assist paramedics, at an incident. The fire service have a great deal of specialist equipment and a skilled emergency team which can be of great assistance to the paramedic, in the extrication and rescue of trapped and injured casualties.

On such occasions, I have found the firemen to be very

professional in their approach to the task. Always willing to do what is best for the casualty, whilst at the same time they are willing to work in tandem with the ambulance crews to reach the common goal. They have the equipment, the muscle, the expertise, and the numbers, to remove and or dismantle any obstacle and thus make a successful recovery of an injured patient.

Some of the actual fire calls that they receive are termed as 'persons reported' and represent a significant number of their emergency calls. Having been with the firemen on many such occasions I can say with absolute confidence, that they truly are magnificent in their attack on a fire when a life is at stake.

Save for a very few malicious emergency calls to the ambulance service, all emergency calls are to people in genuine acute distress. When you hear the audible warnings and you see an emergency ambulance coming your way, with all lights glaring, then please pull over, slow down or stop....give way to them! You can be sure that they are on their way to assist some poor soul in great immediate need and that poor soul could well be one of your own family.

For most people, making a treble nine call (999) is not an every-day occurrence and usually for them it is a once in a lifetime experience, and a nerve wracking one at that. However, there are a significant group of people, for whom making emergency calls, particularly to the emergency ambulance service, seems be their occupation. Although these people are rare in numbers, their existence can be a great nuisance to the service and a cause of frustration to the ambulance crews who have to attend to such calls.

Take for instance the case of a middle aged man, who obviously had some psychiatric problems. He would call for an ambulance for all sorts of vague complaints, sometimes two or three times a day. Upon our arrival, he would then refuse to open his front door. We would then be detained at his address for up to half an hour conducting our conversation with him, through the letterbox, just trying to gain entry to his home.

Eventually having done so, he would refuse our assistance, sometimes even, becoming aggressive.

Over a number of years he made literally hundreds of emergency calls to the ambulance service and gained notoriety for having made more calls than any other of our regular 'multiple callers'.

He once made more than ten emergency calls in a twenty four hour period, none of which, proved to require the attendance of an emergency ambulance. Although it was apparent to many of the people dealing with his calls, that he needed help; it always seemed that we were all powerless to do whatever was necessary and so this fiasco continued. He was not the only 'multi-caller'. We had a few more so that together it was possible in any one week for their combined number of calls to number twenty. This represents a tremendous waste of resources, not to mention the cost.

All these calls were answered by the ambulance service and met with the same response as that to all *genuine* emergency calls. An emergency ambulance would be immediately mobilised with all lights and sirens being used to speed to the scene. Whenever we received a call from one of these 'regulars' we could never risk becoming indifferent due to our familiarity with the caller, for when, inevitably, they do eventually make a genuine call, we will still be there to assist them.

Whenever an emergency occurs there is a brief period of time, when those directly involved or who are witnesses, may be unsure as to what to do. I am often surprised and even saddened sometimes, that the wrong action has been taken at the start of the incident; subsequently resulting in our attendance being delayed and the patient's condition becoming critical, or worse and dying.

I recall responding to such an emergency call, to a house some distance from our station. The emergency was for a gentleman who had collapsed at the top of the stairs and according to his wife, was 'making strange guttural noises'.

Initially the man's wife left him alone, collapsed and lying unresponsive; whilst she went next door to seek the advice of a neighbour. The good neighbour hurried back to where the man lay to ascertain that he had indeed collapsed and was unconscious. There then followed a hurried conversation between the neighbour and the wife, before deciding to telephone the man's daughter who lived several miles away. The daughter eventually answered the telephone, listened to the details, and told her mother, 'put the phone down, and I'll call the doctor, then I'll come over to you'.

Without further delay, the daughter telephoned the doctor's surgery and spoke to the receptionist who immediately told her that what they were really dealing with was an emergency and that *she* (the receptionist) would call the ambulance on 999. Vital minutes had already been lost as we responded to the emergency.

Arriving at the address a few minutes later and grabbing my paramedic kit, I entered the house and was met by distraught lady pointing up towards the top of the stairs. 'It's my husband' she was sobbing uncontrollably and being comforted by a younger woman.

I quickly made my way up and knelt beside an elderly gentleman who was lying on his back halfway between the bathroom and the top of the stairs. 'Hello can you hear me', I spoke loudly to the collapsed gentleman, at the same time I was feeling for a pulse in his neck. I could see that his skin was cyanosed (blue in colour) due to a build-up of Carbon Dioxide in his blood. Checking his pupils, they were dilated and didn't respond to the light as I shone a torch into his eyes. He was a big chap aged about sixty years of age (still quite young) and there were signs that he had vomited. He was not breathing and he had no pulse.

Frank, my crewmate and I quickly ran through our protocols, I listened intently as the younger woman related the story of events. It soon became apparent that there had been a substantial delay in making a treble nine call.

It transpired that the gentleman had called out to his wife

before collapsing. She had tried to rouse him and she recalled that he seemed to be making gurgling sound and had made no more noises or response from that time and up to our arrival, I put the time span at about fifteen to twenty minutes (maybe even longer) since he initially collapsed.

We attached the cardiac monitor, and listened to his chest but sadly there was no sound and the cardiac monitor showed a prolonged flatline. I, therefore, had to conclude that there was nothing we could do to reverse this tragedy - the gentleman was deceased.

Anyone who collapses and stops breathing and the heart stops will soon die; the brain cannot survive much longer than three minutes without Oxygen, except in very rare circumstances.

I made no comment to his wife or his daughter (who by now had arrived on scene) as to the significance of the wrong procedures followed by them, thus causing the delay in our being called. I took them to one side and gently explained that there was nothing that I could do to help the gentleman.

They became very distressed and now I had to treat them as my patients, it was them that I must now care for.

That was a case where the ambulance should have been called immediately; but there is also the other extreme where some people call an ambulance, as simply, as if you or I would call for a taxi.

Take for instance the case of a young man who called an ambulance out at three o clock in the morning. We received his emergency call as 'difficulty breathing'. The call came through the 999 system and as such an emergency response was implemented.

We respond to all 999 calls, using our lights and beacons and siren but at three in the morning there was little need for the audible warning devices to be used, still, we did make rapid response!

Arriving at the house, I was met by a young lady who was, to say the least...worse for drink. She led me into a very dirty and smelly bedsit, where upon I found her boyfriend lying in a bed. Enquiring as to his problem, he told me that he had run out of 'Strepsils' and still had a sore throat and wondered if I might have something to give him! I thought ......a kick up the backside seemed appropriate but I was careful not to voice my thoughts.

Night time seems to bring a lot of unnecessary calls, more so than during day time. In many of these cases I find that I am dealing with people who are living on their own; so it's possible that there is an element of loneliness in their situation. Feeling unwell when you are alone is not very nice and it is even worse in the small hours of the night. Of course the demon drink can often impair a person's judgment when it comes to their health and the need for an ambulance.

I was once called out in the early hours to someone who could not sleep. A middle-aged gentleman explained that he had been experiencing difficulty sleeping at night for many months. 'I think I may have insomnia' he said, as though suffering from a serious illness. I asked if he had spoken to a doctor about the problem, whereupon he replied 'No, I don't want to bother him with it'!

I have long since given up trying to understand some people. This call was a difficult one to deal with, in so far as deciding on what treatment I could offer to this gentleman. In fact there was none I could give, other than perhaps singing him a lullaby, which I didn't fancy doing anyway. Furthermore, I didn't fancy asking my crewmate either because he has a lousy voice. I didn't really think the hospital casualty staff, would thank me for taking such a case to their busy department either.

Ambulance staff cannot refuse to take anyone to hospital and so on this occasion I spent ten minutes advising the patient to see his doctor the next morning.

An emergency call for a broken fingernail may not seem like a very good reason to call for a paramedic; but that's what one young lady did one evening. To be fair, the injury had bled a little, but as is so often the case, there was a friend with her, who had not only had a drink or two, but *actually* knew all about 'The Patients Charter' and the rights to an ambulance too.

'You're entitled to an ambulance, so I'll call one' the knowledgeable friend confidently informed her *injured* friend. And so it was that I found myself racing on another emergency call.

One evening, my crewmate, Geoff, and I responded to an emergency call, similar to those above; this time the patient was, alone, at home surrounded by a lot of empty cider bottles scattered about the room. When I enquired what was the problem that caused her to call the ambulance she became belligerent.

'Because I need to go to F****** hospital, I'm not F****** well. Got pains in my stomach'.

Though I thought the lady had been drinking and that the drink may be clouding her judgement as to her actual condition (in other words there was nothing wrong with her) I still had to be polite and respectful whilst trying to examine her vital signs, pulse, blood pressure and breathing etc. In return, she continued being belligerent and abusive and insisted on me taking her to hospital.

Sometimes it's best to 'go with the flow', so rather than debate the issue further with her, we took her to the casualty department, whereupon, as I had suspected, they were not too happy with her time wasting.

Leaving her in the capable hands of the casualty staff, Geoff and I returned and climbed into our ambulance, outside the casualty entrance.

We were just about to drive off when a car suddenly screeched to a halt across the front of us, just missing the front of the ambulance by inches. 'Bloody lunatic' (I thought to myself). I jumped out of the ambulance again and went toward the offending vehicle. The driver who had got out was now climbing into the back of the car; I could see a woman slumped across the back seat. Realising that this was obviously someone in distress, I called out to Geoff to assist and went to the car door nearest to me and, pulling it open, I climbed into the darkened vehicle.

Then surprised, I heard the driver speak, 'Hi Dale'. I looked up to see who had used my name.

'It's Mum' he said, 'she collapsed at home'.

Through the gloomy interior of the car I saw who was speaking to me. It was my Brother! There on the back seat lay my Mother, seemingly having a heart attack.

My Brother (Steve) had thought it quicker to get Mum to hospital in his car rather than call an ambulance. He actually said that he didn't want to bother us! *Meanwhile,* back in the casualty unit, the woman who had so wastefully called me out a short time earlier was already leaving the hospital after having spent only a few minutes there. In which short time she had been abusive to the nursing staff and consequently had been requested to leave.

My Mother had indeed had a mild cardiac condition and was admitted and (fussed over) by the casualty staff. I am glad to say that she was released from hospital a week later.

There is another group of people who do call us, albeit genuinely, simply because they are not quite sure what to do in certain circumstances. On such occasions it's true to say that I did not mind attending such genuine calls of distress.

Some people will make a 999 call; and having been told that 'an ambulance is on its way' will then have second thoughts and may feel that they have over-reacted. They will then recall the ambulance service to cancel the ambulance. Here on Merseyside, once a 999 call is received it cannot be cancelled and the ambulance will always turn up,

Sometimes when we turn up at a reported emergency we may be met by someone who tells us that the victim has absconded from the scene. On such occasions, we cannot simply turn around and go back to base. We must firstly determine and corroborate the facts and ensure that any supposed victim is accounted for and safe and well. Information received and our observations at the scene will determine our next move: and may involve a search of the area.

For instance, in the early hours of one morning, our control received a 999 call from a man who claimed that he was injured, although he was not too specific as to just how badly, injured, he may be. The call was made from a public callbox in a rather rundown area of town. The man was told 'an ambulance is on its way' and he was told to stay where he was.

Geoff, my crewmate for that night and I were quickly mobilised and en route to the scene. Meanwhile, the man had re-called ambulance control, and asked them to cancel the ambulance response. However, as local policy dictated, his cancellation request was disregarded and we duly arrived at scene a few minutes later.

Arriving at the callbox we found the area was very dark, because of very little street lighting and the street was deserted. There was nobody about and initially there was not much to see. After a brief look around, we informed our control, that the man as far as we could make out, had left the scene. Back came the reply from control, that the caller had seemed genuinely distressed and *was* very probably injured; they passed details of the telephone callbox number from where the call had been made.

Taking a torch we made a close examination of the callbox. Shining the torch to see and read the telephone number, I noticed that the handset was dangling down by its wire and as I reached to pick it up, I felt that it was cold and very sticky and closer inspection revealed that it was covered in blood as indeed, so too, now, was my hand.

On further examination I could see that the whole of the telephone was completely covered in blood. There was a considerable amount, some of it in large congealing lumps with bits of hair attached. Blood was still actually running down the phone mechanism. All this culminated in a large pool of blood on the floor as well as smaller pools trailing off up the street. At this point I asked ambulance control to request the attendance of the police. Something told me that we may need them.

Having summoned police help, Geoff and I set off to follow

a very substantial trail of blood. The trail was punctuated occasionally by a larger pool, of still fresh blood, indicating that the injured person may have collapsed on the ground at that point, before getting up and moving off again. We followed the blood for about two hundred yards, up the dark deserted street before turning down a long narrow alleyway leading into the next street. At this point we were some distance from our ambulance, so Geoff left me alone, whilst he ran back to fetch the vehicle; and meet up with me. I continued, alone, to follow the bloody trail, which now stretched for a quarter of a mile. A few minutes later the darkness and the quiet of the street was broken by the reassuring sight of blue lights, reflecting off the darkened windows of the houses in the street, as Geoff joined up with me again. Moments later we were joined by a couple of our local police officers.

We gave the police officers a brief history, of events as we knew them to be and we together we resumed the search for the injured man. Finally the trail of blood came to an abrupt end in the middle of the road; and no matter where we looked beyond that, no other sign of blood was to be found. The joint conclusion was that, the injured person had probably been picked up in a car.

By now we had been on scene for twenty minutes and we had rightly assumed that there was indeed a badly injured casualty...but where?

As if to answer our questions, a young woman came running out of the dark toward us. Despite the cold of the night she was dressed only, in a thin cotton night-shirt. She was distraught as she told us that her boyfriend, had been beaten up; and he was now in her house, which was in the next street. It transpired that this was indeed, our missing patient. A friend had found him and (as we had suspected) picked up in a car before delivering him to his girlfriend.

A couple of minutes later we all arrived at the woman's house, and entered the front door quietly. But, armed with important information, from his girlfriend that he would react badly to police being present, it was decided that only Geoff and I would approach the injured man. However, the police officers would wait outside the room ready to assist us, should we need it.

Geoff and I followed the young woman into the room whereupon we met a young well-built man who looked as though he had been in a road accident, such was his bloody state. However, far from being glad to see us, he immediately 'kicked off' yelling and offered violence as well as a lot of verbal abuse.

'You lot can F*** off' was his first greeting to us, (the ambulance crew) even before we could say 'Hello can we help you'.

I approached him in a friendly manner, but he kicked out and continued mouthing obscenities and making threats to me. I could see that there was a lot of blood about his head and face and it did seem that he may have a head injury that was serious enough to be causing his aggression, possibly due to some unseen brain injury. There was also a strong smell of alcohol, so his aggression may equally be due to that aspect.

Ignoring his threats, I spoke quietly to him, trying to reassure him whilst I checked his head and facial injuries. Geoff simultaneously held onto his arms, whilst checking them for injuries too. Suddenly the young man lashed out with both feet, screaming and raving like a madman. He pushed us violently away and jumping up, he lashed out at us both. He spat and cursed at us blood and spit seemed to be flying everywhere. His girlfriend managed to push between us, screaming and shouting at him to let us help him. Her interjection seemed only to enhance his anger, he was quite content to hurt us, certain in the knowledge that we would not respond in kind.

Within seconds, the policemen who had been quietly waiting outside the room, upon hearing the screaming and commotion, rushed into the room; and by force of numbers, we all managed to wrestle the man down onto the floor and handcuff him. Now at least I could deal with his injuries... for his own sake.

Putting him down physically like this would not legally constitute assault by us. *Our legal defence is one of 'Implied consent and necessity'*. In other words it would be reasonable to assume that had the man been in a normal mental state he would give us consent to deal with his injuries because it was a medical necessity.

Eventually we managed with some difficulty to dress a rather serious head wound before transferring him to our waiting ambulance. Once inside the ambulance he continued his vitriol toward me and the accompanying police officer. He was kept hand-cuffed for the journey to the hospital. Even in the hospital, despite his injuries, he turned his aggression toward the doctors and nurses, who were attempting to help him.

It later transpired that the man had suffered an assault, by a vigilante group, who were trying to rid their neighbourhood of drug pushers, of which he allegedly was one.

Of all the treble nine calls that we respond to, I have never been able to come to terms with the malicious false alarms (MFAs) It is not only children who make such calls, but amazingly some adults do too. I know not why they do it, but I wish I could be behind them when they were making the call.

MFAs come at all times of the day and night, but there seems to be a common aspect to them, in that they are seldom of a minor nature. Many will report some dramatic incident that requires immediate emergency response.

For instance, one such MFA that I recall, came one very cold and stormy November afternoon at about four thirty, just as we are approaching the evening 'rush hour'. We were ordered to respond to a possible 'major incident' about 15 miles away.

A caller to the treble nine systems reported that he had seen a twin engine aircraft fly low over a motorway flyover, (known as the Runcorn-Widnes flyover) on the M56. And disappear in a downward direction, presumably 'crashing' into the countryside some one hundred feet below the viaduct. Daylight had faded and the weather at the time was dreadful with heavy rain and high winds. To make matters worse the area was difficult to get to. The precise location of the incident was difficult to establish because the caller claimed to have been driving on the motorway at the time and had driven some way further on, before he could safely pull onto the hard shoulder of the motorway to use his mobile phone.

Immediately, as would be expected of such an incident, a whole range of emergency procedures and activities were set in motion, involving all three emergency services, along with hundreds of people to a perceived 'major incident'. In such circumstances first response is to send a significant contingent, from each of the three emergency services, to the general area of the reported incident. Those arriving first would give an all-important 'first report' thus allowing a more bespoke response to the incident.

On this occasion, several ambulances along with the fire service and police were sent along the busy, rain-lashed motorway; a second contingent of ambulances, fire service and police had to make their way to a second location at ground level. Then they had to leave their vehicles in narrow lanes and search on foot through the fields and a wooded area below the motorway flyover. Also, because the flyover spanned a canal, the police underwater team needed to attend too.

Ambulance control set their 'major incident plan' on 'stand-by' and called in other ambulances from outlying towns (some were twenty or more miles away). Meanwhile Manchester airport control tower was informed, so that they could carry out their emergency procedures. Local hospitals were alerted and placed on 'stand-by'. The motorway police began closing the motorway and redirecting traffic away from the scene. The police helicopter was mobilised and together a major operation was soon up and running. Hundreds of people were responding, along with millions of pounds worth of equipment, to this emergency

It is worth stating, that all this was set up, and running, in a few minutes but that is what you the public expect. Isn't it?

The first emergency vehicles on scene at the viaduct, reported that everything seemed normal and nothing could be seen in the fields below. There were no signs of debris either on the motorway itself, or either side of the viaduct. The wooded area below looked intact, but would need to be checked out and searched thoroughly in the darkness, by those crews on the ground.

Eventually Manchester airport flight control reported back that no aircraft had been as yet been reported as lost off their radar.

About thirty minutes after the initial 999 call was made, the incident was declared an MFA!

I hope the idiot who made that call is reading this now and I hope he can see what an absolute prat he really is.

Children make malicious calls, but they also make genuine calls too and for that reason the ambulance control operators make no distinction as to how to respond to a child making a 999 call. We cannot take chances and so we respond as a genuine emergency. Malicious calls from children are more easily understood, they love to see the emergency services drive by, and it is to them very exciting. Never the less it is still a waste of our time and very often it is dangerous for the responding crews.

One afternoon, whilst I was responding to an emergency call (which later turned out to be a 'child MFA') a large black and white collie dog ran out into the middle of the road and tried to attack our speeding ambulance. Given that I was travelling at about forty to fifty miles an hour and approaching road works, I was not going to break violently, and risk skidding, to avoid it. There was a loud thud and sounds of the dog yelping as It caught under the front of our ambulance before being thrown underneath and out again at the back, as I passed over it. We couldn't stop; we needed to carry on to the emergency call, which had been reported as a child run over by a car (child RTA.)

Arriving at the scene a few minutes later, we soon discovered that there was no accident. We were approached by a couple of youngsters who told us that 'some boys had made the call and that they had been laughing at what they had done'. They pointed to a group of young boys, watching us from a distance.

Jumping back in the ambulance we sped up towards the group hoping to give them a telling off. But no sooner had we set off in their direction, they ran off into the maze of nearby streets.

I reported to control MFA and told them that we had hit a dog on-route to scene, telling them that we would return to look for the only real casualty of the incident. We never found the dog, but witnesses said that it had limped away, bleeding and distressed. I felt really upset at the thought that some poor animal had paid a high price for some children's stupid prank. Moreover, that dog may have been the loving pet of some other child.

Another emergency call one day required us to travel through the Mersey tunnel (the tube we called it) to Liverpool city centre, again to a 'child RTA'. Liverpool ambulances were busy and we were the nearest available vehicle.

As is the case with high speed emergency journeys through the tunnel, all civilian traffic is stopped and held back from entering whilst the emergency ambulance is given a high-speed police escort through to the other side. This involves a number of operations to be set in place, but thanks to good co-operation by all concerned, the whole process runs smoothly. However, it is a costly exercise, not to say inconvenient to all those motorists held back to allow us the freedom of the tunnel.

When we arrived on scene, our noisy arrival was greeted with curiosity. Onlookers watched as I climbed out of the ambulance and began looking about for 'the incident' A kindly old gent approached me, to tell me that 'some young children had been playing in the phone box' nearby. It was another MFA!

Thankfully, these malicious calls account for only a very small proportion of our emergency calls, but a reduction would be much appreciated.

2 THE EARLY DAYS

From an early age, growing up in Birkenhead, I had an outgoing and adventurous spirit always wanting to stretch my physical limits; my most notable ambition at that time was to join the Army when I was old enough. And so it was that eventually I joined the Royal Artillery. I chose to train as a surveyor, which relied on a good grounding in maths and a grasp on Pythagoras theorem etc., fortunately subjects that I enjoyed.

As a trainee artillery surveyor I found my work interesting, learning to use various precision instruments such as theodolites, slide rules and a range of equipment designed to accurately point the huge self-propelled guns at a target, many miles away.

I also trained in and worked from helicopters learning to fast rope down from a hovering helicopter as well as all the usual basic soldiering skills.

When I was posted to Hildesheim in Germany, I volunteered to take a 'crash course' in speaking German language; mastering the language enough to converse with the locals within a few weeks.

Upon leaving this exciting, disciplined and well-ordered life of the Army I found it difficult to immediately settle back into civilian life. Trying a variety of jobs I eventually settled into regular employment as a supermarket manager, working at stores in and around Liverpool and Wirral. Although relatively well paid at that time, I found the job boring and every day seemed like the one before; and believe it or not, I found that the job could be quite stressful.

One store which I managed in Liverpool city centre had a particularly serious shoplifting problem with shoplifting gangs working the local area. Generally, when dealing with shoplifters, one of the shop staff has to actually witness the customer pick up and conceal an item. They watch the customer, who having passed though the pay till and actually leaves the store without paying, can be challenged. It is only when that shoplifter has left the premises that they can be (legally) challenged. This is stressful for the manager who may have to do this, but is worse if you are challenging someone who may have aggressive accomplices waiting outside the store. I had many such incidents to deal with some actually ending with an assault on myself or my staff.

Every Saturday evening I would receive s phone call from the area manager, wanting to know the total of that week's takings. If sales were down he would demand to know why? The fact that the week before may have been Christmas week and extremely busy with sales being higher than normal, didn't seem to count. It seemed that the company expected sales to go higher *every* week.

This all made the job as supermarket manager too stressful for me; I needed to get out.

I made a couple of applications to join the ambulance service but all to no avail, not even the courtesy of a reply. One evening I read in the local newspaper an article by The Merseyside Chief Ambulance Officer, complaining that the service was short of ambulance staff.

That prompted me to make a third application but this time I put in a covering letter, asking why the Chief Ambulance Officer (CAO) was complaining that the service was short of staff despite the fact that I had made so many previous applications. I addressed it (FAO) for the attention of the Chief Ambulance Officer. This approach paid off, as I received a letter requesting me to attend for an interview at the ambulance HQ in Liverpool some weeks later.

For the interview I dressed smartly, shoes immaculately polished, trousers pressed to a razor sharp crease and crisp new white shirt. I was determined give the best impression possible to my potential employer. The interview took place in front of a panel of senior ambulance officers, Chaired by the Chief Ambulance Officer (CAO)[1] all of whom were smartly dressed in their respective uniforms and demonstrating to me, that they had pride in their position.

The interview was a little nerve-wracking, but I left the room some time later feeling the interview had gone reasonably well. However, I still had a strict driving test to take using an emergency ambulance but only at normal speed. Driving an unfamiliar vehicle around the streets of Liverpool was a bit daunting. Only a little allowance was made for nerves and few mistakes were allowed. The driving went well, but there would be no decision today as to whether I had been successful or not. I returned home hopeful that I would gain entry into the service, I felt that entry into the ambulance service could provide a secure future for me and my family, as well as offering me an opportunity for exciting career development.

A few days later I received a reply informing me that my application to join The Mersey Metropolitan Ambulance Service had been successful. I was told to report for duty to Ambulance H.Q. at Quarry Street on the outskirts of Liverpool city. The letter went on to explain that I must undergo a minimum period of induction training lasting two weeks before being assigned to a 'base' station. At the base station I would serve as a third man (observer) on an emergency ambulance, prior to going away to residential training.

On the morning of the 7th November 1977, I awoke and dressed early. I didn't bother with breakfast I was too excited to eat. This was to be my first day in the ambulance service which, hopefully, offered the prospect of more security, excitement, interest and job satisfaction than that of my supermarket manager job.

My wife and two young daughters stood on the front step and waved me off, wishing me well as I set off to Liverpool and the Ambulance Service Training School.

On my way to Liverpool I happened to pass a large school still burning and badly damaged from a serious overnight fire. The fire service, though still in attendance, seemed to be packing up their equipment. Meanwhile were a number of 'Green

Goddess' Army fire engines nearby, with soldiers running out lengths of hose-pipe and exchanging places with the firemen. It was then that I remembered, today was the beginning of the first ever fire service strike and military forces were being deployed as a back-up. Little did I realise, at that time, that one day in the future I would be playing a significant role in yet another firemen's strike and working alongside soldiers.

Arriving at the Quarry Street training school, I was directed to a classroom, already part-full with other new recruits sitting at desks. I recognised several of them from the earlier interview and nodded to them in greeting. Looking around for an empty desk I settled for one right at the front and sat down waiting patiently and quietly as everyone else seemed to be doing. Strangely, for the first half hour nobody 'official' came into the room to greet us, we were left to our own devices. Eventually somebody broke the silence by cracking a joke thus giving us an opportunity to introduce ourselves to each other.

A couple of the new recruits were from the other emergency services, the police and the fire service and, as such, they already had an understanding of what an occupation in the emergency services may incur. One of the new recruits (Ronny) informed us that he felt fortunate to have been accepted into the ambulance service at this particular time because this allowed him to resign from the fire service in time to avoid being drawn into the firemen's strike action. Ron went on to assure us that the excitement of fighting fires had worn off, and went on to speak of his great disappointment at never having rescued many damsels-in- distress. He was he said ‘fed up of rescuing cats out of trees’. He was, of course, joking.

I later went on to serve for many years with Ron, not always on the same ambulance but usually on the same station. As for the rest of us new recruits, we all came from a wide range of occupations, shop-keepers, plumbers, builders, mechanics and also one from the navy. There were also two women on this course, one of whom had left the police service in order serve with the ambulance service.

Eventually as we made our introductions to each other, the classroom door opened and in walked a senior ambulance officer. Those of us (like myself) who had been in the forces, automatically stood up, as a mark of respect, and the rest of the recruits followed suit

'Good morning all' the officer greeting us looked imposing, dressed in smart navy coloured uniform, similar to that of a police officer, with braid on the peak of his cap and the insignia of a senior ambulance officer on the epaulets of his jacket.

'I am your trainer for the next two weeks,' his manner putting everyone at ease, he went on. 'My name is Bert, we use first names here in the class but outside you call me sir.' 'First things first' he went on...'tea break'.

For the next two weeks we would all be relying on each other to get through the induction training, for it was widely believed that if we failed this basic course then we would be out even before we set foot in any ambulance. For me, that would mean going back to managing supermarkets.

Induction training was meant to 'kick-start' your brain into believing that you were already an ambulance man/woman. And so it was immediately after tea-break that we began our training.

The first day was mostly taken up with introduction to the service, pay and conditions, introduction to union representatives and management and last but not least, uniform issue.

Later in the afternoon, travelling in a couple of ambulances, we were all transported to Wallasey ambulance station; which served as the main base for all uniform issue for the whole of Merseyside County. Arriving at Wallasey, we drove through a grand Victorian entrance with huge iron gates and into a big yard at the back of the main building (a former fire station but now taken over by the ambulance service).

The front of the old station was very imposing with a one hundred foot training tower standing proud and dominating the sky-line for miles around. Facing out from the front, were four huge green folding doors which could be folded back in seconds to allow emergency ambulances to exit the station directly onto the main thoroughfare of Liscard town centre.

Clambering out of our ambulance we were all led upstairs to the uniform issue office where-upon we were given a card with our uniform allocation printed on it. The list of uniform was quite generous.

Two ambulance tunics
Two pairs of trousers
Two real Leather belts
Two pairs of over-trousers
One raincoat
Six blue shirts
Six black neck-ties (why would anyone need six black ties?)
Twelve pairs of socks
Two pairs of shoes (Doc Martens)
Two pairs of epaulets
One peaked cap.
Two pairs of black leather gloves

By the time each of us had collected our allocated uniform issue and jostled back to our ambulance for the return journey to Liverpool it was near impossible to get everyone back into the vehicle with all their items of uniform.

On day two, all kitted out in our new uniforms, training actually got underway. This really was my first day as an ambulance man; something I already felt proud about.

The induction training course was entitled 'Ambulance Aid' and was basic First Aid by another name. The very first thing that we were taught was basic mouth-to-mouth resuscitation or CPR (cardio pulmonary resuscitation) as it is known. This, essentially, was the first thing to learn, for now that we were travelling, in uniform, to and from training school anyone of the public were likely to call upon us for assistance should the need arise. We, therefore, had to at least have the ability to save a life.

During the induction course we were divided into three

groups and there would be an element of rivalry between each. We were taught about the type of ambulance equipment that we would be expected to use as well the basic rudiments of managing various types of injuries. Using splints and immobilising serious fractures was an interesting subject to those of us who thought a fractured bone was something different from a broken bone.

In those days there few, if any devices that we could use to lift a heavy patient, the only tool was an understanding of kinetics and manual-handling along with the muscle and strength. To make this part of the training, realistic enough; each team had to pick the heaviest person in their group to act as the 'casualty'.

In our group there was no contest, it was going to be big Pete who weighed in at about sixteen stone. The rest of our group weighed on average about eleven stone. Pete thought that he, being our chosen patient, was a great joke and he laughed at our many struggles carrying him up and down several flights of stairs over the course of our training.

However, he who laughs last laughs longest. Much effort was spent by the rest of us in the group, trying to get our 'patient' to lose weight. Indeed Pete complained often to Bert, that someone had been in his locker and stolen his chocolate biscuits leaving only a carrot in place.

As our instructor, Bert, attempted to convince us that it was, actually an advantage to have someone like Pete in the training group, but to be honest none of us believed having to carry anyone that heavy was anything but a huge disadvantage.

The rest of our group including the two women (being comparative weeds) had to learn how to lift Pete's sixteen stone from the floor, carry him up many flights of stairs down again and into the basement. Pete had no end of laughs at our expense as we all struggled with his weight. He didn't make things easy for us. We once caught him putting weights in his pockets. It almost seemed as if he could increase his weight by thought alone. Trying to lift his bulk from the floor was difficult enough but when he acted as an unconscious casualty, he became like a huge lump of jelly.

Would you believe we even had to lower him out of a two storey window using a special device known as 'The Neil Robinson Stretcher'? Meanwhile the other two groups each had lightweight 'patients' to carry.

One day, Bert pulled out a strange looking piece of equipment with a complicated array of straps and buckles. 'This', Bert, told us 'is the Neil Robinson stretcher'.[2] 'It can be used to rescue casualties, from heights, depth or difficult terrain.' Pointing to the equipment, he went on. 'Using ropes which we attach to the metal rings at the feet and head end'. Bert walked over to Pete, our patient, and placed a hand upon his shoulder. Looking at the rest of the class, he went on, 'You are all going to learn to use the Neil Robinson and, as usual, Pete will be the casualty'. 'Furthermore', Bert went on, 'You may wish to know that this piece of equipment actually weighs two stone!' Pete was visibly delighted at our demeanour and burst out laughing; now we would be lifting a combined weight of eighteen stone. Bert too was smiling and laughing as he went on to explain. 'Using ropes and the Neil Robinson, you will be lowering Pete out of a second floor window!'

Suddenly it was our turn to laugh. Pete's face said it all as his smile disappeared as he realised that Bert was serious. We would indeed be lowering him out of a second floor window whilst he would be helplessly strapped into the Neil Robinson. To the 'weeds' in the group this latter exercise would at last reset the balance and put the shoe on the other foot so to speak.

As is still the practise today, each trainee not only had to learn to use the all ambulance equipment but had to sample it too as if being a casualty (except of course the defibrillator). This meant that we all had to take a turn at being strapped into this piece of equipment, thus giving each of us a valuable (and unpleasant) insight as to how a real patient may feel when he or she is being evacuated, whilst helplessly secured in this device; as well as the fact that they may be in pain from some injury.

The Neil Robbo, as it was affectionately called by those of us who used it, was like a canvas stretcher, lined within a strong bamboo frame. The casualty is placed inside and strong canvas sides are pulled up and wrapped about the whole of the body, arms legs etc. Strong straps are then firmly buckled into position securing the patient securely inside and unable to move; the casualty's feet are further strapped so that they cannot drop out of the bottom as they are hoisted upright; the head is placed in a restraint so that the casualty cannot even look sideways.

Actually it's like a strait jacket and not nice to be encased in. Although a patient will be perfectly safe and secure in this piece of equipment when it is handled properly by experts, it can still be a nerve-wracking experience.

Bert continued with his explanations; watching over as each trainee in turn was strapped into the Neil Robinson and man-handled around the room and up and down a few stairs. This gave each of us the maximum 'casualty experience'. It was noticeable that suddenly our heavyweight colleague 'the casualty' was looking pale at the prospect of us 'weeds' now being given such responsibility as might cause him grave damage.

Now came his turn to be encased in this contraption but as promised by our instructor, Bert, he was going out of the window!

Although the situation had not been of Pete's making, he had enjoyed (some say too enthusiastically) playing the role of the casualty and he had enjoyed many a laugh at our expense. However, even though I was now laughing at his dilemma, I could not help feeling some sympathy for him.

As if by some prior arrangement (though I assure you it was not) having secured Pete into the Neil Robbo and as we began to lift him up from the floor - we accidentally dropped him! It was only a couple of feet in height and no real harm was done, except of course, to his failing confidence in our ability to carry out the, riskier part of the task.

It took a little (well a lot really) of reassurance from us, before he would allow us to continue and lower him out of the second floor window. Sure enough as we balanced our casualty on the window ledge two floors up; securely encased in the Neil Robbo. I bet he was wetting himself as we slowly lowered him out and down to a group on the ground. To Pete's great relief the exercise was over, with him safe on the ground. 'Well done lads. Tea-break,' shouted Bert from the upper window. Quickly everyone dashed to the canteen leaving Pete lying, still strapped into the Neil Robbo. After a few minutes someone went to release him.

It seemed no time at all before our two weeks induction training was completed and we were ready to be deployed to our allotted stations. We were by no means completely ready for the road, although we did have a limited capability. At least, we could all carry out CPR and we could also deal with a certain amount of simple trauma, fractures and the like. We were all dispatched to various stations throughout the Merseyside area, where we would work alongside qualified ambulance personnel. The group would eventually be reunited again early new year, when we would attend a residential training programme at Wrenbury Hall training school, just outside Nantwich.

Ronny and I were fortunate enough to be posted together to Wallasey station, close to our homes on the Wirral. This was to be our base station from where we would ride as supernumerary 'third man' observing on what was commonly called 'the crash vehicle'. This being so named because it was the primary front-line emergency ambulance to respond to any emergency and it was also usually the best equipped ambulance.

Our local ambulance station was the large Victorian building where we had come to be issued with our uniforms. It was right in the centre of the town. It had previously been the main fire station and HQ of Wallasey Borough Fire service and Ambulance Service. Both fire service and ambulance were as one, sharing the station and its facilities. Ambulance-men were employed also under fire service management and Home Office regulations.

That all changed in nineteen seventy four; under new Home

Office regulations the services were re-organised, separated and required to function independently of each other. The fire service were dispatched from the old station, which had served as a fire station since the days of horse drawn fire crews, to operate now from a brand new purpose built station, whilst the ambulance service stayed behind taking overall charge of the whole of the old complex.

I learned that the one hundred foot red brick tower, which stood proudly overlooking the town had been used by the firemen for ladder practise sessions and was used also as a hanger for drying out long lengths of hose. During the terrible years of the last war its lofty position was an ideal lookout post for the fire watchers during the blitz by German bombers; there too was the air raid siren (still a functioning machine) Now the tower stood as an empty monument to those bygone days; for we as ambulance-men had little use for such a facility.

I spent about three months working at this station, getting to know the men and machinery before going on to complete full ambulance training. Many times I would be riding as supernumerary on 'the crash vehicle'; thus gaining my first real insight to the emergency side of a job that was to become, to me, the best job in the world. And on those occasions when not on 'crash', I would be on 'sitter ones' working alone picking up hospital outpatients and transporting them around to the various treatment centres.

It was within a couple of days of taking up my post as observer that I sighted my first dead body. I was told later by an 'old hand, that 'you never forget your first one.' He was right, I do remember it well. The two ambulance-men who were with me did not take advantage of my unfamiliarity with the situation but instead guided me through the unpleasant task of handling the body for the first time.

All seemed to be going well as we carefully and respectfully placed the body of an elderly gentleman into a special canvas 'carry sheet' which had carrying handles on each side. This method of removal was necessary because in order to get him out of the house and into the ambulance, we would have to negotiate a difficult, narrow spiral staircase. The steps were wedge shaped, making it all too easy to lose your foot-hold. I was at the 'head' end and holding onto two side straps, with the deceased's body in the sheet held up high against my chest. I was leaning slightly backwards to help ease the weight of the body with one of my crewmates behind me, supporting my shoulders as we began to make the difficult descent. John our other crewmate was facing toward me, holding onto the feet end of the carrying sheet, whilst stepping backwards down the stairs.

A relative of the deceased stood at the foot of the stairs, watching our slow progress down the difficult stairway.

Suddenly as we manoeuvred around the spiral, I felt the heavy body within the carry-sheet beginning to move. I was unable to do anything to stop it, because both my hands were holding onto the side-straps. Suddenly the front of the carry-sheet parted enough for the deceased's head to pop out followed a second or two later by the whole of his upper body. For a moment we all stopped in our tracks whilst we shuffled, pulled and shook the handles hoping to ease his body back into the sheet. Unfortunately our efforts were in vain. Gravity took over and our deceased patient seemed to spring forward falling and head butting John at the feet end.

We sat down on the stairs and managed to regain our composure and secure the deceased back into the sheet. Thank goodness the deceased had not been injured by the event! As for John, he had been struck directly on the bridge of his nose which was now beginning to bleed profusely. We had no choice but to continue on down the stairs passing the grieving relative and out to the ambulance, whereupon I was given the opportunity to practise my ambulance aid skills on my crewmate's bloody nose.

Not a word was uttered by any one of us during this debacle; the relative at the foot of the stairs was unaware of our mishap and did not even notice Johns injured nose. Once our patient was securely in the ambulance and we were all safely on our way to the hospital mortuary we were able to laugh at our mates misfortune, which took my mind off any morbid thoughts about my first 'Dead on Arrival' (DOA).

During these early months every aspect of my working with other qualified ambulance-men had to be regarded as an opportunity to train and learn from them by example. Wallasey Ambulance Station proved to be an ideal training ground for it was here that I encountered an absolute professional attitude from every man. Many of the ambulance staff were older than me and, like me, many had served in the armed forces and so had an integral self-discipline and personal pride. No slap dash approach here, emergency calls were answered and responded to within seconds, (usually the ambulance leaving the station within thirty seconds). Had I ever been too slow to board the ambulance upon which I was meant to be travelling as 'third man' then they would not wait for me.

My first night duty filled me with apprehension as well as a degree of excitement for night time could produce different types of emergencies than those of the day duties. Consequently, unlike my experienced colleagues, I could not sleep – as was allowed back then - and I would sit around hoping (much to the irritation of the other crews) for the red phone to ring out summoning us to some emergency.

During the weekend so called quiet hours, the ambulance crews (three at that time) would set questions for each other based around Anatomy and Physiology; setting up complicated training exercises within the vast complex of the old station buildings and the tower honed our practical skills at dealing with casualties in all manner of difficult situations. These exercises were enhanced by the fact that we had an officer who was very keen on realistic training of ambulance staff and who was particularly skilled in the composition and make-up of fake injuries.

Some of his finished pieces were indeed (although quite horrific) a work of art; using realistic looking blood, bits of bone (supplied by our local butcher) and a liberal supply of plumber's putty he could soon produce the most realistic looking injuries. Having completed his artistry and produced realistic looking injury, his casualty would then be told how to respond to the ambulance crew attending the 'mock-up' incident. The casualty would then be placed somewhere appropriate enough to represent a realistic incident.

For instance, I remember one such exercise where a 'would-be' casualty was made up to have horrible burns as well as a complicated fractured leg and a bone protruding through the skin. He was then being placed under a large boiler in the boiler-house of the old station cellar. He was given further instructions to feign a heart attack during the ambulance-men's treatment of his injuries.

The exercise was set in motion; a report of an explosion was conveyed to the two ambulance men chosen to act as the responding crew. They duly arrived and set about the task of dealing with the mock-up incident, whilst being watched by their peers and a couple of trainees like myself.

I was amazed that they approached the exercise as if it were the real thing; during which they actually showed signs of stress. Although due to my lack of full training and experience, I was not yet able to take part in these exercises I gained a tremendous training benefit just by watching them and later listening to the robust but constructive criticism of the other more qualified spectators at the de-briefing.

Working on 'sitter ones' (working alone ferrying patients in and out of hospital treatment clinics) duty was a valuable training ground and also a most enjoyable part of the job.

Firstly and more importantly it, gave me the opportunity to learn my way around the area in which I would be working. Eventually over the years I gained a vast topographical knowledge of the area; no sat-nav in those days. Not only did I need to have a very comprehensive knowledge of street and road names but also there was an essential need to know all the one way systems, the latest road closures, quickest routes, and shortest routes (these latter two are not necessarily the same).I also learned where all the bumps and pot holes where in the road and learned to avoid them so as to ease the discomfort of patients.

Secondly, working on 'sitter ones' gave me the opportunity to meet many interesting people and to be able to chat with them; I learned to converse on just about any subject under the sun. I have met many what we have called 'great' people in my job over the years and I have learned a lot about life from them. At some point I may write about these great people.

I spent those first months at Wallasey Station and worked on Christmas Day before departing with Ronny to the training school at Wrenbury in the New Year.

◆ ◆ ◆

3 AMBULANCE TRAINING

February 1978 came around and at last the serious business of a full 'Ambulance Aid' course was upon us. It had seemed a long time since my basic ambulance induction course back at Quarry Street Ambulance HQ. I had looked forward, to what was considered to be, real training and had been stuck with my head in medical books for some weeks. Hopefully I had done enough pre-course work to help me in my quest to become a qualified ambulance-man.

A group of us trainees, I along with Ronnie and a couple of men from Birkenhead ambulance station had agreed to share a car to make the journey to Wrenbury. We could come home each weekend, but the rest of the week would be twenty four seven, training and studying.

The training was to be a six week residential course held in and around a beautiful listed building in the Cheshire countryside.

The listed building, Wrenbury Hall, was owned and run as a training centre by Merseyside Metropolitan Ambulance Service. The centre was staffed by serving ambulance officers each of whom had been picked because of their vast experience and knowledge, along with their ability to impart such information to others. The centre and the instructors had a nationwide reputation of excellence in training that was regarded as second to none.

Wrenbury Hall was like a large manor house set in its own grounds and sat at the edge of the village of Wrenbury, just a few miles from Nantwhich.

Upon arriving at Wrenbury Hall, one could not fail to be impressed by the long tree lined driveway which passed over a small bridge and led up to a pair of magnificent ornamental wrought iron gates. We drove through the gates and along a winding path through a forest of trees before coming out in front of a most beautiful old manor house (home for the next six weeks).

We parked our car and entered through the grand entrance into a large hallway, lined with extravagant ornately carved oak panelled walls. Directly opposite the entrance was a wide ornate staircase leading up to our rooms.

Rooms had been allocated for each trainee before our arrival and so having been directed to our respective rooms we were ordered to quickly deposit our bags in the room and meet downstairs in ten minutes. Each room was small and comfortable but without any frills. One man or woman (no mixing the two) to a room; the focus was to be on study.

Ten minutes later, back down in the hall, we met up with other trainees from around UK. There were about fifty of us altogether, some of whom had been on my induction course in Liverpool. There was also a group of about ten men and women from Belfast Northern Ireland.

We were offered tea and biscuits and a brief chance to meet each other before being called to the main hall for a brief history and tour of the manor and surrounding outbuildings. Around to the rear of the manor were two other wooden billet-type buildings which served as classrooms. With the brief tour over, we were then put into four training groups in which we would serve for the full period of our training.

Our particular group trainer was a big jovial chap named Walter. He wore a great grey mustachio and we used to refer to him as 'Wing Commander', for indeed he did fit that image.

All our training would be done in and around the buildings and the surrounding country lanes.

This part of Cheshire was beautiful; we were surrounded by busy canals and locks, which were frequented at weekends by canal-boat enthusiasts in narrowboats. There were (and still are a couple of good) pubs in the village. One of them (The Dusty Miller) sits right on the banks of the canal. Occasionally if we had finished our nightly homework we could just manage to get there in time for 'last orders'. Even today I occasionally return with my family for a pint and a pub lunch. Wrenbury village, with its canal and pubs was a lovely place to do our training.

I soon got to know the trainees from Belfast who were studying alongside us, and I spent many hours listening to the tales of these brave ambulance staff. Listening in awe to their first-hand account of the troubles on Belfast streets I was amazed but marvelled at the risks they took just to do their job. At that time they were dealing with horrific incidents involving multiple casualties caused by an IRA bombing campaign. Little did anyone of us realise, that in the not too distant future, they would be in the forefront of a system that would spearhead and precede the introduction of paramedic ambulance crews to the streets of, not only Belfast but to the whole of the United Kingdom.

Except for weekend leave, we were cut off from our families and any domestic distractions. The training would be intensive and thorough, covering all aspects of modern ambulance aid (such as it was at that time) at the end of which hopefully we would all be rewarded with that much prized professional certificate of competence namely 'The Miller Certificate of Ambulance Aid'. That being the only nationally recognised ambulance proficiency certificate, without which no ambulance-man or woman could practise.

I remember the fear of failing this course was profound; it seemed that my whole future depended on my gaining 'The Millar Certificate'. My family were relying on me too. I spent many hours anxiously re-reading and re-writing my work, hoping that repetition would enhance my memory.

At the end of each day's training and after our evening meal we would return to our rooms to continue with 'homework' hopefully finishing the task in time for 'last orders' in the bar. It was there, over a few drinks, that I enjoyed the company of the Belfast group. Listening to more of their hair-raising exploits as they literally battled to do their job in the face of extreme adversity during the 'troubles' as they called it.

Human anatomy and physiology was studied in a depth that I had previously not anticipated and I found it hard going.

Never before had I studied such a subject. It was all foreign to me, but I had to get through.

Medical jargon was, to me, like a new language, but there are ways to learn to understand many of the complex words. Some words defied my own verbal ability and as for trying to spell them! They seemed to be made up of totally illogical syllables. However, I learned how to break down these seemingly, mind-boggling, tongue-twisting words, into syllables that gave a clue to their actual meaning.

I learned how to remember complex human body systems.

The physiology and anatomical functions and mechanisms of the body, by using mnemonics.

During the days we would learn, in practical training, how to deal with serious injuries such as burns, fractures of bones, and immobilisation techniques. We learned how to safely move people with serious injury Carrying patients took strength and skill. Whenever Walter (our instructor) wanted you carry someone on a stretcher he would always 'volunteer' someone. He claimed it saved time if he did the volunteering for us! Sixteen stone Pete from our Liverpool induction course was still, in my group so Walter, naturally, volunteered him to be carried.

From time-to-time candidates from each group would take a turn at being made-up to look like accident victims, so that the others could learn to assess and treat, accordingly, the particular injury. As usual the 'make-up' was so good that all injuries looked real. On one occasion a group of trainees were tasked with dealing with the aftermath of an explosion. Entering the room full of 'would-be' casualties, the trainees were faced with such realistic looking mock injuries that one of the them, fainted!

One casualty, having been made up to look like he had a serious head injury, had also been encouraged by the instructor, to hold a mouthful of vegetable soup in his mouth. Upon being examined by the trainee the casualty suddenly vomited (soup) all over him. This taught all those watching (and that trainee) to kneel to the *side* of such casualties...and *never* in front!

Many hours were spent learning all the different systems of the body and how they work, along with their relationship to each other. Learning to name all the parts of the body, as well as the parts of the parts, of the body, was a feat in itself. We needed to understand the different functions, the locations, the make-up and the boundaries of all these parts. All the different tissue layers, the inner layers, the middle layers the outer layers, the types of layers and the thickness of those layers.

We learned to understand signs and symptoms, and how to diagnose major illnesses and to provide a pre-hospital treatment regime. High on the list of these major illnesses were heart attacks, heart failure, asthmatic attacks, and diabetic comas, breathing difficulties such as severe bronchitis, emphysema and etalactisis.

We spent many hours learning how to deal with head injuries and the consequences and complications of intracranial pressure. We learned how to differentiate between a Transient Ischemic Attack (TIA), often called a mini-stroke, which is caused by a temporary blockage in a blood vessel in the brain; and a stroke or Cerebral Vascular Accident (CVA) which is more serious and can be caused by a bleed in the brain or a blockage in one of the blood vessels.

We had to understand the difference between sub arachnoid haemorrhages, a sub-Dural or intracerebral haemorrhage as well as understanding how to interpret the signs and symptoms, in order to give emergency treatment to a patient suffering from such an event.

Hours were spent on major incident training. We were taught how to respond in a logical, calm and organised way to such events. We were instructed how to arrange emergency response from all other emergency services, and how to prioritise and triage patients ready for treatment and evacuation.

Emergency obstetrics featured quiet heavily in our training and by the time I had got through trying to remember the various stages of child birth and understanding trimesters etc. I was just hoping it would be many years before I actually got to deal with such emergencies. However, life is not like that but more about that later in the book.

By the end of the six weeks my head was spinning. My nerves were shattered, as they say, as indeed so too were the nerves of all my course colleagues. We took our final examinations over two days; but the exam results would not be forthcoming to us for some days yet. We would have to return to our stations to await the results, which made for something of an anti-climax to the whole course. However I for one was glad that training was over and I didn't actually contemplate failure, I had done my best.

A few days after arriving back on my Wallasey my home station, Ronny and I were called into the Chiefs office and given the welcome news that we had both passed! 'Now', said my station officer, 'Your training really starts!'

Ronny and I left his office, grinning like Cheshire Cats, we'd made it. We shook hands in mutual congratulations and then set about equipping ourselves with the regulation ambulance aid bag, ready for the first job!

That then was the nature of my ambulance training. We would need to take a refresher course every three years and that was that!

I was now fully trained and 'raring to go'; I could not wait to ride as a qualified ambulance-man on the front line emergency ambulance, colloquially called, the 'crash bus'. However it was to be a couple more weeks of outpatient transport before I was let loose on 'crash'.

I had only been out of training school for two weeks and was working on my own transporting outpatients to treatment centres when I encountered what turned out to be (is still today) one of my worst jobs.

The job was what we call 'a running call'. In other words it's a job that we come across, or witness, before any one has actually dialled 999.

I was parked close to the entrance of the hospital casualty department, having just delivered some patients to the near-by outpatient clinic. As I was about to climb back into my ambulance 'sitting vehicle' my attention was drawn to a car which had suddenly pulled up alongside me.

Looking around, I saw the driver jump out and run around to frantically fling open the passenger door. Realising that something was amiss I turned and quickly stepped across to assist a passenger who was struggling to climb out of the car. It was only then that I realised that the passenger was a young boy aged about thirteen. He was dressed in a butcher's overall and apron and struggling to get to his feet before I could actually reach him.

'My arm, my arm', he cried out hysterically, holding aloft all that remained of his badly injured left arm. The whole of the bottom part and some of the top of his arm was missing. A large section of shattered bone (humerus) protruded from the shoulder socket, with some skin and muscle still attached but hanging down. Blood was still pumping out covering the wretched youngster as well as the interior of the car. He reached out to me with his good arm but I wasted no time in acting.

In a split second I had scooped him up in my arms. Then turning around I ran with him, back into the hospital, passing a queue of startled patients, straight into the casualty department. Nurses turned to see me rushing through the heavy plastic screen type doors, calling to the staff as I did so. I continued with him, passed the triage desk, down the corridor and into the main resuscitation room.

No sooner had I placed him on the theatre trolley than he was surrounded by a team of concerned medical staff. Telling them briefly how I had found him outside, I left him being attended to by the very efficient quick assembly of nurses and doctors, whilst I returned to speak to the car driver.

I found him still standing by his blood-soaked car and in a state of shock. I knew that it would be essential to try to retrieve the severed arm and to find out what exactly had happened to the youngster. I had a quick discussion with the driver; who told me that he was a greengrocer. He had been working in his shop when the butcher, from next door, came in saying that there had been an accident in the meat preparation room at the rear of his shop.

The greengrocer ran next door to the prep room to find the young boy (who was thirteen years of age) badly injured, covered in copious amounts of blood and screaming in panic and pain. Feeling that it would be much quicker to transport the boy to hospital himself, rather than call and wait for an ambulance. He put the injured boy into his own car and made a high speed dash for the hospital less than a mile away.

I informed ambulance control on the radio telling them that I was dealing with a 'running call' and that I would give them details shortly. With the car driver safely in my outpatient ambulance I set off back to the butcher's shop. I was driving fast but with caution because this type of ambulance did not have blue lights or audible warnings. I did make optimum use of my headlights and horn to make progress to the shop.

By the time we arrived at the butcher's shop, I had a mental picture in my mind of a severed arm lying on the sawdust covered floor. Having worked for many years myself, managing supermarkets and butchery departments, I was well aware of what such a shop should look like behind the scenes. I had a sound knowledge of all the different types of machinery that could be found in a butcher's prep-room and it had looked obvious to me that the injured boys arm had been amputated by some machine like a band saw.

As I walked into the small butcher's shop I was amazed to see a queue of customers standing at the counter, still waiting to be served. The butcher, a middle aged man, was serving his customers almost as if nothing was wrong. 'Excuse me please', I said loudly. 'Has there been an accident here?'. He looked at me and without saying a word, pointed to a door behind the counter which led into the rear of the shop

Pushing through the queue of customers I made my way into, a small back room, used for meat preparation. My first impression was that it was very clean, and tidy, (a good sign in a butcher's shop). There was no sign of a severed arm anywhere but instantly I my attention was drawn to a meat mincing machine that still had mincemeat hanging from the mouth of the machine. I stepped quickly back into the shop to speak to the butcher who was still serving customers, whilst still more were entering the shop!

'Look', I spoke with an urgent authority, directing my remarks to the customers, 'I'm afraid there's been an accident; the shop is now closed!'.

I ushered everyone out quickly and locked the door before turning my attention to the butcher. 'Where is it?', I asked, without actually saying exactly what 'it' was.

I followed him as he walked back into the prep room; without saying a word he just pointed to the mincing machine. I could see that there was half a tray of mince, with more minced meat hanging from the mouth of the machine.

I examined and smelled the meat hanging from the machine, and that in the tray. I had worked long enough in butchery departments, to know what I should be seeing and this was not it. What I could see was not all regular meat, indeed it was part of the young boys arm. Then looking down the funnel into the lower barrel of the machine I could clearly make out a piece of bone jamming the screw mechanism. I turned off the power supply and set about dismantling the machine. Even in that brief moment I noticed the butcher's surprised look as I deftly and expertly took the machine to pieces in record time.

I took out the main screw-like mechanism (known as a worm) and sure enough what remained of the arm was well and truly wrapped around it. Grabbing a clean white starched apron from a nearby cupboard, I wrapped the mechanism, complete with whatever remained of the damaged arm, and left the butcher with instructions not to re-open his shop and to await the Police.

I returned at speed, to the hospital; where mercifully the youngster had been quickly anaesthetised and was being attended to in the operating theatre. After examining the remains that I had retrieved from the machine, the surgeon pronounced that nothing could be done to salvage the arm, it was beyond repair. The machine part and what was left of his arm was placed in fridge to be disposed of later on.

I returned to the hospital the next day and made a visit to check on the young boy in the ward. Already he was making a remarkable recovery. He was awake and his distraught parents were at his side looking more concerned with him, than he did about himself. He was discharged a short time later and eventually he was fitted with an artificial (bionic type) arm.

The butcher shop never re-opened. The young boy was under the legal age to operate such machinery.

◆ ◆ ◆

4 PARAMEDIC TRAINING

In 1979 the people of Belfast, Northern Ireland, not only witnessed but also became innocent victims of an increase of violent terrorist activity. The IRA were producing horrendous explosive devices made up of nails, nuts, bolts and screws, which upon detonation, caused vast numbers of civilian casualties; many with multiple trauma injuries. It was also found that many victims died at the incident site before reaching hospital. More importantly, it was found that many of those who *did* die before reaching the hospital, had such injuries, that had they received the specialist treatment actually at the scene they may well have survived.

The medical response to the IRA bombing campaign was to set up a mobile intensive care unit (MICU) staffed by doctors and nurses from the Belfast Royal hospital. It was considered that specialist doctors and nurses actually working at the scene of the explosion would save more lives.

For many reasons, it was soon realised that this was not necessarily the best way to deal with the problem; and it was decided, instead, to 'extend" the training of those ambulance staff who held The Miller Certificate and who were already well seasoned to dealing with incidents 'on the street'.

The new idea worked extremely well and many lives were saved by these newly trained 'Advanced Life Support (ALS) ambulance crews. Victims' injuries were stabilised and treated at the scene, before further movement exacerbated the injury. Only then could patients be safely evacuated to hospital.

Advanced Life Support meant that ambulance staff could now give vital fluid replacement therapy, setting up drips and administering life-saving, blood-replacement fluids. They could also carry out intubation of unconscious casualties, whereby a tube is passed directly into the patient's airway to administer Oxygen to the lungs. Something that, previously, was only carried out by anaesthetists. ALS crews also carried a number of drugs to help with various serious heart conditions, including cardiac arrests.

Although they were not called Paramedics at that time, The Belfast Ambulance Service certainly were the pioneers.

Here, on the mainland, a group of ambulance-staff and doctors in Brighton heard about the Belfast idea. Although they (at that time anyway) had no terrorist activity to deal with, they considered that such a scheme could work on a domestic level. And so it was that 'The Association of Emergency Technicians' (AEMT) was founded; and, for some considerable time, Brighton was one of the safest places in The UK in which to have either a heart attack or a serious injury. Such was the level of pre-hospital emergency care provided by a forward-looking Brighton Ambulance Service and Regional Health Authority.

The ALS skills provided by The Brighton ambulance staff at street level, was further enhanced by a public awareness scheme, which allowed voluntary groups to donate funds and or equipment to help raise the standard of local ambulance training, to a level much higher than that of the rest of UK.

To further enhance emergency care at street level, the local AEMT launched a 'Save a Life Scheme' aimed at training members of the public to carry out basic mouth-to-mouth resuscitation and cardiac massage Cardio Pulmonary resuscitation (CPR).

One evening whilst I was watching the news on television, a brief documentary was shown of the Brighton ambulance scheme. Being as keen then, as I still am today, I discussed the Brighton scheme with a friend (John) who managed our local cardiology department and whom I knew was interested in Advanced Life Support (ALS). Also after talking it over with other ambulance colleagues and noting their enthusiasm for ALS training, we decided to write off to 'The Brighton Ambulance Service' requesting further details about their scheme. We received a reply from them a few days later thanking us for our interest and hoping that the scheme could be rolled out across our area.

The Brighton branch of the AEMT furnished all the relevant details of their scheme and offered as much help as we needed in order to set up our own scheme. John, the Cardiology Unit Manager was a tremendous help in the initial set-up. He had access to hospital facilities as well as to doctors and specialists within the coronary care sector. He also had a good relationship with many medical reps who were encouraged to offer whatever help they could to help us get our scheme off the ground.

Back at the ambulance station I began to recruit volunteer members for what would be The Wirral Branch of the AEMT. The local union branch were none too pleased because they considered that the 'they over there' (our bosses in Liverpool) should pay for all ambulance training, and staff should not have to volunteer. However, the union did not understand the personal pride of Wirral ambulance staff who wished to be part of such a pioneering scheme and within a very short time we had well over half the staff committed to join with us. So it was that in 1983 the Wirral Branch of the Association of Emergency Medical Technicians was set up.

John had secured hospital accommodation and also arranged medical reps to donate refreshments, in the form of a very generous buffet, for our inaugural meeting. The meeting was attended by ambulance staff and some officers, from Wirral and Liverpool. We set about recruiting a committee of volunteers, both from the ambulance service and the local hospital. I was voted in as Chairman of Wirral AEMT. Once properly organised I naturally sought the help and advice of our own Chief Ambulance Officer, who unfortunately declined to be associated with us.

With help and advice and some early donations from a few hospital doctors, notably a well-respected casualty doctor, a consultant anaesthetist and a general surgeon we were able to get started. We were also given training facilities within the hospital theatres, with the blessing of the Institute of Anaesthetists. We were also given access to the Wirral Post Graduate Centre and lectures were given by visiting consultants and other specialists in our field.

With the help of Brighton AEMT as well as advice from our committed doctors, we devised a training programme of Advanced Lifesaving Skills (ALS) skills for ambulance staff. The ALS training programme, by necessity had to be so advanced in its structure and required depth of medical knowledge as to allow ALS trained ambulance staff (now known as Paramedics) to be allowed to practice such skills in pre-hospital emergency care.

These skills; airway intubation, intravenous cannulation, fluid replacement therapy, intraosseous infusion, ECG interpretation, administration of drugs; were all previously only performed by doctors and anaesthetists and only in hospital. Those who passed this training programme (paramedics) would be using their skills and knowledge on the street and without supervision.

Therefore, none of the main medical affiliates such as the General Medical Council (GMC) the Royal College of Anaesthetists (RCOA) the Minister of Health would sanction our training or give their blessing to such a programme of training unless they were absolutely satisfied that a very strict criterion was to be met by course candidates.

Our training mandate we agreed to strict working protocols attached to the role of paramedic. One of which was, in any emergency situation, the paramedic should use all his/her skills of diagnosis, formulate a treatment regime, stabilise the patients' acute medical condition and make haste to the nearest casualty department. In other words, not to spend a disproportionate time on scene but get going to hospital and treat en route to hospital.

We relied heavily upon our hospital consultants locally and nationally to steer us in the right direction as far as medical legislation and protocols were concerned.

As a result the devised ALS training programme was strict

and in much greater depth than that which we had been used to. Such training had to be set at a much higher standard because eventually we would carry a burden of greater responsibility.

In emergencies, out on the streets, paramedics are expected to perform invasive therapy techniques which may involve administering a variety of dangerous drugs, intubating a patient's airway or shocking someone's heart, all potentially lifesaving but, potentially, dangerous too.

Unfortunately for us at that time, the local Regional Health Authority (RHA) would not recognise our group, nor did they wish to identify with our aims. That being the case, our own Chief Ambulance Officer had to toe the official line by ignoring our activities; and so we were left very much on our own.

We also had some 'raised eyebrows' and opposition from local GPs who thought we were 'getting above ourselves'.

The local Community Health Council (CHC,) on the other hand, did (quite rightly) see the enormous advantages of ambulance-men and women becoming advanced trained paramedics.

One of the main advantages of this new concept in ALS support training was indeed the cost. Quite simply, it would cost the public purse absolutely nothing! For, it was incumbent upon members of the AEMT to commit to train in his/her own time and at their own expense. Further still, every member had to commit some of their free time to the public education scheme that we were to launch in Wirral. To complement our efforts, we expanded our activities: by organising the public awareness scheme and ran it along the lines of that already running in Brighton. It was to be known as ' The Save a Life' scheme and was designed to teach members of the public the rudiments of mouth-to-mouth resuscitation and heart massage also known as Cardio Pulmonary Resuscitation (CPR). At the end of the two hour course, everyone was able to carry out this very important basic life-saving technique and, as such, each successful candidate received a certificate of competence.

By the end of our first twelve months we had trained over

five hundred members of the Wirral public, to carry out Cardio Pulmonary Resuscitation (CPR)

Eventually our local AEMT became a registered charity and we were then able to raise many thousands of pounds enabling us to buy advanced lifesaving equipment, such as cardiac monitors. These would eventually be accepted by our Regional Health Authority and subsequently fitted into front line ambulances. Eventually other groups of ambulance staff across the UK formed similar organisations, until we all met up to form a single national organisation.

Despite the earlier reluctance of various professional bodies to support our ambitions of ALS training for ambulance staff, we continued to campaign for official recognition by Parliament and health ministers, albeit with little success.

However before the Government accepted the need for ALS trained ambulance staff we, here in Merseyside, were already following the Brighton ambulance design by studying and training in local hospital operating theatres under the guidance of a couple of consultant anaesthetists as well as an Accident & Emergency (A&E) consultant.

Even before the Thatcher Government sanctioned ALS training, here on Merseyside we had four ambulance-men who had qualified as ALS-trained and registered through an AEMT affiliated group.

It was these four people who then went on to train paramedics under the NHS Scheme. These four, John, Ken, Peter [3] and Boyd were the 'first' paramedics on Merseyside. *

Then came the Brighton Bomb!

> In October 1984 the Conservative Party (the Government of the day) held their annual conference in Brighton. Prime Minister Margaret Thatcher, along with many of her ministers, was accommodated in the Grand Hotel. At 2.54 am on 12th October a massive explosion ripped through the building, killing five people and injuring 31 others. That had been an attempt by the IRA to assassinate The Prime Minister and members of her cabinet.

In the immediate ensuing major incident response many people were rescued by the fire service and medically treated by the only officially trained ALS ambulance staff (paramedics) in the UK.

Such was the level of medical expertise offered to seriously injured victims that night by Brighton paramedics, that many lives were saved. In the wake of that tragedy The Government decreed that there should be a paramedic on every 'front-line' ambulance throughout the UK, and so it was that Merseyside Ambulance service came 'on board' with the AEMT to offer paramedic training to all staff. The majority of the public had never heard of paramedics before and thought that it was an American idea, albeit a good one. WELL NOW YOU KNOW THE TRUTH!

Paramedic training is 'something else'. It is extremely intensive, with a great depth of knowledge required in anatomy, physiology and human biology.

Basically the course can be described as having four parts'. Part one is home study, part two is training school, part three is in-hospital and part four is your final on-road assessment with a paramedic trainee assessor (of which I was one). It is only then that you are free to practice as a registered paramedic.

Special life-saving skills have to be learned and honed to perfection. For instance, the pass rate on the paramedic course, for resuscitation of a patient is 100%. Paramedics must understand the effects of the dangerous drugs that they may need to administer to a patient. As a paramedic your combined knowledge should be such that you are able to make an accurate diagnosis and life-saving treatment decisions based upon your assessment of a patient's signs and symptoms.

There is little advantage in describing, in full details for the benefit of the reader, exactly the depth of study that one has to go to in order to pass the written side of the paramedic training. However it is worth remembering, that the paramedic can be called to absolutely any incident; anywhere at any time and will be expected to cope without the aid of a doctor. As such, this will involve making a correct diagnosis and then responding with the correct form of treatment.

Paramedics are expected, as a matter of course, to be able to equate a patient's signs and symptoms, with a medical diagnosis that we are then able to treat and stabilise before transporting, without unnecessary delay, to hospital.

When a patient is taken by ambulance into hospital, say with a cardiac arrest, they will be treated at the scene by just two people, one paramedic and an ambulance technician. The pressure and stress on an ambulance crew in such circumstances is quite simply immense. When they get to the hospital the patient is then handed over to a *full team* of doctors and nurses numbering as many as seven or eight. Each of that team will be gainfully employed in trying to save the life of the patient, who previously had been attended to by just two ambulance staff.

The Merseyside Ambulance Training School in Liverpool was, without doubt, second to none. The training regime was tough and relentless. Emphasis was on your ability to think and work out the problem no matter how complex. Even before a candidate was accepted for paramedic training they needed to have already studied long and hard enough so that, in theory at least, they were amply qualified to become paramedics. There was then only the need to test that knowledge and to back it up with practical training in advanced life support and life-saving techniques and skill.

The motto at this training school was 'We train 'thinking' paramedics'.

Here trainees were expected to cover all medical subjects and all skills pertaining to pre-hospital emergency care. In doing so the knowledge should all link together at once, in a comprehensible manner, leading to a complete grasp and understanding of the science of emergency medical aid.

As you may expect, dealing with doctors and medical consultants during our day-today work is essential. Their involvement comes early in the training of a paramedic and it is in the training school that their contribution is essential and immeasurable.

With such training the paramedic completing the course will be able to provide a successful diagnosis and pre-hospital treatment for all patients. Mind you, the training is mind-boggling at times and many course candidates 'hit the wall' at some point during the course.

Hitting the wall is a description of a mental state, whereby no matter how hard you try and no matter how much someone explains to you; you just cannot understand, grasp or remember some particular element of something you have been told. No amount of careful logical explanation can get through to you. Your brain seems to be unable to absorb any more information, everything seems to be in a haze and at this point many may wish that they had not even started the course at all. Some (only a few) even consider dropping out altogether. However, the prize is so great that we carry on until we do eventually qualify.

So it was that the 'thinking paramedic' was trained. It speaks volumes about the Merseyside Ambulance Training School, that Ambulance Authorities from far and wide, across the UK sent their staff to this centre for training.

Once the paramedic is in the back of an ambulance with a patient, the care and welfare of *that* patient is exclusively dependent upon the skills and knowledge of the paramedic. Meanwhile the other crew-member will be engaged in driving in an appropriate manner to the nearest casualty department.

One paramedical skill we learn and practice many times, is what size needle (cannula) we may use in any given situation and where on the patient to insert it successfully. This takes a certain amount of skill and judgement and the paramedic will always be under pressure to get it right first time. After all, needles are sharp and painful so if you don't insert the needle in the correct place, and in a suitable vein at the first attempt, then the poor old patient is not going to like you 'having another go'.

Having successfully inserted a cannula into a suitable vein, it is then necessary to connect a line (transparent tube) to it in order to administer either drugs, or some type of fluid through it.

Intubation is a delicate but sometimes essential advanced life-saving technique and is one which the paramedic practices many times. Essentially it is a technique whereby a tube is passed down the back of the throat, through the larynx (voice-box) between the vocal chords, into the airway; the lower end of which has an outer inflatable balloon structure which is then inflated enough to hold it in place Thus securing a viable airway free from the risk of vomit entering the lungs.

The paramedic must also learn how to use a cardiac monitor and defibrillator, so as to check a patient's current heart condition.

When it came to learning how to interpret the ECG (electrocardiogram) readings, one has to spend many hours learning to understand (read) the oscillating line on the paper strip that feeds from the cardiac monitor. The paramedic then has to make an accurate diagnosis as to what, if any, heart condition the patient may be suffering. No two patients will display the same cardiac rhythm, (almost like a variable fingerprint) and the paramedic must be able to understand what each peak and trough on a cardiac readout means.

In the case of a patient having a cardiac arrest, then a powerful electric current is passed across the heart. This is a very dangerous technique and there are stringent safety procedures which have to be maintained at all times, even during a sometimes frantic life and death resuscitation emergency.

If you, as the paramedic, make a mistake things could go disastrously wrong. You can either kill yourself or even your colleague or some innocent bystander and, of course, your patient will not survive.

That is why it is absolutely essential that paramedics must have good and well-rehearsed skills, always with an eye to safety.

Training school is where we are taught and practice, for

hours on end, the actual mechanics of advanced life saving techniques. Every day, as we entered the classroom we had to first carry out CPR before we took a seat at our desk.

At the end of every paramedic course there are final examinations. These examinations were spread over two days. The first day was taken up with written exams testing our medical knowledge. Day two involved thorough and, essentially ruthless, testing of our diagnostic skills as well as our practical ability to, urgently, implement an immediate life-saving protocol.

The resuscitation side of the examinations carried a minimum pass rate of 100% (no room for error).

During the practical examinations there will be no allowance made for mistakes. Mistakes mean...failure. The trainee paramedic cannot go back and have another go. Everything has to be done right first time.

You are on your own; no-one to help or encourage you as you enter the examination room. Your years of experience, months of late night home-study and weeks at training school will all be tested to the limit because ultimately LIVES ARE AT STAKE!

The practical exams were arranged in four different examination rooms, each set up with a different scenario and controlled by a medical consultant.

One of the tools that the examiner uses is a computerized mannequin (used as the patient). The mannequin is linked to a central control unit and operated by the examiner allowing him to instigate a myriad of complex, realistic medical conditions, from unconsciousness to various sudden cardiac changes right up to full blown cardiac arrest. This particular mannequin can be given various drugs and or fluids intravenously, any of which may bring about radical physiological changes to the patient's condition. The mannequin could also be intubated and used with a defibrillator. It is very realistic and offered the maximum testing of a would-be paramedic's knowledge, skills and nerve. The minimum pass mark...100%.

Another part of this test involved giving our patient (the

mannequin) a number of different drugs. Having first decided upon the correct drug, we must then administer the precise dose and administer it in a very precise manner; all the time monitoring the patient and watching for any sign of adverse change in their condition.

None of this is straight forward, because the consultant may throw in a 'wild card' and try to catch you 'on the back foot' by changing the patient's response to the drug that you have just administered. As in real life and death situations the paramedics response, to any drug induced physiological change in his patient, has to be immediate and confident. The consultant may even question your treatment of the patient, in a manner that may cause you to doubt something that you have done, when in fact you know that what you have just done was correct.

In other practical examination scenarios we used real people who could use special make-up so that they looked as though they had realistic looking injuries. Fake blood and bits of bone from the local butcher were sometimes used. However, we could never get volunteers for the examination of cardiac defibrillation (shocking the heart) scenario...it's a bit dangerous!

Finally after all the examinations and practical testing has taken place; there is the long wait while special examiners are brought in to mark and assess your individual result. This takes a number of hours, during which time the candidates are kept in one room anxiously awaiting the final interview with the head of the training school, at which point they will learn as to whether or not they have achieved paramedic status.

Eventually we all drew lots to decide in which order we would go into the final interview and out of twelve candidates, I drew number ten. By the time I went into my interview, all except two of the candidates before me had passed; entering the interview room I was as nervous as hell, more so than on any emergency that I may have to deal with.

The training school senior instructor and one of my course

tutors sat together behind a desk, inviting me to sit down on the lone chair opposite. They didn't beat about the bush; I felt a lump in my throat, as I heard the senior instructor announce that I had gained a 'creditable pass'. For one of the few occasions in my life I was speechless, it was an emotional moment for me. At last I had earned an award that I was proud of, one which I had worked so hard to achieve.

It is only if you pass all these stages that you can then advance onto 'stage three' of the paramedic course. This involves working in the A&E casualty department and in the hospital operating theatres, all under the watchful eye of various doctors, consultants and nursing staff. And of course you will be working on real patients with your newly acquired skills. It is here that you actually practice the skills that you have been taught in training school. You have only one month to acquire and perfect the skills of 'invasive therapy'.

Invasive therapy covers such things as: intubation, which is carried out in the operating theatres on patients, who are about to undergo surgery, under the watchful eye of the anaesthetist. Which basically means that we pass a tube down a patient's throat, through the larynx (voice-box) and into the trachea (wind-pipe)? This will allow us to ventilate the patient's lungs. We often need to use this procedure on unconscious patients or in cardiac arrests.

Another invasive treatment is intravenous cannulation. This is a procedure whereby we introduce a hollow needle (cannula) into a vein, so that we can administer drugs and or fluids into the body. We can also take blood samples this way.

On rare occasions, if we cannot gain access to a vein when there is an urgent need for fluid replacement we may need use a different technique known as intraosseous infusion. This procedure involves the paramedic using special equipment to enter, by drilling into, the bone using a special instrument and needle, thus enabling him to administer life-saving fluids into the bone-marrow.

Defibrillation of the heart (shocking) is the procedure involving passing an electric charge across the heart during a cardiac arrest. There are different power settings but all are dangerous and can be lethal if you make a mistake.

During a cardiac arrest incident, the paramedic will be very busy carrying out multiple invasive procedures, and quickly too. For instance the patient may need intubating (for Oxygen) as well as cannulation (for drugs/fluids) and defibrillation and or basic CPR.

All the above are practiced in the real hospital environment on real patients (with, of course, their permission).

During my in-hospital training I had to perform, successfully, 25 intubations, 25 cannulations, 25 fluid replacement therapies and

25 drug administrations as well as attending any cardiac arrest calls that came in during my time on duty. Each paramedic was issued with an audit book so that after successfully completing each of the above procedures it would be signed off by the consultant.

I recall an occasion which emphasises the need for paramedic training to be so in depth and well-practiced.

It was whilst I was training in a Liverpool University hospital, alongside trainee doctors. In the operating theatre everyone (except the surgeons) are all dressed in the same theatre white gown, hat and facemask; there was no way I could be distinguished from any of the trainee doctors. One day after I had just completed another successful intubation on a patient, a trainee doctor came over and commended me. 'Well done, you made it look easy,' he said, going on to enquire 'how many have you done?' (meaning, intubations). Opening my signed audit book, I turned to the page relating to intubations. 'Twenty two with just three more to do,' I replied.

He looked at me, surprised, 'why do you need to do as many twenty five intubations?' 'Because I'm a paramedic' was my proud reply. He seemed suitably impressed, before informing me that he only needed to intubate FIVE patients. 'Why so few?' I enquired.

'Because I'm training to be a doctor!' he replied.

Intubation in a hospital theatre is a very different practice than outside, on the streets, where I would be working. In the sterile environment of a hospital the patient is obviously lying on a theatre trolley at a convenient waist-height, in a warm, well-lit room and all instruments easily to hand, and sterile. They will have fasted for their forthcoming operation, reducing the likelihood of them vomiting.

Out 'on the street' many patients are found in the most difficult locations, usually on the floor, indoors or out, in weather hot or cold, wet or dry, light or dark, nothing like the hospital environment. The paramedics will have to perfect their skills to a degree that few doctors will ever have to match.

Imagine, if you can, that we are dealing with an unconscious patient who has crashed his car during a snow storm on a dark country lane. He has lost a lot of blood and his breathing is impaired due to his serious injuries. He is wrapped up in a couple of layers of winter clothing making it difficult to even raise his sleeve to take a blood pressure or insert a needle into his arm. It is also impossible to move him because he is so severely trapped.

We will have to deal with him in-situ, until he is freed. Our only source of light is from a hand held torch. We are in a non-sterile environment because there is blood and car-refuse all over the place. With petrol leaking and battery acid giving off fumes, along with the smoke and heat from the driver's airbag the environment is hazardous.

At such an incident, after struggling to enter the crumpled wreckage the paramedic has to function at a near perfect level of expertise. He must intubate the unconscious patient no matter how difficult that may be. He must also try to find a 'good' vein on the patient and then, in all this mayhem, he must carefully insert a cannula into it. Then he must decide what fluids and or drugs to administer. Throughout all this he will be ably assisted by his crewmate who will be a highly qualified ambulance technician.

One of the problems with intravenous cannulation for the paramedic is finding a suitable vein on a seriously sick or injured patient. All too often veins collapse and may be almost impossible to see and thus difficult to insert the cannula into the tiny blood vessel.

In hospital training we deal with real people (patients) all of whom seemed to have a high regard for the ambulance staff. They were only too willing to let me cannulate them and take blood as part on my training. I had to learn how to decide on the size of needle, that I was going to use, and then find a suitable vein in which to insert it. Having done that I was sometimes required to take blood for sampling and then set up a drip, having first decided the correct fluid of choice. Thanks to all those who offered themselves to me.

As with all paramedics, there is a lot of pressure on you to perform to your optimum and very often you know that it is imperative that a patient be cannulated before you set off for the hospital. The patient may be deeply unconscious, with peripheral shut down (veins collapsed) but needing life-saving fluids and or drugs. All eyes would be on you as you carefully try hard to find a vein; even then the vein may only be a tiny one, not much bigger than the needle that you are about to insert into it. Carefully I would insert the needle, watching for the all-important 'flash-back' of blood into the end of the needle.

'Thank you God' I would mutter to myself as I saw the tell-tale sign of a successful insertion, for to fail to get a cannula into a patient, who may be in desperate need was viewed as a failure by ones-self.

No paramedic likes to fail to get a cannula into the vein of a patient who needs it. We cannot stay at the scene too long trying to get the needle in, if after the third attempt you couldn't do it; you would quickly evacuate the patient to hospital.

Finally, when you have completed the first three stages of paramedic training you then move onto 'stage four', whereupon you work on a front line ambulance with a qualified Paramedic Trainee Assessor (PTA) of which I was one.

It is only after successfully completing this final 'stage four' that it is deemed that you are now ready to be 'signed off' as qualified and then you can at last...call yourself a paramedic!

That then completes paramedic training. Following all that, every three years a paramedic is required to re-attend the training school for a Post Proficiency Course (PPC). Also every twelve months they must also attend a local emergency department to have their invasive therapy skills re-appraised by medical consultants. It is little wonder then, that paramedics do have a high degree of skill.

Looking back on my days at training school in Wrenbury Hall in Cheshire and to my fears and difficulty in grasping and remembering all that was taught of anatomy and physiology, I am pleasantly surprised that my love for the job gave me the incentive to want to become an instructor. It became easy for me to read and understand medical text-books, preferring a book for instance on 'Head Injuries' rather than a novel. I find anatomy and physiology a truly fascinating subject; marvelling at the human body and its workings.

During my last six years in the ambulance service, I set up and organised regular weekly night classes, for those staff primarily employed on outpatient duties but who wished to make the difficult transition to the accident and emergency service.

Running this night school gave me the opportunity to learn the art of teaching and training people. I also enjoyed having the influence to promote a professional attitude to potential ambulance paramedics. I am glad to be able to say that I did help many candidates to pass their entrance exams, with better than average marks, thus gaining a valued place on a Merseyside Ambulance. It gave me a tremendous amount of pleasure, to see someone join my night classes, then take their first struggling steps, (as I had done years earlier) getting to grips with the foreign subjects of anatomy, physiology and life-saving resuscitation, in order to take the emergency ambulance service entrance examination. I felt privileged that they sought my opinion as to whether or not they had what it would take to become a paramedic. I would tell them of my own struggles to gain a strong understanding and wide knowledge of our subject.

Occasionally one of them would fall at the first fence (fail the entrance examination) thus denting their delicate confidence; but I am glad to say that they all dusted themselves down and came back to re-sit the entrance exam and to pass on another attempt. I am proud to say that one of my early trainees went on to become a university instructor in Paramedical Science.

My strong instinct for enhancing the public's perception of the ambulance service and particularly the men and women working in it, did from time to time cause some people to take umbrage with my methods. There were those for instance who were strongly union-minded and viewed my voluntary and unpaid off duty night-school training programmes as some form of treachery.

'Why?' they would ask, 'Should ambulance staff have to train in their own time when it is the employer's job to see we are trained to a higher standard'.

That in my view was nonsense. Surely it is every ambulance person's responsibility to learn as much as they can about the pre-hospital care of sick and injured patients. It is imperative to give the absolute best service to those in need. Anyone who does not believe that should get out of the job and make way for someone who will offer that level of commitment.

I do not care what a person's attitude may be toward the bosses, it matters most what attitude and service you present to a patient in distress! Your own personal pride should drive you to present your very best...and nothing less!

Ambulances are run daily around the clock, three hundred and sixty five days a year. As such, despite their high mileage, they have to be mechanically fit to roll. Consequently, when a station takes delivery of a new and more modern vehicle and it is immediately put into service on the front line, the older vehicle that it replaces is still serviceable but may be used as secondary vehicle.

Naturally, if the need arises the older vehicle may become a spare and will get shunted around from station to station covering for ambulance breakdowns. Consequently, the older vehicles are not 'loved' so much by some crews, who prefer to use the nice new shiny ambulance.

Seeing an opportunity to enhance my work as paramedic trainee assessor I sought to hang onto to one of the older ambulances on a permanent basis and to use it as a dedicated training vehicle. My station boss and my area manager gave their blessing to the idea, and allocated an ambulance that had only just been replaced by a newer one. I set about getting it spruced up, painting and polishing, until it was looking impressive. Then rummaging around the store-room where all sorts of damaged, dirty and dysfunctional equipment had previously been dumped, I collected as much suitable equipment as I would need to fully replenish the newly dedicated training ambulance.

Once all the equipment that I had secured from the stores was cleaned, and in some cases, repaired it was placed on the ambulance ready for any emergency.

I was pleased with my efforts and the vehicle was (as we used to say in the Army) immaculate. Thereafter, those trainees who went out on that vehicle with me, felt rightly proud to present such a professional image to the public.

Unfortunately this seemed to antagonise one particular individual. He was a paramedic with many years of experience, but unfortunately, he was known for his extraordinary ability to be a pain in the backside. He had a big mouth and a bigger ego and purely out of spite he took several opportunities to vandalise both our ambulance and items of the equipment. A popular act of his was to empty our Oxygen and Entonox bottles and, disgracefully, on one occasion damaged box-splints so that they could not be repaired. This happened when I was off duty but was witnessed by other less senior staff who felt obliged to 'turn a blind eye'.

One would assume that such behaviour would not be found

in the service and may indeed present a prosecutable offence. However, witnesses to such incidents of vandalism were of course decent people and had no wish to see him on the dole.

'After all it's not his family's fault that he's a prat', they would say and so they were reluctant to become involved in any official complaint. Presumably this little chap with the big ego is still getting up to his childish tricks should anyone be unfortunate enough to arouse his jealousies.

I must point out that behaviour of that particular individual actually served as a useful example for my trainees. For instance I would use him as an example of how *not* to behave. Whenever he had been on duty in my absence the trainees and I would have to be extra vigilant with the routine vehicle checks. Consider the fuss there would have been if we had found a piece of equipment damaged only when we came to use it on a patient, thus placing a detrimental element of care upon the patient.

Once a paramedic is fully trained and qualified, he will be expected to return to the training school from time to time, to be taught new emergency medical techniques, as and when such new skills are deemed necessary.

◆ ◆ ◆

5 ROAD TRAFFIC ACCIDENTS

The term Road Traffic Accident (RTA) offers an infinitely wide spectrum at which to look, and, therefore, I propose only to touch the tip of a very big 'iceberg', for to do otherwise would involve writing a whole book on this singular subject. However, I will cover the subject in vehicular group. Motor Vehiclesand Motorcycles

Road traffic accidents (RTAs) account for only a small percentage of the day-today work of the paramedic. Furthermore most RTAs do not always result in serious injury, although all have that potential; minor injury is more common in most cases. Because of the minor nature of their injury, many casualties will refuse to go to hospital by ambulance, consequently an ambulance may leave the accident scene without the patient, hence the term vehicle not required (VNR).

Most road accidents are caused by someone's carelessness, but some are also caused by illness of the driver. Some accidents are caused by criminal activity of the driver such as car thieves, speeding and of course the 'big' one, drink driving.

The highest risk of having a road accident is held by the 17 to 30 age groups with men being the greater risk in that group, hence the higher insurance premiums for that group of drivers. Sadly, some young people who pass their driving test gaining a road licence at the age of seventeen, sometimes go on to show off, trying to impress their friends. All too often, such drivers tend to over-reach their driving ability often by driving too fast for the road conditions. Consequently I have had to deal with many of them and the victims with mangled injuries or...dead.

For many years I have been saddened by seeing and dealing with the horrendous aftermath of such 'young driver' accidents. I have seen babies, young children, teenagers and adults, seriously injured or killed in, and by, vehicles driven by some driver who was not yet 18 years of age.

I recall one incident (which I personally did not attend) in which eight young people, four girls and four boys, all under the age of 18 were killed in a road accident involving two high powered cars. Both vehicle drivers were under the age of 18 years of age.

Another similar accident involved a 17 year old driver who lost control of the car on a wet road, crashing and killing himself and his four teenager passengers.

One such accident (which *I did* attend) happened on a lovely, sunny evening and involved a 17 year old driver who had been allowed to borrow his parents, high powered car. Accompanied by his friend, this young driver drove down the motorway before leaving on the exit road to join the roundabout. Although he claimed that he was only travelling at 30 mph, he lost control of the car as it entered the intersection, and careered across a very wide grass verge, onto the opposite carriageway; colliding with a smaller, oncoming car, about fifty metres away, then continued on further up the road and overturned onto its roof.

I, too, needed to take the same motorway route to reach the accident and upon reaching the exit road I reduced my speed to enter the roundabout safely. From my first observation I could see two cars on the opposite carriageway about 75 metres apart; from each other; effectively two separate crash scenes. The car furthest away was on its roof, whilst the car nearest to us was at an angle with the doors hanging off.

Pete, my crewmate, jumped out of our ambulance and ran across the grass verge to the nearest car whilst I drove up my carriageway then turned and drove over the grassy central reservation to reach the overturned car. There, two young men were sat at the side of the car looking shocked and bewildered, but being comforted by another motorist who had stopped to assist. After a very quick assessment I established that they were from the car but were, fortunately, uninjured.

Leaving them in the care of the kind motorist and with instructions to him, to call me if either of the boys became worse,

I jumped back into the ambulance and drove quickly back to liaise with Pete. Priority dictated that I call for immediate assistance (more ambulances, fire service and police) before rejoining Pete in our efforts to save lives; little over one minute from our arrival on scene I was requesting emergency backup from ambulance control.

Pete had managed to clamber into the back seat of the wrecked car and was trying desperately to save the life of a child who was trapped inside, with terrible head injuries. It was obvious to Pete and that the car driver had died instantly and that there would be no chance of resuscitation. The front seat passenger, a young teenager, also displayed no sign of life but there were no visible signs of external injury so I took the decision to resuscitate; with the help of another motorist, I set about carefully (with extreme caution to any potential neck injury), removing their lifeless body from the car and onto the road. Now on the side of the road I began resuscitation until another paramedic crew arrived a few minutes later to take over.

Unfortunately there were *no* survivors in that car; mercifully they would not have known what hit them!

In these few instances I have covered the deaths of *16* young people under the age of eighteen. *What a terrible tragic waste of life. What a terrible nightmare for their families* and friends.

This is only the tip of the 'iceberg' for I have had to deal with too many similar accidents resulting in various degrees of injury, disfigurement and permanent disability.

I have written to various members of parliament including, the sitting Prime Minister of the time, Tony Blair suggesting a change in the law governing the granting of driving licences to young people. I re-produce part of that letter (which was sent in 1996) here for you now. Judge for yourself, if it is an unreasonable suggestion?

'Dear Mr Blair

I would like to make two suggestions for your future policies, one of which is a new idea.

The suggestion is that a future Labour Government would alter the minimum driving age to 18 years of age. This would produce many great advantages, and I believe it would prove to be very popular, particularly with the older age groups. I could not for instance imagine any parent, complaining. Complaints would only come from those aged seventeen; and even those complaints would cease after a short period.

The advantages:

a. At a stroke....many lives would be saved.
b. many serious injuries would be avoided
c. many families would be saved the terrible heartache,
and
lifelong burden of grief.
d. There would be savings within the NHS services
e. There would be savings to benefits agencies.
f. There would be savings for the insurance indusTRy
g. Most people in this high risk group would not gain a full license until they were nearer to the age 19 or older.

Young people becoming eighteen would look forward to their birthday being special because

a. They would be old enough to apply for a provisional license
b. They would become eligible to vote.
c. They would be eligible to drink alcohol legally.

With regard to their eligibility to drink alcohol, in the same year as they could acquire a driving licence; I believe that the 'Drink Drive' message would not be lost, but would gain more meaning to the young people learning to drive; they would be more prone to the idea of not risking their driving licence.

After they had passed their driving test, they would be obliged to display a green coloured sticker 'P' for the following 12 months, and would be restricted to certain power ratio vehicles (to be decided).'

I did not receive any reply; nothing was done, and so the carnage continues. Many young lives that *could* have been saved...*have now been lost!*

When a road accident happens it can often look and sound spectacular, screeching of brakes, the noise of impact and vehicles ending up on its roof, yet may produce no apparent injury to the participants who may walk away with little more than a scratch. However, a significant number of RTAs do result in serious injury to one or more people, and at worst may even result in someone's death.

It will be obvious to the reader that paramedics do indeed see many horrendous and sometimes grotesque sights. Over the years of dealing with the aftermath of some RTAs I have had to pick up the pieces of severed limbs, deal with truly horrible burns, open head injuries, disfiguring facial injuries and life threatening abdominal injuries, some of which could have been avoided had the victim been wearing a seatbelt. I have even had to scrape brain tissue from my uniform before I would place it in our washing machine at home.

I have never understood why people reject wearing a seatbelt. It makes no sense. I have seen adults and children seriously injured because they didn't put the belt on. One incident involved a car hitting a wall. The driver (wearing a seatbelt) survived; the front seat passenger (not wearing a seatbelt) went through the windscreen and died, with their body lying across the bonnet of the vehicle.

Because of the potential for serious injury, ambulances always respond to RTAs as a full emergency, making haste to the scene, ignorant at that moment as to the exactness of the accident details; sure only of the potential for serious injury.

It would not be the first time that I arrived at the scene of an accident in a crescendo of noise with blue lights flashing, headlights full on, only to find that our ambulance was not required (VNR). People near to the incident looking perplexed because of the high profile of our arrival. Wondering why 'on earth' we had arrived making such a noise, seemingly in such a fuss.

'After all there is no-one hurt,' I have heard them remark, sarcastically.

Ambulance crews will not usually be fully aware of the full and accurate nature of the incident until they actually reach the scene. Only then will they have the opportunity to make an accurate assessment and evaluation of the situation for themselves.

The caller who makes the initial 999 call may very well have been a witness, but it is unlikely that they will made a thorough check of the incident, with regard to severity and number of injuries before they called for the ambulance. For instance a caller will request an emergency ambulance to attend an accident, but when that ambulance does arrive, the paramedic may request additional ambulances or fire service attendance. This may be due not just to the number of casualties, but also to the seriousness and nature of injuries.

If a paramedic arriving at the scene of an accident finds, for instance three casualties, two with minor injuries and one with a more serious injury, then he will require more ambulance help for the other patients; en-route to hospital he will be unable to deal adequately with more than one serious casualty at a time.

Motor Vehicles:

I was, working with Brian when we received our first emergency call of the day. It was 08:30 on a bright summer morning when the call to attend a two vehicle RTA at a busy road junction, a few miles away from our station. With such sparse information it was impossible to predict what we may find at the scene.

Less than 30 seconds later, we left the station, making our

way through the busy morning rush-hour traffic in our usual emergency manner. Blue flashing lights, intermittent flashing headlights and horns blaring we commanded the road.

Five minutes later we were faced with a long line of stationery traffic which was obviously caused by the accident we were attending, so it became necessary to travel the last quarter of a mile on the wrong side of the road. The accident was in the middle of a busy road junction at the foot of a hill.

Even before our ambulance came to a standstill I could see a mini-bus in the middle of the road, with a car 'head on' into it. As Brian and I stepped out of the ambulance we each, automatically, went our separate ways, one to each vehicle.

I went to the car which was nearest to me and quickly established that there were two elderly casualties inside. One, a woman in the front passenger seat (the most dangerous seat in a car) had sustained a fractured knee along with chest injuries, which were giving her some problems with her breathing. The driver (her gentleman friend) complained of severe chest pain and his face was pale, cold and showing signs of cyanosis (blue). He too was having difficulty breathing and was looking very poorly and looked as though he had possibly suffered a form of cardiac event.

Less than a minute later I was re-joined by Brian who informed me that there were multiple casualties (six in all) in the minibus, three of whom would need stretchers. One male casualty was unconscious with an open wound to his head, two people had severe lacerations to both knees (one of whom looked likely to faint due to his state of shock) and the driver who was complaining of neck pains, possibly a whiplash injury. Brian had managed to get someone to look after the unconscious man whilst he was briefing me.

With the two serious casualties in the car we had a total of six casualties all of whom would require a stretcher.

Leaving Brian with my two casualties I quickly returned to my ambulance and called ambulance control to 'make vehicles six'. The total made up of a further five more ambulances plus our own.

Then grabbing my paramedic case along with drugs, from the security locker in the vehicle I returned quickly to the car and set about dealing with the car driver, who had suffered some cardiac emergency and his elderly woman passenger, with chest injuries. Brian, meanwhile, returned to the mini-bus; I was confident that he would be ok with his triage and treatment of his casualties until other ambulances arrived on scene.

At that time of morning, ambulance control would have some difficulty mustering an extra five ambulances but we had little choice if we were to give the maximum beneficial treatment to each of our patients. Two of whom had conditions from which they could die.

On occasions such as these, when there are a number of casualties we are glad to be able to use the help of the 'man in the street' and that is what we did here. Indeed, on this occasion, we were lucky for a nurse came out of the nearby factory with one of her first-aider's; she was able to deal with a couple of the less seriously injured until reinforcements could, make their way through the traffic chaos and, arrive to help us.

All credit to The Merseyside Ambulance Service, for we soon had on scene the other five ambulances, and paramedics that I had requested, as well as a senior ambulance officer (duty manager they call them now). All patients were being attended to and were soon being evacuated from the scene with expert pre-hospital care.

A short time later as I was clearing up at the hospital the duty manager pulled me to one side for a 'quiet word'. He himself was not para medically qualified but seemed somewhat upset that I had requested so many ambulances at such a busy time of the day. His attitude seemed to suggest that I had over reacted in my request for another five ambulances. Thankfully I was judged to have made the right decision by others more qualified than him, namely my paramedic peers. The technicians and paramedics who had attended the incident thought that it was *he* who was out of step.

As one paramedic quipped, 'He's probably narked because they (control) had to call in ambulances from Liverpool'. 'It serves them right, for cutting the service', another piped in.

At the time the service was going through some changes in relation to ambulance 're-deployment' (management jargon) for cuts in service.

Sadly the heart attack victim died in hospital one week later. It also transpired that it was his vehicle that had actually caused the accident when he suffered the acute chest pain causing him to lose control of his car.

Sometimes what you see is not always what it may seem to be.

Receiving a call to a serious road accident, sent me and Brian racing to a location that didn't quite fit in with our knowledge of the area. The location, which we, both, knew well, was a small cul-de-sac about 25 meters in length, in a very quiet part of town.

Arriving at the scene and turning into the cul-de-sac we were faced with a stationary car at right angles across the roadway. On approaching the car I could see only the legs of a man sticking out from under the front, his head and shoulders hidden under the vehicle. A couple of yards away, was a bicycle lying in the roadway.

Initially I got down on my belly and crawled under the car to make a quick assessment as to his condition and vital signs and to establish if we could get him out, move the car or call fire service to lift the vehicle off him.

My quick and close examination established that he was not *actually* trapped beneath the car but lying under it. However it was obvious that he was seriously ill for he was having great difficulty breathing and he was turning blue in colour.

With the help of a few bystanders I had the vehicle pushed back off the man's body so that I could assist him and examine him further. In the meantime Brian had returned to our ambulance and called ambulance control, requesting police attendance with the message, 'confirming pedestrian RTA.'

With the car now clear out of the way I was able to deal with the man's breathing problem by giving him a high rate of Oxygen whilst Brian carried out a quick but thorough body check looking for any sign of injury.

We found no immediate signs of injury caused by the car, but anyway the old man was deteriorating so fast that we decided to quickly load him into the ambulance and make a dash to the hospital, carrying out life support en route.

Two police motorcyclists and Range Rover arrived on scene just as we were loading our patient on board. I left Brian to speak with them whilst I set up the ECG monitor and an intravenous line in case I needed to administer drugs on way to hospital.

Suddenly the old man went into a cardiac arrest. I called out to Brian who dived back into the ambulance to assist. I already had an intravenous line set up and inserted into a vein in the old man's arm, this would allow me to administer life-saving drugs. I turned to grab the defibrillator paddles whilst Brian ran a pair of heavy duty scissors up the front of the man's clothing, baring his chest ready for me to administer a powerful electric charge to his heart.

After two or three shocks and a number of drugs we managed to restart his heart. 'Right', I said 'let's get going...fast...but steady on the corners!'. Brian jumped out and made sure the ambulance doors were securely closed. I braced myself in such a position that I was able to continue with cardiac compressions whilst we travelled to the hospital, helped by the two police motorcyclists providing a very fast escort.

We were soon arriving at the hospital with our patient still in cardiac distress, yet no outward sign of injury, no bruising, no swelling, nothing. I concluded that he had in fact had a heart attack without suffering any injury at all. But I wondered why the car had been on top of him and his bicycle?

Sadly our success in restarting his heart were short lived, for the old chap died in hospital the next day without regaining consciousness.

The police investigating the accident concluded that the incident was not after all an RTA. From witness statements it was established that the old man had suffered his heart attack whilst riding his bicycle and had fallen in front of a slow moving car, which had been turning from a side entrance onto the street. The driver had stopped the car and jumped out to help the old man. Unfortunately in the panic the driver had not engaged the hand-brake and so the car simply rolled forward over the prone body of the man, without actually touching him but for all intents, making it look like an RTA.

At all road traffic accidents where injury is sustained the police are obliged to attend to deal with investigation of the incident. For that reason, whenever receiving RTA emergency calls the ambulance control officer will automatically inform the police of the incident so that they too can attend. More often than not the ambulance will be in attendance well before the arrival of the police. However, there is the odd occasion when they 'make the scene' before us.

On one such occasion in particular the police had arrived at the scene of an accident almost as it happened and as such they were in a unique position to witness the stupidity and arrogance of one particular car driver who was creating problems for the emergency ambulance.

Ambulance control informed us via our radio that two cars had crashed into the central barrier on the motorway and were now blocking the outside lane. The police were already on scene and reported that one of the drivers was injured; they were laying out cones around the accident and motorway signs were imposing a thirty miles per hour speed limit.

With the information coming from police actually on scene, I knew that the details that we had been given about the accident would be accurate.

On this occasion I was in the driving seat as I entered onto the M53 and automatically entered onto the outside lane, noticing as I did so, that the speed restriction signs were already showing 30mph (but obviously not for us). Accelerating quickly I deliberately positioned my ambulance so that we straddled the white line between the middle and outer lane, thus hoping (in vain) to indicate to those driver's behind, not to overtake me. I was travelling above the national speed limit (70mph) with my blue flashing lights and horns and klaxons switched on.

Knowing that the accident was in the outside lane about a couple of miles mile ahead, it was essential that no-one should pass me at this stage.

However, some idiot driver had other ideas (as many often do) he wanted to overtake me. Ignoring the speed restriction signs and even at this high speed he drove his red Sierra dangerously close to the back of our ambulance, tailgating as if to get me to move over to make way for him. He made a number of attempts to overtake me, trying to pass down the off-side between the ambulance and central barriers.

Realising that I would not move over to allow his dangerous manoeuvre, he then moved across to my near-side and tried to force his car between me and the traffic in the inside lane; in so doing he almost caused another accident. Again he swerved across and back to the outside lane. Now he was really angry! He began flashing his headlights furiously trying to intimidate me to move over.

By now I was needing to concentrate on his foolhardy antics, as well as having to gauge my safe approach to the accident blocking the lane ahead. He continued with these crazy antics for a couple of miles, causing me some distraction from my main purpose. Somehow he was so stupid or arrogant that he was not going to give up his attempt to overtake an emergency ambulance.

What happened next, gave those of us who witnessed it, a smug sense of satisfaction and; and even if I say so myself, my timing was impeccable.

By now we were approaching the scene I could see the accident about half a mile ahead, two cars completely blocking the inside lane, just where the red Sierra driver wanted to go. I could see also that that the police were on scene and watching our approach, and presumably the idiot driver behind me.

As I slowed down and moved over across into the middle lane (no longer straddling the white line) the Sierra driver seized his opportunity and accelerated from behind me and into the outside lane. Roaring up alongside of me, he took the time to glare at me and give a two fingered salute...before suddenly he saw the accident in the lane ahead of him.

Now the idiot realised he could be in trouble. He began to rapidly decelerate hoping to drop back behind me again, but to no avail. I took the opportunity to synchronise my breaking with his so that he was unable to slow quickly enough to pull in behind and was now trapped in the outside lane, between me and the central barrier, where he had been so eager to be.

To those witnessing, it was like manna from heaven as I calmly drove in the middle lane right up to the accident before stopping, with him now trapped, embarrassingly, alongside our ambulance. As I alighted from my ambulance I grinned at him scowling at me, for I could see that behind him was another police car which had been following us up the motorway, videoing his high speed antics as he tried to bully me out of his way.

My crewmate and I dealt with a minor injured patient from the crashed car, and left the scene for the hospital. A few weeks later, I learned from one of the police officers dealing with the accident, red Sierra driver had been fined heavily and banned from driving for his dangerous driving.

I have often been amazed at the sheer bloody-minded arrogance of some drivers who will not give way to emergency ambulances (I bet the police don't suffer this problem). I have travelled at high speed (above the national limit) only to have some driver refuse to give way or alternatively trying to overtake me. Believe me these idiots are still out there and many of them seem to drive white vans or some posh fast cars. (Before anyone complains, I should point out that I too own quite a fast car...I just don't race ambulances or fire engines).

Alcohol: It is a sad fact that despite our 'Drink Driving Laws' most RTAs occurring in the evening and early hours of the morning will probably have an element of alcohol or drug use by the driver.

Personally I have no time for drunk drivers! Over the years I have dealt with the innocent victims of these selfish morons, but also with their own, well-deserved, injuries. I sometimes took a perverse pleasure by reminding them that their insurance would not pay out if they were over the alcohol limit.

Christmas is a busy time of year not just for road accidents but also incidents involving alcohol, drugs and violence?

The next incident had them all. It was a couple of days before Christmas, about 02:00 on a windy and bitterly cold night, when Brian and I found ourselves responding to an RTA on the seafront at New Brighton.

The accident was on an unlit and isolated section of road. Well away from all the clubs and night-life. In the summer this particular section of road is, occasionally, used for motor cycle and car rally racing. Consequently we do get 'boy racers' driving well above the speed limit and well above their personal driving ability on this race-track type surface.

There was a strong high tide running on the river Mersey at the time; huge waves were crashing against the sea-wall sending plumes of freezing cold spray up into the air which was then blowing across the roadway and reducing visibility even further.

As we approached the scene we could just make out the shape of a black car which had overturned and come to rest on its roof.

The area was deserted except for the lone driver of another car; he had witnessed the accident and stopped to try to offer help. Having called 999 he then stood well back, away from the overturned, fearing that 'it may explode or go up in flames due to the fact that petrol was pouring from damaged fuel tank'.

Brian quickly returned to the ambulance to request the attendance of the fire service, whilst I approached the overturned vehicle. By the headlights from our ambulance, I could see that the roof had collapsed inwards on impact, with most of the side windows shattered. There was a substantial amount of petrol all around the vehicle. Peering through a broken side-window, I shone my torch and shouted to anyone inside.

From within came the muffled reply of a man who said that he was stuck and couldn't get out. I soon established that he was alone in the vehicle, but was trapped between the seat and crushed roof of the car and unable to get out.

I knew that it could be another ten minutes before the fire service arrived, in which time there was a very serious risk of a fire or explosion if a spark were to ignite the petrol.

Making a calculated decision I got down on my belly and eased my head and shoulders through the broken side windows, just enough to reach the driver who was trapped upside down and twisted in an awkward position between one of the seats and the roof.

Due to the high personal risk, I kept both my legs well out of the vehicle with strict instructions to Brian to drag me out if the petrol caught fire, thus leaving the trapped victim to his own fate.

Having got the top half of my body through window and using my torch to try to find the seatbelt clip, I was literally face to face with this guy. There was a very strong smell of alcohol on his breath and his demeanour was aggressive. Suddenly he tried to punch me, effing and blinding at me even as I tried to calm him down; making it difficult for me to help him. It occurred to me that he may be drunk but equally he may have some injury that is causing him to be aggressive. Struggling in an up-turned car is difficult at any time but with a violent casualty it was frightening. If this car did catch fire I reasoned that he would probably grab hold of me in panic. I shouted to Brian to pull me out, I had done my best. The man would have to wait for the fire service to rescue him.

Fortunately, they appeared almost as I was being pulled free by Brian. The traffic police arrived just as the crash victim was being released from the damaged car.

We placed the crash victim into the ambulance before giving him a thorough examination, throughout which he was belligerent and aggressive. Remarkably he had not suffered any injuries. He was then arrested by the police, when it proved, after a breath test that he was well and truly over the alcohol limit.

Brian and I booked 'off air' so that we could go back to base to clean ourselves up.

It was a Friday evening, and I was on a night duty from 18:00 to 06:00 (12 hours) working out of the very busy Birkenhead station. My crewmate for the night was Julian, a very keen trainee paramedic who was with me for assessment.

As usual, Julian arrived on duty in a happy and enthusiastic mood, ever willing to project the best image of the ambulance service. Together we set about our routine vehicle and equipment check, making sure all medical gas cylinders were full, electronics functioning, medical hardware stowed securely and drugs in date. Once we had finished, we retired to the mess for a coffee.

'Right Dale', he said laughing and wringing his hands as if in anticipation 'what do you think we'll get tonight'? 'Friday night, Birkenhead town centre?' I thought aloud. 'It's a nice evening, end of the month so everyone's been paid. We could be busy' I replied.

'Well let's hope it's something interesting' he went on. 'Friday night in Birkenhead is bound to throw up a few good jobs.'

He was right. Birkenhead is a medium sized town of about a quarter of a million people; many of whom live in the outlying housing estates.

Typical of many other towns around the UK, the town centre there is a wealth of so called 'Fun Pubs' (in some cases, the 'fun' being a misnomer). As well as the pubs there are a number of nightclubs catering for the thousands of young people who travel into the town centre for an evening's entertainment. There are also a substantial amount of fast food outlets which stay open until the early hours of the morning. Put this all together and we have a recipe for fun and frolic. But all too often it becomes pandemonium, with hooliganism ruling the streets for a while.

This whole night-time scene provides a 'buzz' for the new ambulance paramedics when they are called upon to respond to the varied and sometimes violent incidents within this field. Tonight Julian was looking forward to his shift at Birkenhead.

We just managed to enjoy a cup of tea before our first emergency call of the night, came in. It was just 18:30 when we left the station and set off through the busy town centre, blue flashing lights flashing horns and klaxons sounding terrifyingly loud as we pass through the early evening traffic. Another Friday night was under way!

As it would turn out, it would be a few hours before we would get back to the station for a meal break. We were back and forth to hospital all evening with various emergency admissions. We did manage to grab a quick cup of coffee in between calls, whilst at the hospital.

It was approaching midnight, when having booked 'clear' at the hospital we were given permission, by ambulance control, to return to station for a meal–break.

The distance to our station was about five miles, so we wasted no time returning, for we knew that if another emergency call came in whilst we were still mobile (on the road) then control would pass the job to us and we would have to forego our meal break.

Our route back to base took us to a fork in the road, either direction leading to our station, I took the left fork. Two minutes later, and just seconds from the station, our ambulance emergency bleeper sounded signalling an incoming emergency call.

'There goes our meal-break' I thought, as Julian began to take the message details from control. I listened intently as the emergency message was transmitted; Julian busy writing down details. 'Emergency call to RTA outside No.74 Stoneglint Avenue' The ambulance controller continued, 'we are getting several calls of people trapped and car on fire' he went. 'Give me a first report ASAP, time 23.58hrs' (two minutes to midnight).'

I switched on our blue flashing lights and threw the switch to sound our klaxons, as I began a tight 'U' turn in the town centre, by now very busy with club revellers and night-time traffic, and headed back in the direction from whence we had come. En route, we received a second message from control, to the effect that they had received more calls to the accident; it sounded like this would be a 'bad job'.

'Thank God I have a good man with me' I thought to myself. Julian was very keen and already a well-liked trainee paramedic. He was showing signs of heightened awareness and seemed exhilarated at the prospect of dealing with such a serious accident. His Saturday night was about to deliver on the 'Richter Scale' of Excitement.

I knew that Julian was likely to be facing one of his most serious jobs; and one that (if reports were true) would tax us both, for that reason I gave him hurried specific instructions to stick by me no matter what and to listen and follow my instructions precisely.

Because of the reported seriousness of the accident, and the chance of fire at the scene, I kept the sirens and warblers switched on, knowing that people at the scene would hear us coming, and as such reduce their acute anxiety. Foot hard down on the accelerator I drove back to the fork in the road that we had passed only a few minutes. Reaching the fork in the road, I swung the ambulance hard left into the long winding road, and slowed my approach so as not to run into the accident myself. Rounding a sharp bend, our headlights illuminated a scene of carnage.

The whole area was poorly illuminated due to crash damage to street lamps and the road was made narrower with parked cars all down one side. Lying across the middle of the road, at right angles to the pavement, was the wreckage of a car with a small fire burning in the engine compartment and a man, who looked unconscious from my view, hanging head down out of the front passenger door with what appeared to be other serious injuries. I stopped the ambulance momentarily to let Julian jump out to attend to that casualty, telling him that I would arrange backup for him.

I could also see that about fifty yards further down on the opposite side of the road was the wreckage of another car smashed into a tree and surrounded by a crowd of people, plus there seemed to be a number of bodies lying in the roadway too.

I quickly grabbed the radio hand-set from its holder and called ambulance control asking them to send another ambulance as this incident appeared to be 'serious RTA', I also reminded them that I would be sending a ‘First Report’ when I had done a thorough recce of the scene. The time was 23.59 (about one minute after we had first received the call, in the ambulance).

Driving down to the second area of the incident I stopped and made my way immediately to two young women lying several yards apart; having been thrown out of one of the cars during the crash, they were being comforted by people who had come out from the nearby houses. Both women were conscious, and I established that they both appeared to have multiple serious injuries. I had no choice at this moment, other than to continue with a vital recognisance of the whole accident site; I, therefore, left them with their unknown guardians, along with clear instructions for the girls not to be moved.

Turning my attention to the other site of the incident, I made my way across to the car which had crashed into a large tree. There was a group of people milling around and trying to pull the doors open. I had some difficulty making myself heard with all the shouting going on. In the end I just bent down low and pushed between everyone there so that I was able to get limited access to the car driver.

I could see that a middle aged woman (the driver) was on her own in the car and had sustained serious head and leg injuries. She was trapped firmly by the steering wheel into her chest, with her legs trapped by the tangled wreckage. I knew that we were going to need the expertise of the fire service in order to extricate her safely. From my experience I could also reason that she was likely to remain trapped for some considerable time and, therefore, I would request the attendance of the Hospital Emergency Medical Aid Team (HEMAT). They would give her life saving treatment on the scene during, what may be a long extrication process.

My mind was still on Julian and his casualty and I hoped he was coping with, what had looked like complex injuries; indeed I knew, in a macabre way, that he would be relishing his part in this very serious incident.

I had been on scene for less than two minutes (it was now one minute after midnight) when I ran back to our ambulance and transmitted the following message to ambulance control.

'322, (my ambulance call sign) to ambulance control. First report. I am acting as 'incident officer' for serious RTA. Two cars involved. Please make ambulances five, and request attendance of the fire service, police and HEMAT. We have four casualties, all multi traumas. One unconscious, head injury. Two females lower limb injury and one entrapment.'

Having transmitted the vital 'first report', I briefly

checked on Julian with his casualty. As I expected, he was doing well, administering oxygen and treating the injuries of his patient. I informed him that I was 'Incident Officer' and that his casualty would be first to be evacuated as soon as another ambulance arrived. [4]

I left him to carry on whilst I returned to the centre of the accident site and set about organising the people around who were offering to help.

One lady approached and told me that she was a retired nurse so I knew she would know what to do with the ambulance dressings that I handed to her. I directed her to take charge of the injured driver, trapped in the wrecked car until such time that the fire service and HEMAT arrived to take over. A man and his wife from a nearby house offered to help, so I sent the man back to our ambulance to fetch blankets whilst I introduced his wife to the two young women lying injured in the road, reassuring them that more help was on its way.

Everywhere was bedlam, with people shouting and crying. A policeman arrived at my side and grabbed my arm, interrupting my examination of the young women. 'Hello, can I help what do you want me to do?' he asked eagerly. Informing him of the imminent arrival of another three ambulances, the fire service and HEMAT, I asked him to arrange for more police assistance, to provide escorts to hospital, and to close roads off to oncoming traffic.

In the distance I could hear the reassuring sound of sirens making their way to us. First to arrive was the fire service followed very quickly by the first paramedic; together they would work to treat and free the woman trapped in the car. A few moments later HEMAT arrived with their team of doctors and nurses. Now I was able to take stock of the overall situation. Looking around I could see that the trapped woman was surrounded by paramedics, doctors, nurses, and firemen. All working together, illuminated under brilliant arc lights, and surrounded by a crescendo of noise from cutting gear and generators.

More police were arriving on scene, one of the policemen waving an ambulance through the road block that he had set up; the blue flashing lights, a welcome sight. I recognised the ambulance crew as they approached me for instructions; Davy, a paramedic and his crewmate, Geoff, a highly qualified ambulance technician.

I asked them to take over from Julian and to send him back to me; I would need his assistance with the two injured women lying here in the road.

Both young women had been covered in blankets and were still being comforted by the husband and wife couple when I tasked Julian, who had just re-joined me, to take over their care. Speaking calmly and reassuring them that they would be all right, I asked their names and ages, whilst at the same time taking note of their responses to questions. I was particularly concerned more about one of the girls, because she was in shock and showing slow response to my questions her levels of consciousness seemed to be deteriorating and she appeared to have internal bleeding. I decided that she would be the next casualty to be evacuated from the scene. Her friend, though badly injured, was complaining a lot with pain in her legs, which did, indeed, look as though they were both fractured (broken) Pain in some circumstances is a good thing. It indicates that you are alive!

It was not long before another paramedic team took over the care of the quiet young woman from Julian so that he then turned his attention to the young woman with the fractured legs.

The whole incident was in full swing, having taken only about twelve minutes to fully implement.

Davy and Geoff (the first of the extra crews to arrive on scene) were already leaving the scene with their casualty; along with police motorcycle outriders to escort them to the hospital, three miles away.

My task had been to bring it all together, and to co-ordinate the different services on site. All the pieces of this dramatic jigsaw had been put in place in the space of just 12 minutes, an achievement that the service could be proud of!

By now I was the last available paramedic on the scene, the others all being too busy or en route to hospital with other casualties. Now I was able to assist Julian with his casualty.

The young woman's injuries included two fractured femurs. As such she was in a lot of pain as well as severe shock from blood loss. Our pain killing gas, Entonox, seemed inadequate in relieving her pain we would need to immobilise her broken legs before getting her on a scoop stretcher and moving her. It was apparent that I would need to put a line in to her vein in order to give her drugs and fluids.

Unfortunately, where she lay was away from the arc lights of the fire service; in an area of relative darkness. This made it difficult for me to see to find a decent vein in her arms. Eventually, with Julian holding a torch, I was able to find a vein and insert a cannula (hollow needle). We set up a fluid drip and were fortunately joined by a one of the doctors from HEMAT who attempted to ease her pain with drugs, but to no avail. He then made a decision to anaesthetise her fully before we could immobilise her injuries and remove her to hospital.

Amazingly, some weeks later, I read in the local newspaper that one of the young women had actually gone into the local fire station to thank the firemen for their help that night! To my knowledge no firemen even saw this young woman, but it seems that none of them thought to enlighten her, preferring instead to be photographed, with her, for the local press. If she reads this, she will now know the truth.

Motorcycle Accidents:

The problem with motorcycles is that there is nowhere to put an ashtray, consequently, one day I found myself dealing with a young motorcyclist who had fallen off his machine and broken his leg after his lighted cigarette (which he was smoking as he rode along) had blown from his mouth and lodged inside his crash helmet, causing him to lose control and crash.

Another problem with motorcycles is that they offer little or no protection against injury to either the rider or pillion passenger. Once a motorcycle becomes unstable, it is virtually impossible for the rider to recover control and avoid parting company with the machine. Anyone falling off a moving motorcycle is immediately in danger of very serious injury or death in the worst cases. The faster the motorcycle is travelling the faster and further the dislodged rider will travel toward his destiny.

Without doubt it was the motorcycle rider/passenger that presented to me some of the most hideous injuries with which I had to deal. Dare I say it was mostly young men! Speed was the major factor in many of these serious injury accidents. I dealt with riders who had come off their motorcycles at speed and been thrown high into the air before landing head first onto the road (a crash helmet is of little use in such situations) Another rider was thrown through a shop window, injuring shoppers within. I have had to attend to young men who had crashed their prized motorcycle before they themselves had been projected at great speed into the wall of some building, sustaining serious injury.

In some cases the dead ones were the lucky ones, such was their injury. Many motorcycle casualties suffer leg injuries, which in many cases may require several operations in an attempt to repair the damage. Some unfortunate victims suffer such injury that they may be crippled for life.

The scene of one such serious motorcycle accident turned out to be a nightmare for two witnesses of the incident. After hearing the initial impact of a motorcycle crashing into a car, they had seen the rider fly high through the air before his body slammed into a brick wall, falling into a lifeless heap on the roadside.

Running across the road to join other people gathering around the unconscious rider, the couple soon realised that the victim was their own son! They were distraught with grief, unable to offer any help to their precious offspring they could only await the arrival of the ambulance.

Upon my arrival at the scene I found that the young man was unconscious and appeared to have broken his pelvis and both legs, one of which was behind him with his foot at the level of his shoulder. Amazingly the young man recovered over a period of many months.

When I visited him in the hospital ward he seemed to take a somewhat immature macho approach to his accident. Grinning to me and a couple of his friends he recounted the details of his accident and subsequent operations. He failed to comprehend the tremendous impact upon his parents as he boasted that he would soon be back on a bike. No doubt his parents suffered longer with emotional and psychological anxiety.

On one approach onto the M53 there is an entrance link with a very severe bend leading onto the motorway. This particular bend has a low maximum speed limit which is all too often ignored. One motorcyclist travelling around this bend, lost control of his bike and slammed into the steel barrier at considerable speed. Such was the effect that he was thrown many yards over the barrier into thick shrubbery and almost out of sight of anyone from the carriageway.

Upon our arrival on scene, my crewmate and I had to scramble slipping and sliding, down an embankment thick with shrubbery and brambles to reach him. His main injury was to the leg that had been in contact with the steel barrier. Wearing a pair of jeans, as opposed to leather trousers, offered no protection and as such he had a wide open leg injury which had caused considerable blood loss. Struggling to maintain my foothold on this uneven surface I lost my balance and slipped backwards with my hand falling onto some brambles and a sharp piece of wood.

Lifting my arm from the brambles and looking at the piece of wood, I realised that it was in fact a section of his tibia about fifteen centimetres long. How fortunate...for him that I should fall and find that piece of bone.

Taking it with us to hospital, surgeons were able to replace it and so greatly aid his recovery.

◆ ◆ ◆

6 INDUSTRIAL ACCIDENTS

Accidents only happen to other people! At least that's what the great majority of the population prefers to think. Unfortunately the opening statement is not true. Accidents can, and will happen to everyone, at some point in their life. Everyone reading this book will have had an accident of some kind at some time, even if it was only a minor knock on the head or a cut finger, in your own home. Indeed, your home is potentially the most dangerous place of all; presenting a wide and varied range of hazards - not just to you and your family - but also to people visiting your property.

However it is within the workplace that many people receive injury, serious enough to hospitalise them. The more serious the injury, the more likely it is that your boss won't take you to hospital in his car, instead an ambulance will be called and a paramedic will respond.

If your home can be a hazardous area then so too can your place of work, and so it's true to say that no industry is completely safe; which is why we have 'factory inspectors'.

Most people go to work each day never expecting the unexpected; never contemplating that they will be involved in some work- related accident which will either change their life completely - or end it!

Having dealt with all manner of 'industrial' accidents, in various types of industry, over the years I became accustomed to dealing with horrific injuries and sometimes fatalities. Not only did I deal with injuries, but very often I was involved, jointly, in the rescue and extrication of many of the trapped victims, working in tandem with the fire service.

Generally, being 'first on scene' placed an obligation upon the paramedic, not only to provide emergency care, but also to organise and co-ordinate the rescue of an injured casualty. On rare occasions this did necessitate my involving members of the public. But more often than not, I would request the expert services of the fire service.

Dealing with any rescue situations can be dangerous. The inexperienced or untrained person will not notice or be aware of potential dangers and may 'rush in; possibly exacerbating the situation and may, themselves even become another victim.

As with all paramedics, it became a necessary second nature to 'think on my feet' when dealing with someone injured and trapped in or by some machinery. I would do my absolute best for the injured patient, applying all my skills to relieve their, pain, anxiety and suffering; ready to act instinctively to any life-threatening changes in their medical condition.

Due to the number of patients that I dealt with, it was impossible to dwell too often upon every accident victim and the problems that they and their families may later experience.

Delivering the accident victim to hospital was usually the end of the matter for me, except for the usual post-accident discussion with my crewmate. Every paramedic and ambulance technician will take time, after a particularly interesting event, to question his or her handling of the incident. We were never complacent with our endeavours; always looking to improve...for the next time...always looking to perfect our level of pre-hospital care.

Of the many factories within our area, there was one which was the cause of many (more than average) calls upon the emergency ambulance service.

The factory, small by comparison to many in the area, dealt with the construction and maintenance of heavy plant and machinery; as such you would be unrealistic not to expect the occasional accident.

However, my colleagues and I attended to so many emergency calls at this particular factory that the place gained certain notoriety amongst the ambulance staff.

On my first ever call to this factory I entered the premises with the usual ambulanceman's caution, watching out for signs of danger to myself or to bystanders. I was so busy watching that

I didn't hit my head on several heavy steel objects which were, either suspended or protruding dangerously, at head height around the factory, that I walked into a piece of steel plate which was sticking out across the walkway, at ankle height! Suddenly I experienced a searing pain as my ankle caught the sharp corner of the metal. No serious damage was done, but I cursed to myself as I clutched my ankle and rubbing it to ease the pain, before hobbling over to the casualty nearby.

The casualty, a young man, was lying on the floor clutching his ankle too. He seemed amused at the coincidence of my misfortune and that of his; for he too had struck his ankle on the very same sheet of steel plate; although his injury was more severe, enough to need hospital treatment.

Sometime later, at the same factory, the ambulance service attended to no fewer than five accidents in one week, at the rate of one a day, some of which resulted in serious injury to the victim.

About midway through this particular week, I responded to one of those calls at the factory. Upon arrival I jumped out of the ambulance and was met by several employees' (whose faces were now becoming familiar to me) directing me to the incident. Leaving my crewmate to negotiate the ambulance into a suitable parking position, I followed one of the workers into the factory, this time, taking great care for my own safety.

As I rounded a corner I was met with a middle-aged man lying face down on the ground. He had a very serious 'open' fractured skull, and was unconscious. Nearby was a large piece of heavy machinery suspended by chains from a mobile crane. The machinery was still swaying precariously about ten feet off the ground, whilst two men were arguing over whether to move it or not.

It was pointed out to me, that as the crane was manoeuvring about, one of the chains had come adrift from the machine with such a force, that it had whipped down with ferocious speed hitting this unfortunate worker on the back of the head, inflicting very serious injury (a case for the factory inspector and the police to attend immediately!). I noticed that none of the workers were wearing hard-hats; come to think of it *neither was I*! This would be something that I would have to deal with back at base.

With my crewmate by my side and we set about dealing with the seriously injured casualty. Time was of the essence - for in those days we did not have paramedic skills and our patient needed expert 'advanced' life support.

Whilst still dealing with the casualty I instructed the other workers not to move the machinery. They should stay clear of the overhanging machinery, cordon it off and await the arrival of the police and factory inspector - this being normal protocol in such serious factory accidents.

I encountered objections to my instruction from only one particular worker, namely, the foreman; who totally ignored me. Instead he issued his own instructions, to the men working there, to move the machinery, regardless of any danger that it may impose upon them. I informed him, firmly and in front of his colleagues, that moving it was tantamount to interfering with evidence.

As we left the scene a few minutes later, I saw that he had persuaded someone to move the offending object before any investigation could take place

The patient did recover but only after many weeks in hospital; whether or not he ever received proper compensation I do not know.

A short time later the company closed down. In my view not before time, for it seemed only to be a matter of time before someone died working there.

On a similar occasion, a factory director interfered in such a way as to place myself, my crewmate, Alan, and an injured casualty in danger of serious injury, later resulting in a huge fine for his company.

Responding to a 999 call for someone trapped in machinery, sent us speeding to a local factory where, upon arrival, we were met by a large group of workers congregated outside the factory gate. Usually the presence of such a large crowd is indicative of a serious incident, and so my crewmate and I were, in some small way, pre-warned.

Alan went ahead to deal with the casualty, escorted into the factory by one of the workers, whilst I positioned the ambulance ready for a safe evacuation of the premises before following after him. Moments later, I quickly followed and found Alan in a heated debate with three smartly dressed men who were, apparently preventing him from approaching the casualty; a young man crouched upon a long rubber conveyor belt.

The young man's arm had been pulled into the mechanism of a second, identical conveyor belt which ran overhead and parallel with the one on which he was on. He was firmly trapped with obvious serious arm injuries and a significant amount of blood loss, in shock and yelling and cursing, clearly in pain. These three men in smart suits (part of the management) were more concerned with protecting the rubber conveyor belt than they were about the welfare of the injured man.

Although unqualified to do so, one of them had been attempting to undo some of the bolts of the upper mechanism which in turn was causing more fear and pain to the casualty.

I was astounded to learn that Alan, who was still in his probationary period - and as such lacked authoritative experience, had been told to stand to one side, while they attempted to dismantle the mechanism. This situation was totally unacceptable!

'Excuse me please', I said, firmly as I pushed passed them to make my way to the casualty. Their response was to tell me too, stand out of the way and wait! 'I will do no such thing' I replied angrily.

'You lot get out of *my way* now! Let me see the casualty' and pushing roughly between them I climbed up on to the belt beside the injured man. Alan took the hint and jumped up to join me.

The injured man was crying in pain, his arm looked crushed and broken. His arm was trapped between two heavy steel rollers of the overhead conveyor belt, which was about one and a half metres above our heads. It was obvious that we could not remove the damaged arm from the machinery without professional help.

I climbed onto the belt and crouched beside the young man and arranged to stay with him and to administer Entonox (pain killing gas) whilst Alan returned to the ambulance to call for rescue assistance from the experts - the fire service.

Meanwhile the group of managers had held an impromptu meeting, before approaching me in a manner that was probably normally reserved for their own work-force.

'This is our factory and you are on our premises, we are going to dismantle this belt ourselves' I was told arrogantly.

Before I could do anything else, two of them, clutching big spanners, proceeded to undo part of the roller mechanism, despite my protestations and demands to stop, they continued unbolting the roller which was just above my head. Just as I suspected, something went wrong.

There was a loud clang and whole belt unit shuddered violently as they attempted to remove a large bolt from the roller. The heavy belt shifted as one side of the roller dropped crushing the man's arm even more. Their ill-conceived efforts, not only resulted in exacerbating the injury to the entrapped arm and causing more pain to the young man, but had now put me in danger too.

It was obvious to me that they were more concerned with preventing damage to the conveyor belt, than they were with preventing further damage to the arm of the young man.

Eventually, tired of their ignoring my instruction to stand clear, I actually physically pushed the managers away from belt; telling them all - in front of their employees, 'That's it. Get off this belt now, and stop what you are doing', I shouted at the bosses. Now it was my time to give the orders

Alan re-joined me, and between us we supported our casualty until the arrival of the fire service.

In the meantime we both had to endure verbal hostility

from the factory management team...despite the fact that I warned the director that I would be reporting him for impeding our treatment, and for putting my own safety in jeopardy.

Thankfully we were soon joined by the fire service. As the senior fire officer approached he witnessed the behaviour of the management and naturally asked me what was going on. I explained about the trouble and hindrance that I had encountered from this belligerent group. Their understandable anxiety about damage to the belt had caused them to interfere with a proper rescue of the casualty. Both conveyor belts ran the length of the factory and were essential to the daily routine of production.

Unfortunately due to the inappropriate action of the managers, the casualty's injury was worse and of more immediacy. The mechanism had now shifted so much that his arm was jammed to the point that I could not feel a pulse. There was now a danger of 'crush syndrome'[5] which could result in renal failure. The belt needed to be cut!

Within a couple of seconds a firefighter had cut the belt which in turn allowed the arm to be lifted free.

Why was he on the belt in the first place? Some said he had been larking about. Others staff admitted that it was an unofficial transport, practice for some employees to travel along the long belt from one end of the factory to the other.

The belt was off for some days whilst expensive repairs were carried out. Had the management team responded favourably towards me and my crewmate, taking our professional advice, then it is likely that the fire and rescue team could have had more time (given consideration of the casualty's condition) to dismantle the mechanism in manner that they the management would have appreciated.

The company were later prosecuted under the Health and Safety at Work Act and had to pay a hefty fine.

Fork lift trucks look like good fun to drive, but they can be dangerous if you are not careful. I know because over the years I have attended many accidents involving such vehicles, most of which could have been avoided with a little more care.

Responding one day to an emergency call to a local food processing factory, we arrived at the scene to be met at the main gate by a man, one of the workers, who directed us to the entrance of a large warehouse within an industrial park. 'What's happened...what's the problem?', I enquired from the worker.

'There's been an accident involving a forklift truck' he said.

I jumped out of the ambulance and put on a hard-hat before heading inside and leaving Dave, my crewmate, to park the ambulance before following on after me.

The warehouse was a large modern building with a high roof. Inside, there were many rows of floor to ceiling heavy duty steel shelving each of which ran along the entire length of the building. Each huge shelving unit was loaded with wooden pallets stacked with heavy boxes of dried fruit. I calculated that there must have been hundreds of tons in combined weight in each row of shelving.

As I reached the site I could see that, between two of these tall units, about half way down the aisle, there was a huge pile of pallets and packing cases, some of which had burst open and the contents of dried fruit spilled out. The whole unit was twisted so that the top was almost at ground level, whilst the far end was still up-right and intact. It put me in mind of a section of roller-coaster with its long sweeping curve down to ground level. In between the two extremes, the heavy pallets were still moving and depositing more and more heavy cases into the aisle.

A group of workers were standing well back out of the way whilst another small group were on top of the pile frantically pulling boxes and trying to remove the pallets from the top.

Upon seeing me, one of the men shouted. 'There's a forklift truck and the driver underneath this lot'.

My immediate assessment was that this was a very dangerous situation with a potential for more danger to me as well as those workers struggling to reach whoever was trapped beneath the pile.

As Dave arrived to join me, I asked him to request from ambulance control, another ambulance and the fire and rescue service, meanwhile returning to the pile of packing and ordered everyone off for safety sake. The would-be rescuers climbed down from the pile and stood back allowing me to make a proper assessment of the situation.

It was confirmed to me that trapped under the pile (which was estimated as weighing about ten tons) was one man *and* his forklift truck. Witnesses claimed that the truck had caught the top of the shelving units, causing it to twist and buckle, shedding its heavy load onto the poor unfortunate driver who was now some-where underneath.

From somewhere within the pile of cases the man was, desperately calling out for help. He was in severe pain and fearing for his life as the loads on the shelving continued to slip and fall.

Dave arrived back with the message that fire service were on the way. But we considered that there was a need for us to act immediately to help the victim.

Quickly but carefully so as not to dislodge any more cases we both scrambled to the top of the pile and looked over onto the other side. The pile was shaped a bit like a volcano, in so far, that there was a hollow in the centre where we could just make out the arm of the casualty sticking out from under some cases. All the time more boxes were falling onto the heap and we were alarmed at the fact that another full pallet of cases was hovering precariously above the casualty, and seemed almost ready to fall upon him...and now, us too!

As protocol demands, we must remove the patient out of immediate danger and to safety before we can attempt to treat any injuries. And so with instructions to the watching workforce to watch and, call out a warning if the pallet looked like it was moving, (and likely to fall onto us), Dave and I scrambled down into the centre of the pile. We were now able to remove a number of cases to one side and locate the driver still trapped, by his legs. Looking up, I could see that the pallet loaded with half a ton of dried fruit was still sticking out over the edge of the swaying and creaking shelving, threatening to fall upon us all at any moment.

Reaching down and grasping his outstretched arms Dave and I heaved him out of the cage and, unceremoniously, pulled him alongside us. He complained of severe pain in one of his legs. A quick glance told us that he had a badly broken ankle. He definitely could not climb out, but nor could we stay here.

Suddenly we heard the welcome sound of fire engines arriving outside the factory. Moments later, all three of us were being helped back out of the pile by several firemen, whilst others took hasty securing measures, with the pallet threatening to fall onto us at any minute!

Had more pallets fallen before the firemen arrived, then it is likely that the driver may have sustained further and more serious injury. For that reason, Dave and I had taken a calculated risk to get him out, rather than await rescue services.

In my day, paramedics didn't wait around; they generally did what it took to get the job done, even with some risk to themselves. It worked! I lived to tell the tail.

The fork-lift truck driver went to hospital and was released later, on crutches. He was lucky to get away with a relatively minor injury.

Ladders or scaffolding accounted for a substantial number of industrial accidents that I attended, most of which involved *professional* users and most were avoidable! Accidents involving window cleaners, builders, roofers, decorators and dare I say - a fireman - by far, outnumbered similar accidents by the average DIY enthusiast.

I once dealt with a seriously injured contractor, who had climbed a ladder against the advice of his workmates who, fearing that the ladder was unsafe, had refused to use it. The ladder *was* faulty and the unfortunate man suffered serious spinal injuries which confined him to life in a wheelchair.

Window cleaners don't have the time or inclination to 'tie ladder's off', hence I attended many such calls whereby the ladder had simply slid sideways and fallen; depositing the window cleaner in a heap on the pavement. I recall another occasion when a DIY enthusiast hired a scaffolding platform to carry out work on his house. Unfortunately the platform did not reach the height which he required and so he hoisted a ladder to the top of tower hoping that would give him the extra height. With the foot of the ladder resting on the platform of the tower, he set the top against a tall chimney that he was about to work on, and climbed up. As he neared the top of the ladder (he was about sixty feet above the street) the bottom of the ladder began to push outwards against the tower which was NOT tied securely - as safety and common sense would dictate. The result was that the unfortunate climber fell sixty feet to the ground below, whilst the scaffolding tower fell over and crashed through the roof of a nearby garage.

On this occasion the ladder climber was relatively lucky, in that he only broke his leg and sustained serious bruising to his body as he bounced off the falling tower. He could so easily have been killed.

At about 08:00 one cold frosty morning we received an emergency call to reports of a man fallen from the roof of a house. Upon arrival at the scene we were met by a group of roofing contractors standing in the street. Climbing out of the ambulance, I was met by the foreman who led me to the back of a house where they had been working.

There on the ground was a middle aged man lying spread-eagled on his back in the garden. He was dressed in heavy over-coat and sweaters to keep out the morning cold. A small group of anxious workmates surrounded him, all of whom were advising him to keep perfectly still, and not to move; good advice in such circumstances.

Looking up at the roof, I could see that it was covered in a generous layer of frost and, incredibly, there was no sign of any roof ladder.

The man was conscious and able to speak coherently, as I knelt down beside him. 'What happened?' I asked, taking care to monitor his responses s to my questions. 'I fell off the F****** icy roof 'he said turning his head to look at me. I made a mental note of his head movement. 'Have you got any pain anywhere?' I enquired. This time he shook his head, 'no mate...no pain at all...I feel fine'.

I carried out a thorough check of all his vital signs and asked all the relevant questions, and then eventually I asked him if he had any tingling or pins and needles or could move his fingers? With methodical assessment I established that he could move his arms, and legs. All worked well.

'Look' he said, with some irritation, 'I'll do a ******* dance for you, if you'll let me get up off this cold, damp ground'. 'Okay, let me see how well you can move'.

I was confident in my own mind that his fall had been cushioned by the mound of soil that he had fallen onto. Now as if to emphasise his miraculous escape he jumped up and did a jig around the garden, to the amusement of us all.

One of his workmates confirmed that he had, indeed, fallen clear of the roof and landed in a mound of freshly delivered soil. Had he fallen from the opposite side of the roof, he would have landed on the pavement, and the consequences would have been far more severe.

Occupational or works accidents, certainly made me put my 'thinking cap' on and on some occasions gave me some of my most harrowing jobs. People removing safety guards from machines, placing their hand or fingers into machinery, falling down unguarded holes or off ladders, all receiving injury; most were avoidable!

Put a man where a machine is and you have a potential for a major personal disaster. So be warned...take notice of all safety instructions, they are designed to save your life!

◆ ◆ ◆

7 EVERY PARENTS NIGHTMARE

I sometimes deliver Child Accident Prevention (CAP) lectures to schools and other interested groups. One of the questions I put to children is this; what is the most dangerous place in *your* world?

Some of the answers can, as you may expect from children, be strange and fanciful. Such answers for instance have been; 'Walking on the edge of a volcano, Fighting a Ninja warrior, Crashing in a car' to name but a few. However, most children are usually surprised when I tell them that the most dangerous place in their world is...actually *their own home.* This is true!

The problem with children is that they don't understand many of the dangers in their world of play. They have little perception of hazard awareness, nor do they understand risk assessment and so sometimes they pay a terrible price. They suffer an accident that may cause them at best an injury or at worst, death.

As a paramedic, dealing with child accidents was a part of my job that presented some of my most difficult challenges emotionally, mentally and medically. Dealing with a screaming, frightened child, who has had an accident, can tax even the most experienced ambulance crew, many of whom will have children of their own. Often there will be a distraught parent with the victim struggling to control their own emotions, trying to put a 'brave face on' as they anxiously try to soothe their injured child. In such situations the paramedic has not *only* the child victim to deal with but also the welfare of the parent has to be considered as a secondary patient, who may be in need of support and reassurance too.

On such occasions the paramedic must act impeccably, setting aside his own emotions whilst he tends the injured child. Quietly, gently, reassuringly he will try to gain the confidence of the child (and parent) whilst administering the essential medical aid.

I recall one occasion when I was treating a little girl who was lying in the road with a broken leg. Having being hit by a car, she was in great pain, frightened and screaming and was difficult to reassure and comfort. She was the same age as my own youngest daughter and I had to control my own natural emotions, but I couldn't help picturing my own child in such a situation as I dealt with her.

Imagine, if you can, this scenario. My crewmate, Mike, and I were on duty at Wallasey ambulance station. Both being family men with young children, we were looking forward to spending this warm summer evening with our families. As previously planned, I was looking forward to joining up with my wife and young daughters at their friend's birthday party.

Suddenly, the station alarm sounded throughout the station complex, signifying a most inconvenient 'late call', It was getting on for 18:00, our finishing time, on a lovely warm, sunny evening another five minutes, (I reflected) and I would have been on my way home.

Now picking up the red phone (dedicated emergency emergencies only) I listened as the ambulance controller related the brief details of an emergency call. 'Hello three zero one, will you respond to a Child RTA...it sounds serious we have had multiple calls to this'.

Within seconds Mike and I were in the ambulance and heading out of the station and into the rush hour traffic. I was the driver this time around with Mike the attending paramedic. With all lights blazing and in a crescendo of noise from the siren, I knew that our response could probably be heard at the scene which was only about a mile away. Already the adrenaline was beginning to pump around my body, my senses alerted ready for whatever I may be called upon to do. For this emergency call is special; one that all ambulance staff dread. 'Child RTA'.

Travelling at speed we reached the scene of the accident within a couple of minutes. As we approached the scene, I could see a large crowd of people, standing well back on the pavement, and well away from a small bundle of humanity lying in the middle of the main road. I knew instinctively, that this was a bad sign.

I slew the ambulance across the road to block the traffic and protect the scene and booked 'in attendance at scene'.

Meanwhile Mike was out of the vehicle like a flash and soon at the side of a small boy aged five or six years old. The child had run out onto the busy main road chasing a football, and had been hit by a van, which had then gone over him, dragging him for about one hundred feet, before his broken body was thrown clear.

It is suffice to say that our primary examination indicated that there was little we could do to save him for; his injuries had been instantly fatal. My colleague and I spoke softly to each other, and to the child, even though we knew he couldn't hear us, as we gently lifted his small broken frame onto our stretcher and into the ambulance out of 'the public gaze'.

There was no sign of the little boy's parents, and his other little friends were seen to run off-- presumably in shock. No-one in the vicinity knew who he was.

The police arrived on scene very quickly, as we prepared to leave for the hospital; it would be left to some unfortunate police-officer, the task of locating the parents in order to break the devastating news to them of their child's accident and death.

Mike and I left the scene, with the child alone, his small frame seemed even smaller on our stretcher, no mum or dad with him.

Arriving at the hospital a few minutes later, we handed the little boy over to the casualty nurses and doctors. Each of them, in turn, handled him with complete care and compassion and the love that one feels for any injured child. They too all spoke softly *to him*, as though he could still hear them.

I commented that some mother somewhere is about to experience her worst nightmare. The nurses at the hospital set about their preparations, with the child; awaiting that most daunting task of greeting his distraught mother, father and family.

Mike and I both felt numb, and helpless; as we returned quietly to base, and didn't say much to each other about the incident.

I booked off duty, and set off for home; alone now in my car I could reflect on that awful last call of our day. I had to pass nearby the spot where the accident had occurred. The police where still there investigating the circumstances and events leading up to the accident. I wondered about the boys' parents, had they been located? Did they know yet of their child's fatality?

It was still a warm sunny evening as I arrived home, a few minutes later. I was met by my own two young daughters, Eleanor and Susan along with their friends, all shouting excitedly, laughing and tugging at me, to join in some their friend's birthday party fun in our garden.

I wanted to talk to someone, I wanted to sit quietly and try somehow to deal with this acute grief that I was feeling, but the opportunity was not now it would have to wait. I looked at my daughters and their mum and wondered how I would cope, if such terrible tragedy should ever befall my family. I couldn't tell them about the awful incident that I had just been dealing with and joining in all this fun and games seemed an impossible demand on me at that time.

Many ambulance staff have similar experiences of similar terrible events and may sometimes have to cope with psychological after- effects. We may have to put our own emotions, stress, fears and anxiety on the 'back burner'; and so it was that I joined in the celebrations of the children's party that evening. I never liked to tell my family of the terrible things that I encountered during my work; it didn't seem right to burden them with such details. Instead, like so many in the emergency services I kept many terrible eventful details to myself. But that awful job pervaded my thoughts throughout the rest of that evening and following days, right up to this very moment of my writing.

Every child looks forward to the summer holidays, loads of free time and fun away from the strict rigors of school. However, the other side of the coin can be very tragic. At the end of the holidays...some children will never return to school or at best may do so with life changing injuries.

Many child accidents happen when the child is having fun. Sometimes having fun can mean taking risks or simply not being aware of dangers. Children are not very good at judging speed or height and often overestimate their own ability to carry out a particular activity. They climb trees collecting conkers, swing from ropes, run across roads, swim in inappropriate waters, and play with fire, run madly around crowded playgrounds. They carry out activities on park playground equipment that it was never designed for...kids just want to have fun!

Paradoxically some parents (these days) tend to steer their child away from any and all risk and so the child gains no experience or appreciation of everyday knocks and bruises.

What then should the parent do? Keep the kids at home?

Hang on! Didn't I mention, at the beginning of this chapter, that home is *the most dangerous* place in a child's world?

Sometimes the only comfort that can be gleaned from a child's tragic accident is the thought that they were at least having fun when it happened; if they survived then maybe it would serve as a valuable lesson to them.

It seems to be mostly boys who suffer accidents when playing and having fun. They have a tendency to compete with their peers or accept challenges that they cannot hope to achieve. Consequently, it was never a great surprise to be called to an accident caused by someone swinging on a rope from a tree. I recall that in one week no less than three young boys were victims of such a rope swing.

There was (and still is) a very old tree on the banks of the River Mersey at New Brighton. The tree was part way up a grass bank, with huge branches extending out over the promenade roadway. Someone had attached a thin nylon rope to one of the branches in such a way, that if you held onto it whilst jumping from the top of the slope you got a better swing. However, when kids swung out in an arc they would just skim the top of a three foot (one metre) brick wall at the bottom of the bank; at its limit; they could be about ten feet (three metres) high over the promenade. Of course, this was the type of challenge that boys, mostly, would attempt.

No sensible adult would try this...but plenty of kids did just that, and many to their cost. Alarmed by the child accident rate, local people did cut down many ropes only for another one to soon replace it.

It was during the school holidays that I was called to a 'child accident' at this particular tree, to find a group of young boys standing around one of their friends who had been injured after losing his grip on the rope. Apparently, just as it reached its limit his hands slipped causing him to fall onto the promenade below.

He was about 12 years old and his injuries included two broken legs as well as cuts and bruises. He was in a lot of pain and, as with such fracture's, he had significant blood loss which was apparent by the amount of swelling around the injury site and his obvious signs of shock. Even whilst we were attending to his injuries the rest of his pals had resumed their rope swings seemingly oblivious to what had just happened to their friend.

We got his fractures immobilised with the help of some Entonox (pain relieving gas) then carefully placed him on the stretcher. Once inside the ambulance and out of sight of his friends, I inserted a cannula (needle) into one of veins so that I could put him on a fluid drip before leaving for the hospital.

By the time we got to A&E his parents were already there, anxiously waiting for us, having been alerted by a neighbour who had witnessed their son's accident. He himself was by now (after inhaling generous amounts of Entonox) quite chirpy and full of bravado promising to go back and have another go. His mum and dad on the other hand were not so chirpy.

Derelict buildings can be an obvious dangerous playground for children, boys and girls alike. Unfortunately, they can also seem more like an exciting adventurous playground to some kids. Over the years I attended several child accidents in and around such locations, some of which were serious and others less so.

One summer evening at the beginning of my night shift, just as I was about to carry out the 'vehicle check' (thorough check of equipment, gases, drugs and ambulance lights horns etc.) the station emergency bell rang out. I took the call from ambulance control.

'We have received an emergency call from a child saying that his friend has fallen from a wall' the controller went on to give me the address of a street full of derelict properties in a redevelopment area. He added the comment that he thought the call (made by a child) may be a hoax.

Nevertheless, we still treat such calls as genuine, and so it was that within a few seconds I was in the driving seat, with my crewmate, Ray (attending) heading off to the location. Lights and horns helped to clear the traffic ahead and we were soon on scene in a street of boarded up houses.

As we pulled into the street there was a man stood in the middle of the road waving frantically at us, but as we drew close to him he ran off down a rubbish strewn back alleyway, yelling loudly for us to follow him. Immediately Ray and I sensed that this was going to be something serious.

We were not wrong. All the old wooden back gates of the houses had been removed and the entrances bricked up to keep people out. The man whom we had followed, stopped at one of the houses and pointing to the bricked-up entrance; 'There's a young boy in there. He fell off the wall, but I can't get to him.'

Without a word being spoken, both Ray and I instinctively and simultaneously jumped up and scrambled over the wall dropping down into a small back yard strewn with rubble and broken glass.

Lying on his back amongst all the rubble was a young boy

aged about ten years old, crying and in deep shock, due to what we could immediately see were, extremely serious injuries that he had sustained. His injuries were caused when he had tried to jump from the backyard wall onto an opposite window ledge; the security boarding had been removed leaving only the glass window frame exposed.

Leaving Ray to deal with the injured boy I climbed back over the wall to return to the ambulance to fetch the stretcher and other essential equipment to deal with the injured child.

As I dropped back into the alley-way I found that there were another couple of men who were now kicking at the wall in a desperate attempt to demolish it. Leaving them to it, I ran to the ambulance and grabbing a passer-by got him to help me get enough equipment together and carry it all back up the alleyway to the backyard. By the time I returned with our equipment, enough of the wall had been sufficiently demolished by the men kicking at it, that I could easily scramble over the mound of bricks to assist Ray with the injured boy.

Ray was leaning over the boy and talking softly to him whilst making desperate efforts to deal with the injuries. The young boy was now very quiet and was drifting into unconsciousness. Looking up at me Ray shook his head with a look of despondency.

'Let's go now…fast!' He instructed. Working quickly together, we did what we could to stabilise the boy's injuries before physically moving him, from where he had fallen and placing him onto the stretcher. Meanwhile, the men who had heroically kicked the wall down had now lifted our stretcher atop the mound of bricks and were supporting it enough for Ray and me to gingerly lift our patient onto it. Ray would continue to treat the child on our way to hospital, once he and the boy were secure in the back of the ambulance; I set off to the *new* hospital several miles away. Our local hospital which would have been only two minutes away had been closed down, just *one week* before.

I radioed through to our control room and asked for the

casualty staff, 'to stand by to receive a young boy aged about ten, with (too graphic for description) injuries'

This was a situation when I would need to get to the hospital very quickly. *But I had to get there!* I could not afford to have any mishaps on the journey and I had to allow Ray to be able to carry on with his crucial medical treatment of the boy. It would no good if he was getting thrown about in the ambulance. There were a few serious bends in the road as I made my way through the traffic. Using all lights and horns I commanded other drivers to keep out of my way. Occasionally I needed to drive on the wrong side of the road at speed, but always with great care. On that particular emergency I distinctly remember praying to God to give us a safe journey to our desperate endeavour.

Within ten minutes we were arriving at the hospital where a reception of doctors and nurses were waiting for us at the entrance to A&E. As I pulled up and stopped one of the staff was opening the back doors and in a flash we were all racing down the hospital corridor to the resuscitation room where, already an anaesthetist and surgeon had been summoned and waiting.

Sadly...it was already too late. The young boy had passed away in the final few hundred yards of our journey.

The most dangerous place in the world, for a child anyway, is the home! Over my years as a paramedic I attended many calls to accidents in the home, some of which were serious and others not so. From a child falling down stairs and breaking a leg to a child with a piece of Lego stuck up their nose. The child's home environment is full of dangers and hazards...if only they knew it.

Bumps, cuts and grazes may seem obvious and regular daytoday child accidents, but how many people realize that some cosmetics can be dangerous to children?

I recall incidents of children playing, too liberally, with mums' hairspray or spray-on-deodorant resulting in severe breathing difficulty and the child being very sick. Children climbing and running around the house brought in several cases of concussion. Some rather nasty cuts from knives and scissors as well as drinking bleach or other damaging fluids all kept the child accident rate at a worrying rate.

Children finding and taking their parents' prescription drugs was also problematic because very often the child would be found unwell or vomiting and unable or unwilling to tell anyone what they had taken. In some cases, with younger children, they may have thought the brightly coloured sweets (pills) that that they had eaten had tasted unpleasant and may not associate their sickness with the tablets. Having swallowed pills, there may be no accurate record of the amount that had been in the container *before* the child had swallowed them and so it may be that they undergo some rather unpleasant treatment to expel and treat the effects the drug.

Very young children explore their world by trying to taste or drink whatever new and interesting substances they discover in their home. Drinking bleach, trying to eat dishwasher tablets, finding alcohol or even a supply of illicit drugs within easy reach, accounted for some very distressing emergency calls.

I recall another 'home accident' which happened at bath time when a child's mother filled the bath with hot water *first!* The child, a little girl aged about four was not in the bathroom at that time: but when mother was unexpectedly called away, before she could *add cold water to the bath,* the little girl entered the bathroom and jumped into the hot bath. The result was horrific. The child suffered very severe scalds over much of her body and had to undergo many, many months of painful treatment.

Despite many tragic accidents, and minor ones too, many children bounce back with remarkable tenacity. Some even relish their moment in the 'limelight'. As time passes the memory of the event may fade. For the parent though there may be a longer and more difficult journey of recovery. The parent may feel a number of different emotions from guilt to hopelessness or even despair. One parent may even blame the other for some perceived lack of care of the child... Family harmony may be irreparably damaged. They may be engaged in a lifetime of caring for a child accident victim. They may be embroiled in long protracted legal matters followed by years of medical and social care of their child. A terrible price, for that one moment in time, when your child has an accident. Your nightmare!

◆ ◆ ◆

8 CHILD ABUSE

Dealing with an acutely sick or injured child is, more often than not, a very distressing time for all those concerned with their welfare; be it in the pre-hospital treatment, by paramedics or later in hospital by the doctors and nurses. The distress felt by the carer is usually more profound when there is a reasonably strong suspicion that the injury or illness is due, in some part, to a form of abuse against the child.

During my time in the ambulance service I have had to deal with many incidents which, in my initial assessment, lead me to believe that I was dealing with a case of child abuse. In all but one case being proved right. The spectrum of child abuse seems infinitely wide, and seemingly there are no clear parameters to the range or nature of abuse, or to its effects upon the abused child/children. Abuse can be physical or mental and may inflict serious injury (non-accidental [NAI] or serious mental and physical disabilities, upon the child.

What may seem like its simplest form, a 'lack of care', may result in serious deprivation and so may ultimately be deemed to be a case of abuse.

Generally speaking, battered or abused children are children who are deliberately injured physically or mentally (usually) by adults. About two thirds of child abuse victims are under the age of three years. In many cases having been singled out from the other children in the family they are then abused by an adult family member.

Each year in the United Kingdom there are many thousands of these cases reported; occurring at every social and economic level. There are no class barriers; victims can come from very poor backgrounds, or from a very wealthy one. Sadly some of these children die each year from their injuries, many more will remain permanently disabled physically and scarred emotionally. For various reasons not every case reaches the public domain.

The abuse of many children can go on for years without other family members, friends or neighbours being aware that anything is going on. Hence there can be a strong disbelief of the child's accusations and sometimes a real hostility toward the professional dealing with the event.

Not all non-accidental injuries (NAIs) are due to systematic abuse, sometimes an adult may wish no more than to chastise a child, but unfortunately, they forget that they are much stronger (heavy handed) and often can be very angry at the time. Consequently, if a child injury, emergency call is received the paramedic may arrive quickly, but not before the abuser may have coerced the child to give a different story as to how the injury actually occurred.

It is only by trained and very careful observation that the paramedic may be able to 'pick up' on something he hears or may see.

I am a great believer in body language. It may be instinct, intuition, a sixth sense, call it what you will, but I have been right on too many occasions where I have dealt with NAIs. None of that is evidence and that is where the police come in, for by necessity always they will be involved.

I can recall one afternoon, just after the local schools had finished for the day, being called to a large detached house, and shown into a bedroom to find a young boy of thirteen lying on his bed with a head injury. His mother, who had met me at the front door, looking very distressed and looked a bit 'knocked about' herself, led my crewmate and I to an upstairs bedroom where a young boy was lying on a bed with head injuries and bi-lateral black eyes. She didn't say much, nor did she look straight at me, instead she left the room leaving us alone with him.

Upon examination I suspected at best that he had a severely broken nose, but the signs that he presented to me indicated that he may actually have base of skull fracture. He told me that he had been beaten up by a couple of boys in the street, on his way home from school.

I attended to his injuries, reassured him that he would be okay and went on to explain about going to hospital and the treatment he could expect. Now I needed to see his mother, she would need to come with us to the hospital. I left the injured child with my crewmate, whilst I went to look for the boy's mother. It was a big house and I had to look around for her, in doing so I bumped into another boy in the house who told me that he was the injured boys' younger brother. This child looked distressed too and looked as though he had been crying.

Eventually I found the mother, also crying, leaning over the kitchen sink. I had already began to wonder about the degree of distress that I was seeing within her, but her body language indicated that she didn't want to face me or be questioned by me. Most mothers in such a situation would be hovering over me whilst I dealt with her child, but here she was, downstairs in the kitchen her distress seemed most unusual and more than I would expect to see in an incident of this kind.

Patiently and quietly I questioned her as to what had gone on, how had her sons injury had happened, why was her son not wearing school uniform (I knew that this local grammar school had a strong uniform regime) if he had sustained the injury outside why would he change out of school uniform before an ambulance was called.

She was his mother she loved her sons and obviously felt very upset about her injured son's condition. Suddenly she broke down; telling me that her husband had got between his two boys who were fighting in order to break them up. But then he too lost his temper and set about the older boy (our injured patient) and beat him severely. She then went on to tell me that it was quite a regular occurrence, for her husband to beat the boys, but particularly the eldest, and that she too was often the victim of her husband's attacks.

Her husband had left the house when the ambulance was

called. Incredibly, the injured boy was more concerned about his dad; but sadly he was blaming himself for the fact that he had caused his father to do this to him! This event took place in an upper middle class family.

At the hospital the injured boy stuck to his original story of being attacked outside school by other boys. I took the senior nurse to one side and gave my version of events along with my findings; she in turn informed the hospital social services who would investigate further.

The child abuser is usually an adult and either a parent, guardian or some other carer; very often one who themselves, was him or herself, abused as a child. The parent who abuses their child tends be poorly prepared for a career of parenthood and all too often may have unrealistic expectations of a child's behaviour.

Consider for instance the situation when a mother brings her new child home for the first time. Placed in a cot and sleeping quietly, the parent initially longs to hear the child communicate, usually by crying. The novelty of a crying baby can soon wear off, however, and for the unprepared parent this can often be the start of the slippery slope to child abuse. Many child abusers have little or no social support, and may be heavily involved with alcohol or; more commonly today, drugs. There are many other reasons why a child might become the victim of abuse, particularly of a violent nature. Some specific events, anxieties or stresses may be a pre-cursor to an attack on a child or for that matter upon groups of children; for there are many examples where more than one child in a family had been abused.

There are many stresses in today's modern world, which can create a domestic trigger for child abuse. For instance, long term unemployment, sudden loss of employment, marital breakdowns, family deaths, poor housing, financial worries, alcohol or drug dependency to name but a few. All of these and many more factors have been linked with incidents of child abuse.

Rarely, if ever, will an emergency call, come in neatly termed 'child abuse', nor will the abuser admit openly to his actions. Child abuse is like any other emergency call, in so far as the paramedic has to make a diagnosis, based upon his or her findings at the scene. A diagnosis of 'child abuse' is usually based upon the paramedic's suspicions rather than on outright evidence, and will include a diagnosis of whatever injuries may also be found. Foremost in his suspicions may be the mechanics of the injury, in other words the experienced paramedic is used to seeing certain types of injury, and has a thorough understanding of how certain injuries can and do occur, relative to the severity of the injury. It may, therefore, be the case that a child has a particular injury, which does not relate to it happening in the way that has been described.

For instance there may be a marked discrepancy between the history, and the physical findings; if the child fell off a stool in the kitchen, then one would expect to find sign of injury either on the front of the child, or on his back, depending upon how he fell, it may be unusual to find a broken leg from such an accident.

There were occasions when I have been involved with such cases that may have been termed 'NAIs' (non-accidental injuries). My initial suspicions have been aroused, not by something the child has said, but by something far less tangible - a sixth sense - a feeling that 'something was not quite right'; maybe I could not quite put my finger on it. But my rule of thumb is to go with my instincts, and to tread tactfully and carefully, in the hope that I would eventually secure a positive evidential idea, as to the true events surrounding a child's injury.

I have found that if the abuser (be them parent or other carer) is on the scene with the child, then usually he or she will be evasive in their manner and will be unhelpful in so far as they will not actually volunteer any information as to the history of events. All too often they will stand well back, even to the point of going into another room, leaving me (a stranger) with the child who is confused, in pain and frightened, by my appearance on the scene. These parental indicators, show a lack of care or concern for the child, and are a great 'give away'.

Often the abuser will give contradictory details, either contradicting themselves, or more often than not, contradicting the child; who having been told what to say (before our arrival) has not quite got the story right. As well as what we are told, we also become extremely aware of our surroundings, and we are required to remember as much detail as possible, and of course to look out for clues.

Having established the child's chief complaint I would deal accordingly with it; and give whatever treatment was appropriate. If I suspect that it was a case of NAI, then I would continue with a more thorough head to toe examination of the child; always in a matter of fact way, keeping my suspicions to myself. Very often, the abuser would never show any signs of guilt, but instead would show outright hostility toward the child; accusing them of telling lies; or alternatively they would be hostile toward the ambulance staff; that way they could 'clam up' and say nothing.

Whenever one suspects' child abuse has taken place, it is easy to find yourself feeling angry and hostile toward the person deemed responsible for the child's demeanour. We were supposed to be non-judgmental, and we had to keep an open mind, and if necessary be supportive of the abuser

In that part of my job which involved training other ambulance staff, I used to advise them not to feel hostile, but instead to be canny, and to act friendly and sympathetic toward the alleged abuser. Talk about anything other than the event. The fact that the abuser wishes to talk about the more mundane things in life at this time, and not to be concerned about the child, speaks volumes in itself. By befriending the abuser, one may gain all sorts of information that may lead to the eventual truth of the event. You gain nothing from showing hostility or disbelief in their explanations of the cause of the child's injury.

Attempted suicide calls represent a significant percentage of all our emergency calls; but I recall one such incident which involved a woman who had taken an overdose of tablets, and had decided to take her three year old son with her to the 'hereafter'. Fortunately for all concerned, the woman was found, by a neighbour before it was too late; sitting in a chair at home, but with her child asleep on her knee.

When I arrived on the scene, the woman was initially quiet and subdued, but lucid and informative, telling me what tablets and how many she had taken. Then in a matter of fact way, went on to inform me that she had given her child a quite considerable overdose of her tablets too.

My main concern immediately switched to the sleeping child; who was not sleeping but was in fact unconscious. She went berserk when I tried to take her unconscious child from her. No amount of persuasion by me would make her hand the child over, and she was becoming more and more threatening, screaming abuse at both me and my crewmate. Time was of the essence and so only a little time was spent trying to reason with her. In the end we had no choice but to call for immediate police back-up. They arrived within a couple of minutes and assisted me with gaining security of the child.

The woman was later charged with attempted murder, but the outcome resulted in her receiving psychiatric treatment. It later transpired that the woman who had taken the overdose had a recent history of mental problems, but had shunned help from the social services department, soon after moving to the area.

Responding to an emergency call one day to 'a child fallen', found me with my crewmate, Chrissy, looking down at a small boy aged about three years old, who was lying on a settee and fully dressed, with his head slightly inclined to one side.

We had been called out by the child's mother. The little

boy appeared to be distressed and in pain; and was very reluctant to move his small body; but it appeared to me that he also seemed unusually quiet.

My crewmate, Chrissy, who was a trainee paramedic (but with years of previous nursing experience) questioned him carefully. Making a physical examination was a little difficult because he was dressed in nice clean clothes which included a tight fitting woollen jumper. Whilst Chrissy examined the child, I took the opportunity to speak to the mother. She told me that she had left her son at home with her boyfriend whilst she went to the local shop. On her return she found her son had been washed and dressed, but was laying here, 'Like this complaining of pain in his shoulder' she explained pointing to his shoulder. When I asked her what had happened to her son, she said that she didn't know! 'Where's your boyfriend now?' I asked. 'He's in the kitchen' she replied pointing to another door and calling out to her boyfriend. 'Danny, come in here, the paramedic wants to speak to you'. I could just make out a muffled voice of a man, saying something to the effect that he didn't want to come in to speak to me. The woman persisted 'come on, he wants want to know what has happened to young Andy'

This time the voice from the other room was more aggressive, F**** off will you, I'm not speaking to nobody'.

I looked down at Chrissy, and we made the sort of eye contact that says we are both thinking alike. If the boyfriend was the one with all the answers, then I needed to speak to him. I went through into the other room, just in time to see a man about to leave by the back door. 'Hold it, mate', I said firmly. 'There's a young kiddie out here who is injured, and I want to know why and how it has occurred.' He turned again to walk out, but I told him in no uncertain terms that I would not let him leave the house (I meant it, and he sensed it). He turned back to face me, but would not come into the room where the injured child lay.

At this point I knew that I would need to remember

exactly what he said in reply to my questions. He told me that the child had fallen in the bath, whilst he had been bathing him.

'But', he went on, 'he (the child) was okay afterwards, because I dressed him, so I don't know what's wrong with him'.

I went back to Chrissy, and assisted her to deal with the injured child; we established that the he had a broken collar bone (which can be very serious even life threatening if it cuts through the nearby artery). As if to further strengthen my suspicions of non- accidental injury, I had noticed that the child was clean, hair combed and dressed in a tight fitting woollen jumper. I reasoned to myself, that it would have been almost impossible to dress the child properly with such an injury and I, therefore, reasoned that the injury probably occurred when the child was dressed; so concluding that the child may not have fallen in the bath, as I had just been told by the boyfriend.

The child's mother stood close the child, looking as any mother would, anxious and concerned for her child. Chrissy gently and quietly asked the youngster again, 'Andy, how did you hurt your shoulder?'. The child looked at us both, and despite his tender years he seemed to know that what he was about to say was some serious, He whispered one word only 'Danny' (the boyfriends name).

Chrissy and I made no more fuss. We immobilised the child's injury, before evacuating to the ambulance.

Once inside the ambulance with the injured child, I turned to look for his mum who had not followed us. I went back into the house and found her engaged in heated conversation with her boyfriend, who apparently didn't want to come with us to the hospital. But at my instigation he did eventually come along with the child's mother. I treated him kindly and with respect, as did Chrissy, and he climbed aboard the ambulance for our journey to hospital.

With Chrissy and our passengers safely stowed in the back of the ambulance, I was able to contact ambulance control by radio and request the attendance of the police to deal with suspected 'NAI'. Chrissy, meanwhile, would occupy the journey by attending to the child; but also by engaging in friendly conversation with the two adults, trying surreptitiously to glean any evidential information about the child's injury.

Arriving at the hospital a short time later, I was glad to see that the police were already there ahead of us; they were tactfully staying a discreet distance away, until we had handed over to the casualty receiving staff.

Chrissy and I detailed the events as we knew them to be, but when I came to tell the doctor what I had been told by the boyfriend, as to how the child had sustained the injury, (falling in the bath) Chrissy interjected. 'He (Danny) has told me something completely different' she said, and went on to recount that Danny had told her and the mother, during the journey, that the child fell off a chair after getting dressed

So there we were already two differing accounts as to young Andy's injury. Later, we gave our statements to the police before leaving the hospital to resume our normal duties. Sometime later, when we arrived back at the hospital, we were met by one of the nurses, who told us that the boyfriend had now given a third and different account of how Andy had sustained injury.

This incident may have been a 'one off' for that particular family, in so far as the abuse may not have been of a prolonged systematic nature, but more an unfortunate sudden impulse to smack a seemingly naughty child. However, if such chastisement causes physical injury, then whatever the rights or wrongs, it is the paramedics' legal (and in my view, moral) duty to inform the authorities, in such cases.

Some years ago I attended an incident at about 10:00 in the morning; where a child had reportedly fallen from his pushchair, sustaining a facial injury. Upon arrival at the address, which was a house in a run-down part of the town, I was met at the front door, by a young woman in her early twenties. She led me into the house, whereupon the first thing I noticed was a horrible foul smell. Inside the house and everywhere was dirty and untidy; the carpet seemed to stick to the soles of my shoes and had obviously not been cleaned for a long time (if ever).

I was shown into a back room, where there was a young man, (the woman's husband, and father of the child) he too being in his early twenties. He was sitting by an open fire, with no fire guard on it, and watching television, drinking a mug of tea.

He said something like 'Hiya mate' to me as I entered the room; and merely nodded towards a child nearby. The child, a little boy, aged about eighteen months old, was sitting crying on the carpet, he rubbed his eyes; his nose was running and he seemed totally miserable. He was wearing a very dirty 'baby-grow' and he smelled of urine, and vomit, and was himself unwashed (today at least).

I approached the crying child and gently tried to gain his confidence before picking him up; making an examination of his injury, which initially seemed to be of a minor nature. I could see a bruise and slight swelling on his forehead, but nothing more.

The child's father carried on watching television, and drinking a mug of tea, whilst the young mother, explained events to me. This was her only child, with no history of previous hospital visits. Strangely she told me that she thought the child had fallen from his pushchair, and hit his head on the floor as he landed. 'Why do you *only* think he fell from the pushchair'? I asked her. 'We (she indicated her husband) were in the kitchen when we heard him crying, when I came in here he was on the floor' she answered.

When I asked if the child had been unconscious, or vomited, she looked startled, and turned to ask her husband if he knew. Without actually looking at me, the husband answered, saying something to the effect that the child had vomited, 'but not much' he added.

I had already registered a few things in my mind, one

of which was the husband's apparent lack of concern for the child. It was also strange that his wife was unable to answer some simple questions about her child's injury and any possible after effects.

We would need to take the child to hospital. I organised both parents to secure the house, before coming with me and their child. Both parents came along as I carried the child into the back of the ambulance and as Geoff, my crewmate, closed the back doors, he gave me a nod, as if to indicate that his suspicions were similar to mine (maybe NAI).

Once inside the ambulance with the child safely placed on the stretcher, I began to chat with both parents in a friendly and jovial manner, whilst at the same time carrying out, what the parents may perceive as a somewhat, casual but more thorough examination of the child.

En route to the hospital both parents seemed more content to converse about all sorts of mundane subjects, this despite the fact that their child had been injured enough for them to call an ambulance. My examination of the child revealed a number of bruises of differing degrees of severity and age, both on his back, his legs and his front.

I made no comment to the parents about my visual findings, but continued to chat to them in a friendly and open way. During the journey they seemed to relax more, and at one point they were laughing and joking with each other. At no time did either parent offer any words of love or comfort to the still crying child. No touch of a caring mothers hand, no caring word.

At the hospital, I asked both parents to go to the reception counter to book their child in whilst gave my report to the receiving casualty staff, indicating my concern that this may be a 'child at risk' possibly NAI. I also entered my concerns on my ERF[6]**

It is suffice to say that later that day the child was discharged into the care of the parents. Apparently the hospital doctor had considered that the child was *not at risk,* as I had earlier reported in my handover to them.

Several months later, a colleague from another station attended an emergency call to that same address, and the same family. Upstairs in a cot, was the body of a little boy, well beyond the possibility of resuscitation. My colleague immediately called the police, and a full scale investigation took place, the result being that the father of the child was charged, found guilty and jailed for the systematic abuse and subsequent death of the child.

Child deaths are amongst the worst incidents that we have to deal with, but the event is even more harrowing when the death has occurred due to someone's deliberate act. Not all such incidents are necessarily the end result of systematic or prolonged abuse.

There are some cases where a sudden and impulsive attack upon a child can be catastrophic in its consequence, leaving the perpetrator to carry the terrible burden of their guilt for ever.

At about 05:30 on a bright, sunny summer Sunday morning and nearing the end of a busy night shift my crewmate, Robbie, and I were both dozing in a chair when the station 'red phone' rang out.

I took the call from the controller informing me of the emergency to deal with 'some sort of domestic incident'. He went on 'We've received a call from the police, of a woman threatening to kill her baby' before adding 'police on scene'.

Within a few seconds we were out to the ambulance and set off with Robbie driving. Soon we were speeding through the deserted town centre. It was a beautiful morning, sun low in the sky, streaming through the branches of the trees as we sped by, not a soul on the road.

Having been to many and varied domestics incidents, I had a mental picture of what this particular incident may involve, and if things were true to form there would probably be a lot of shouting and swearing, before we managed to calm things down. At least that's how these things often went.

Despite our fast speed, I was surprised when two police cars overtook us; disappearing out of sight ahead of us. Robbie and I exchanged remarks to the effect that they (the police) may also be going to our job.

A few minutes later we pulled off the main road and into a quiet tree-lined side street, in one of the better areas of town. I booked in attendance on scene; it was just coming up to 05:35.

Half way down the street, I could see several police cars, and a couple of police vans, all blocking the road ahead. Robbie parked up close to the address that we had been given, and as I as made my way through the maze of police vehicles, I was approached by a senior police officer. 'Good morning' he said ruefully, 'we have something of a siege going on in this house' he pointed to a large nearby house. 'A woman is threatening to kill her baby'; he turned and beckoned me to follow him. We stopped outside the gates of a large Victorian house, and looking up the gravelled driveway, I could see the front door which was open and guarded by a policeman.

The senior police officer informed me, that upstairs inside the house were some of his officers, trying to negotiate with a young woman who was threatening to kill her child. He was not sure as to what the full circumstances were at this time; but pointing toward a middle aged woman, who was standing on the front lawn, he suggested that I speak to her as she was a witness to the event.

As I walked up the drive and through the garden, to speak to the woman, I noticed that there were about twenty police officers around the house, along with a dog handler. The woman neighbour (the witness to events) was in her fifties, and dressed in a flowered dressing gown and although she seemed shocked and upset, she was able to tell me quickly, the chain of events.

She lived next door. She had risen early that morning because she could not sleep, and was picking the milk up from her doorstep, when she heard the sound of breaking glass.

Looking up she saw that the bedroom window of the house next door, had been smashed, and (what she took to be) a bundle of rags, falling onto the front lawn. This was followed by the sound of a woman screaming hysterically inside the house; followed a moment or two later by a young woman coming down the front steps of the house, shouting and crying, and going to retrieve the bundle from the lawn.

It was only when the young woman picked up the bundle that the neighbour realised that it was, in fact, a small baby. Who later turned out turned to be the young woman's baby.

The, shocked, neighbour ran around and confronted the young woman, who by now was climbing the front steps to go back into the house, still clutching the 'bundle'. There was a brief altercation between the two women, before the younger woman, along with the baby, disappeared back inside the house. The neighbour had seen that the baby seemed to be injured, with blood on its head. She did not know just how bad the injury may be. She also told me that she thought the baby was about six months old.

As I listened to her account, I looked up to the broken window and made a rough calculation that as well as the baby being thrown through the glass of the window, the child had fallen in arc of about twenty feet. I very quickly approached the front steps of the house, and there on the top step was a small pool of fresh blood. 'Is that from the baby?' I asked the neighbour, pointing to the blood.

She could only nod her head in response. I knew that *that* amount of blood loss for a six month old child could be fatal; I had absolutely no time at all to waste. Negotiations were an encumbrance at this stage. I made an instant decision as to my action, I would go in and snatch the baby from the mother come what may!

I did not know the layout of the house, there was no time anyway, to bother with detail, nor to discuss my plan with the police, and I would just 'act on the hoof'.

Passing quickly by the policeman standing by the front

door, I entered the house. Immediately to my left was a staircase lined, with police officers. Not stopping, I moved quickly and quietly up the stairs without hindrance or challenge from anyone. I heard someone say 'here's the paramedic' and people moved aside as I hurried by.

It took but a few seconds to sprint up the stairs, I knew already what I was going to do. As My line of sight drew level with the top of the stairs, I could see a room opposite, with the door wide open, and a number of police personnel (men and women) kneeling down inside, to the left of the open door. Their attention seemed focused on the incident which was obviously behind the door and currently out of my sight.

As I was later told, and commended upon, I came in 'like a bat out of hell'. Reaching the top of the stairs, I pushed passed everyone and barged noisily in through the open bedroom door; making a loud announcement 'Ambulance service coming through' as I did so. Turning quickly to my right, not knowing what I would find; I saw a young woman on the opposite side of the room. She was sitting cross legged on the floor, holding the body of a small child in her lap. The child, dressed in a pink babygrow, was lying face down with the head in the woman's lap and feet towards me. The woman, who had her hands around the child's neck, looked up at me briefly, startled and dismayed. Still moving quickly, I moved toward her, she was now screaming, as I pushed my wide open hand directly and forcibly into her face, knocking her backwards and causing her to lose her grip on the baby.

With my free hand I quickly scooped the small pathetic limp body of the baby from her lap; turning around quickly, I marched out of the room. It had taken only about four or five seconds to rescue the child; audacity had been my weapon of choice.

As I left the room with the baby I was aware of the woman jumping up behind me, in a vain effort to reach me, screaming and cursing hysterically by which time the police officers on the opposite side of the room were jumping from their feet and diving behind me to apprehend the still screaming woman.

As I dashed back down the stairs I clearly heard audible gasps and comments of 'Oh my God' from those police officers on the stairs. Once I reached the outside of the house I was met by Robbie who was waiting with the doors open on the ambulance. It was only then that I could look at the injury to the child.

The immediate sign of injury was of a horrific head and neck wound, the baby (a little girl) was deeply unconscious and was only just breathing with great difficulty.

We ran to the ambulance and jumping onto the seat in the back, I wedged my feet up against the opposite stretcher, put my seat belt on and placed the unconscious baby, face down, in my lap. Grabbing a large absorbent sterile dressing I placed it gingerly over the injury which covered the whole of the top of baby's head.

Using the ambulance radio my colleague arranged for our controller to ask 'the hospital to be standing by to receive a baby with serious head injuries... likely to prove'.[7]**

In the back of the speeding ambulance I worked hard to maintain the infant girl's airway in order to administer life-saving oxygen. During the journey to the hospital, I managed to make some further limited examination of the little girl. It was only then that I noticed an ominous bruise appearing around the base of the baby's neck, suggesting the possibility of a fractured (broken) bone.

Now as we raced through the quiet Sunday morning streets; the early morning sun was shining brightly heralding the beginning of another perfect summer day. The whole thing seemed horrible and unreal, for me this was a nightmare demanding the best of my skills. I felt alone with this wee mite. I prayed (as many ambulance staff, sometimes do). To Almighty God to give us a safe journey to the hospital, and to spare the life of this little girl.

Robbie did well to get us to the hospital within about 5

minutes.

The pressure on the driver in such dire circumstances is truly immense; for he too was aware this baby's dreadful plight. One mistake by him, or his failure to correctly read the road conditions, or to anticipate the actions of other road users, and we could end up in an accident ourselves; then none of us would get to the hospital in time to save this little girl.

As we pulled up outside the accident and emergency department, I unhooked my seat belt and, cradling the baby in my arms, still face down, I stepped quickly toward the back door of the ambulance which was being thrown open, by waiting nurses and a doctor. 'What's happened?' asked the doctor.

I gently held out the injured child to him and the waiting nurses, hoping that they could see the obvious, for suddenly (and for the only time in my career) I was so choked up I was unable to speak. There was a terrific lump in my throat. I felt like crying, but knew that this was neither the time nor the place.

The doctor and nurses realised my situation and took the baby from me without further question. Fortunately Robbie was much older than me, and had many more years of experience in the service; he was able to relate the dramatic details surrounding the baby's injuries to the doctor and casualty staff.

I heard later, that the mother of the little girl, had been taking drugs prior to the incident. She already had mental health issues, and may even have had 'post-natal depression' so it was unlikely that she would face a charge of murder. Later that beautiful summer day....the little girl died.

NB: Even recalling this event years later gives me a lump in the throat, this incident like many others involving children still remains vivid in my memory.

Drugs are something of a modern day phenomena in child abuse cases, very often resulting more in neglect, of the child, rather than outright assault. Personally I have been sickened and amazed at how much effort was applied to maintaining the so called 'family unit' in order that some drug addicted parent may retain control of their children, regardless of the risks associated with that policy. All too often I have attended incidents where very young children have been left in the sole care of a drug abusing parent.

Some well-meaning social worker has deemed it a reasonable risk that a child or children be left with such a parent or parents. The social worker probably finishes work at 17:00 and is invariably off duty at weekends or may be unavailable when a serious child abuse or neglect incident is needed to be dealt with.

It seems that we must protect the rights of the parent at all costs. We must protect their 'human rights' not impinge upon their parental credibility, by doubting their drug dependent aptitude for parenthood.

Even as I write, there are measures afoot to legalise some drugs, which in my view will equate to even more abused children. The trouble with these protectors of the problem parent is that *they* don't have to deal with the aftermath of their liberal ideas, or indeed pick up the shattered and injured children.

At about 16:00 one bitterly cold February afternoon a woman called the ambulance service because she was concerned about her neighbours four year old daughter, whom she had noticed had been standing alone on the front doorstep of the house for a considerable time. Furthermore the child was dressed only in a thin nightdress, totally unsuitable for a cold February afternoon.

Along with Jules, my crewmate, on that day, we arrived to find a little girl aged about four years old, who was crying, confused and very cold and dirty standing on the doorstep of her home.

She told us that she had come out of her house but was unable to get back inside because the front door had shut behind her. She had stood crying on the doorstep 'for a very long time' until found by the neighbour.

The neighbour confirmed that she had tried in vain to get an answer at the front door, before calling the ambulance.

Jules scooped the child up in his arms and carried her into our ambulance; wrapping her in a warm blanket (which we kept in heated storage locker during cold winter spells) left her with the neighbour in the warmth of the ambulance. Meanwhile I was making attempts to contact anyone who may be in the house, I banged and shouted and peered through the letterbox and windows, all without response from within.

Jules returned to me and after a quick discussion, we decided that he would return to the ambulance radio to request the attendance of the police whilst I would go around to the rear of the house to see if I could discover another way into the property. I found the back-gate of the property down a narrow, rubbish strewn passageway. The gate was locked so I wasted no time in climbing over the wall and dropping down into a small backyard. The small yard was dirty with rubbish strewn about from an overfilled refuge bin.

I noticed that the windows were dirty behind which, hung some rather dirty greyish net curtains; in all, the place looked neglected.

At first, banging on the back door and calling out, I tried to get access to the back kitchen but the door was locked. I then I tried to peer through the windows but the shabby net curtains made it difficult to see inside.

Just when I was beginning to think that the house may actually be empty; I heard the crying of a baby from within. There was a small side window by the back kitchen door also covered with a net curtain and although I had difficulty seeing through it if I pressed my face against the glass I could just make out a tiny baby inside, lying, naked, on the kitchen floor.

That was it! I shouldered the door, which gave way quiet easily allowing me into the kitchen area. The infant (a little boy aged about four months of age) was naked from the waist down, lying on a cold and dirty kitchen floor. I picked him up and quickly ran through the house to the front door and opened it. Jules was already there. He looked totally surprised when I opened the door and handed him the baby. 'I will check the rest of the house' I told him.

He wasted no time in taking the freezing cold tot from me and, returning to the ambulance, calling over his shoulder to me that the police were on their way.

After a quick search of the house I eventually found the mother. She was a young woman, crouched behind a bedroom door, totally oblivious and out of her head on drugs.

A short time later, while we were still at the house with the police, a middle-aged woman arrived in a very distressed state. She had been informed by another neighbour about the events at the house. She was the mother of the young woman and grandmother to the youngsters. She was very angry and upset. She informed us that she had been overruled by the social workers, when she had wanted custody of the children. She claimed that she was told that social services prefer to keep children with the mother!

This was not the only case of its kind, but it was one of the more distressing for me and my crewmate. I dealt with a number of other drug related child neglect/abuse over the years.

Drugs and all the related issues seem to divide society as to how to solve this problem. It may be worth mentioning, but I have family who live in the Middle East, where there is little or no such drug abuse problem. Maybe there's a lesson to be had from there.

◆ ◆ ◆

9 VIOLENCE AND THE PARAMEDIC

You could be forgiven for believing that as a paramedic, we enjoy some immunity from violence being directed toward ourselves; our skills being paramount to the health of the casualty. You may think that people's hidden decency and sense of fair-play will shine through, and restrain the beast within them. Not so I'm afraid. All too often our presence has offered someone another focus of attention for their violent behaviour, and we have become either a supplemental or secondary target. Our involvement can be seen as an intrusion likely to light the 'touch paper' of someone's warped sense of injustice.

I have encountered and been the victim of so many incidents of violence during my career that I have had to restrict this chapter to cover just a few, but be assured...there were many more!

When I first joined the ambulance service, very little was said about violence; even then the subject dealt singularly with those being in need of psychiatric care. Somehow there was something not quite 'normal' with such people. Their mental state or their social attitude, it could be said, was one of inherent violence. I was taught to be careful when dealing with psychiatric patients; they could be an unknown quantity capable of anything and at any time, without warning.

Well dear reader, I can tell you now, that after twenty years at the 'sharp end' of the emergency services, I never had cause to be afraid of anyone who had a psychiatric disorder, of whatever nature, quite the opposite proved to be true.

However, I did have many occasions when I had just cause to be afraid of those in society who would term themselves 'normal'; on a few occasions, enough to fear for my life. It was Mr and Mrs 'normal' citizen who sometimes, gave me my biggest concern for my own safety and at times making my job very dangerous and frightening.

Violence in today's society knows no bounds; paramedics have to endure it every day of their working lives. No thug gives a quarter to the emergency care worker, be them paramedic, nurse or doctor. During one particular violent incident in which I was trying to deal with a badly injured patient, some young drunken yob nearby was being abusive, and referred to me as 'just a f****** paramedic'.

Ambulance staff do not enjoy dealing with violence, be it from a patient or some other source. Those who choose a career in the emergency ambulance service are people who are usually oriented toward care and rescue, not toward some form of martial art, or any use of force. All ambulance staff are caregivers, not 'heavies'. I am, what I consider to be a pacifist, I do not believe in violence for violence sake, but, having been in the forces, I am not averse to facing it head on when I have to. Many a time, I have been afraid of a situation involving a potential for violence, *but* I was more afraid to turn my back, and so it was very often a 'fait accompli'.

Any call that involves ambulance staff dealing with aggressive or violent patients can leave one or both of the crew injured in some way, either serious, or minor. Such violent encounters can present a risk of physical as well as mental injury such as 'post-traumatic stress'. This, in turn, may lead to a premature cessation of the ambulance person's career due to the debilitating effect of such injury.

The paramedic always has to be psychologically and tactically prepared to deal with violence at any time, and from any quarter; whether or not he/she is scared, they cannot abandon a patient. If they do, then in my mind they should not be in the job.

In the aftermath of a violent incident the crew may even find themselves feeling, tired, angry, guilty or just plain upset. In the past, I have been left badly bruised, feeling bewildered and angry; sometimes still visibly shaking, through a mixture of fear and rage, long after the event has subsided. I have had feelings of incredulity, disbelief and scepticism, about the behaviour of some 'normal' person who has attacked me, whilst I was attempting to assist them. All too often such attacks upon ourselves are totally unexpected, and as such a well-aimed blow from the assailant has offered some rather painful stimulus to some part of my body.

In an ideal world, crews that had been involved in a violent incident would have some sort of debriefing about the event -- a time for those who were involved to talk about it together -- thus allowing for a 'stress' break, before being called upon to continue the rest of their shift.

Unfortunately, 'stress' breaks (in my paramedic days) were never regarded as a priority and after such violent incidents we were simply expected to carry on, 'business as usual'. Even after a particularly harrowing event, we would usually be expected to report 'available' ready for the next job; when in fact we may well have been in some form of 'post incident' anxiety

Over the years I have been witness to an increase in violence within our society; an increase not only in numbers, but also in the degree and barbarity and severity of injury. An increase in the use of weapons has made obsolete, the fist; instead we now have gun and or knife culture. Even our DIY culture has been hijacked. The humble pickaxe-handle, once a popular weapon, has been replaced by such items as craft-knives, ball-peen hammers, screwdrivers and most heinous of all...drain cleaning fluids, so that, in the minds of the idiot thug, they too can be looked upon as legitimate weapons.

In my early days, most 'street' violence was related to drink, and its effect upon the consumer; often making normally placid people belligerent, along with an increase in their bravado. At most, bloody noses were the order of the day; when a man was felled; his opponent stepped back and either awaited a continuation of the fray, or accepted the peaceful hand-shake of the floored contestant. Now-a-days new rules apply. If someone is knocked down, the assailant will try to 'finish him off ' or at least commit some serious injury. Kicking someone in the head has become the 'norm'.

'Give him a bit of brain damage, that'll teach him a lesson', I heard one man say.

Sick isn't it! Some young man leaves home for a good night out; he'll meet some other young lad, and one of them ends up with brain damage, or worse.

On the other hand, patients who are hostile and angry and offering physical violence, or even verbal abuse towards the paramedic, may present difficulties that are sometimes difficult to overcome.

One of the first, essential, considerations that the paramedic needs to make when dealing with an aggressive patient is to determine whether or not their aggressive behaviour is actually due to an injury or illness.

Initially we have to give the aggressor the benefit of the doubt, and treat as if their aggression has a medical origin, and treat accordingly.

Paramedics must always avoid the temptation to respond with reciprocal anger, for doing so rarely serves any useful purpose, and may even further inflame the situation. Most angry patients can be calmed by a trained person who conveys an impression of confidence that the patient, is caring for, will behave well. It takes a lot of experience to understand that anger can actually be a symptom of injury or illness, and aggressive behaviour may be the patient's way of dealing with feelings of helplessness. Their anger may have a physiological basis, due to some sudden change in the body's equilibrium, caused by injury or illness.

For instance anyone who loses sufficient blood will become hypovolaemic (low blood volume), thus starving the brain of its usual supply of oxygen, and causing cerebral hypoxia (low Oxygen to the brain). Such a condition may cause a normally placid person to become aggressive, and confused. There are many other medical emergencies which may cause a patient to become aggressive or violent. It is not uncommon for an ambulance crew to be called to an emergency where the patient may be acting strangely, and becoming more and more belligerent whilst the crew try to attend to them.

For instance, diabetic emergencies occasionally present the paramedic with difficult challenges from a belligerent patient. Due to hypoglycaemia (low blood sugar) there can be chemical changes in the brain activity which may impair the patient's ability to comprehend or understand their current demeanour. As a result they may become disoriented, confused and stubborn: refusing the immediate help that they need to save their life.

As the paramedic you will endeavour to be sympathetic, kind, friendly, and good humoured but sometimes even a firm commanding response may be tried, but all to no avail. You cannot get impatient, or aggressive, despite the fact that you can see your patient becoming increasingly agitated toward yourself, and to the point where they may offer violence to you. You know they can't help it because they are diabetics; they may go into a coma, unless you can give them the help that they are currently trying to avoid.

Alternatively, there may be some psychological reason behind the aggressive manner of a patient. An aggressive patient may be suffering from some form of depression which can also cause otherwise placid people, to become extremely aggressive, and they can be very difficult to control. I have seen people who were probably normally easy going, suddenly become angry and aggressive, when learning of the sudden death of a loved one; their initial anger, born of grief, aimed at the person nearest to them at the time.

Then of course we come to 'Mr or Mrs Normal'. After a good night out and, having consumed too much 'El-vino Palonko' (alcohol). Tonight the world was their oyster, until they started arguing and screaming at each other. When the shouting stops - the fighting begins; after slapping her about, he is now ready to take on 'all comers'.

Unfortunately, some of those 'all comers' may be ambulance staff, called by someone concerned for the woman's safety; the crew are just trying to do a caring job, against the odds. It will take all their tact and diplomacy to talk nicely, calmly and patiently to the man, whilst at the same time deal with his injured wife, who - it must be said - may also be equally abusive to the ambulance crew.

Even violence not directed towards me, could still make me angry and frightened. Some such incidents in the past did leave me feeling insignificant, guilty, and a failure.

One such violent incident involving a group of club doormen (bouncers) which caused me such outrage happened in the early hours of a Sunday morning, whilst I was attending an emergency call at a local nightclub. After the event, I felt guilty, useless and insignificant, but most of all I felt a profound anger; so much so that I instigated further action through the police and licensing authorities, later in my off duty time.

The event started innocuously enough, with an emergency call just around 02:00 in the morning. My crewmate (Tony) and I were just enjoying a cup of coffee back on station, when we received a call to attend to a young lady with 'a cut foot' at a local nightspot. Being night time, and with our knowledge of the area we would be attending, we took the precaution of wearing our yellow fluorescent jackets; this would give us maximum visibility; it's the only way to be sure of standing out in a crowd.

Arriving at the seafront nightclub, a few minutes later, and right on closing time, we were met with a large number of rowdy revellers spilling out into the street. Manoeuvring carefully through the noisy but good natured throng I pulled up close to the door of the club and allowed Tony to make his way inside to locate the patient. Meanwhile I retrieved a 'carry chair' and blanket from the back of the ambulance and followed after him.

Carrying the blanket, and the carry-chair, I made my way through the crowded club foyer and into the main bar room. Over the heads of the crowd, I could just see Tony (thanks to his fluorescent jacket) with his back to me. Ignoring all the friendly banter from some young women dressed in their brief Saturday night outfits, I pushed through the crowd to join him

He was talking to a young woman who was sitting on a chair with her injured foot up on a stool. Displaying a, very nasty looking, laceration, caused when she had trod on a broken beer glass. Tony was now bending over the young woman, dealing with her injury; she giggled nervously and laughed as her friends joked, trying to reassure her.

There were still a few stragglers in the club room. Outside I could hear the boisterous laughter of people calling to one another as they made their way out of the club. It seemed the end of a perfect night out for some. The club was winding down for the night. A few staff were busy collecting the empty glasses from the small wrought iron tables with imitation marble tops, which surrounded the dancefloor. The shutters were up on the bar, the music had stopped, and the main bright lights had been switched on. I imagined the club looked completely different just a short while ago.

Suddenly, without any warning, I saw a young man aged about 18 years of age came crashing heavily onto the floor beside Tony and our patient. Both she and her friends began to scream as the young man, reached out toward them for help. Immediately, one of the club doormen set about kicking him in a frenzied attack with scant regard to the safety of us bystanders. He was kicking the young man about the head and body. I estimated the weight of this bouncer to be in the region of about 14 stone or more; he was built like the proverbial outhouse. Very muscular build and with a thick neck, which was red with rage.

Time seemed to slow as I watched, dumbstruck. I still had

the metal carry chair tucked under my right arm, but I had dropped the blankets. Our patient was now screaming hysterically, due to the close proximity of the attack, and the very real danger of further injury to her. Tony had also been forced to abandon (for the moment), his treatment of her injury; moving away for fear of being kicked himself, by this thug.

Within a couple of seconds another bouncer joined the affray, and he too began to kick the young man, unmercifully. Both men (I use the word loosely) seemed to be in a terrible uncontrolled rage. They were wild without consideration for their victim, or for those of us watching the event unfold.

Nearby tables and chairs were sent flying, as these two men continued their cowardly attack.

I realised that I could do little or nothing at this time, they were like wild animals; if I tried to interfere the likelihood is that they would beat me up (a 48 year old, ten stone weakling), before realising who I was. I decided that the best and only action that I could take at that moment was to try to remember as much of these events as I could; I was sure that I was going to be a witness to something serious. For a while, I was transfixed. I stood and watched, the young man as he lay on the floor, with both bouncers kicking him hard. I had never been so close to such a ferocious attack. I had never been witness to such graphic and grotesque barbarity.

Incredibly, the second bouncer picked up one of the small wrought iron tables, and to my amazement, held it aloft before deliberately slamming it, feet first, onto the young man on the floor. The young man was clearly unable to protect himself and was desperately trying to avoid heavy blows from both sides. I saw the table bounce off his upper body, only for the bouncer to repeat the offence again. Amidst all this commotion, I became aware an eerie quiet about the room. People were standing watching; they were obviously afraid to intervene. The only noise seemed to be the grunts and heavy breathing from the enraged bouncers.

From my right hand side I noticed a third bouncer running across the room to join in the melee. He arrived with a well-aimed, Karate type, kick which connected to the side of the young man's head. His head was knocked sideways as he tried to sit up, and to fend off anymore kicks.

My own mind was now in turmoil. It was my job to protect people, I thought...to care for them...to help them...to dress their wounds, NOT to stand by while someone murdered them. For this now seemed the most likely outcome, unless someone put a stop to events.

Just as the newly arrived, third, bouncer was about to aim a second kick at the young man's head, I intervened! I had seen enough! I could no longer stand by and watch these thugs working out on this young man.

Using the metal carry chair (that I was still holding) as a defensive shield, and shouting loudly, 'Paramedic coming through'. I shouldered my way passed the doorman with his back to me and stood with my legs apart straddling the young man., and shielding him from further attack. I was relying on my uniform to protect me. These bastards had all gone berserk; there was no knowing what they would do. But they had injured me too...my pride! I had never allowed anyone to be physically attacked in my presence before. Now I had made my move, I was committed. 'Back off...Now' I commanded to them. 'Back off, I am reporting you to the police for endangering me and our patient and for assaulting this young man' I spoke angrily and directly into the face of the initial aggressor,

At first he seemed oblivious to my presence, so I reached out and pushed his left shoulder (not too hard... I'm no hero) and he looked up at me; my face, defiantly, less than six inches from his. His bulging neck and face was red, his eyes staring straight at me with pinpoint pupils. Suddenly I was not afraid of him. I too was angry! But I had now established my authority and power to make him and his other thuggish colleagues back off. I put that round down to me!

His face seemed red and his eyes stared at me. It seemed that he would have loved to give me a good kicking too; now I was humiliating him and the other two thugs.

It was certainly not my physique that halted their cowardly attack, but the fact that I was in uniform.

For reasons of good taste I cannot tell you, actually, what I said to him at this point, but it was one hundred percent Anglo Saxon. 'Scumbag' was one of the milder expletives that I used, as I kept my eyes focused on him and the other two thugs.

To my side I could hear the young lady crying, Tony having now resumed his task of dealing with her injuries. He called across to me 'come on Dale, let's go'.

I looked down at the young man, lying between my feet, his face was badly swollen but he was not unconscious. I stepped across to some other young men nearby, and asked them quietly, if they would help him out to the ambulance, whilst I assisted Tony with our patient.

I was visibly shaking and I was angry inside, I wished I had been able to punish these thugs, but my priority was to get out of here and to get our patients to hospital. I helped the young man to his feet, so that his friends could assist him safely out of the club and to our waiting ambulance.

Turning around I saw the three bouncers, standing well back in a dimly lit area of the club. I could see (or sensed) that they were smirking, at me. They had enjoyed their bit fun, a ' bit of a buzz'. Still angry, I walked across to them, and once again voiced my opinion of their behaviour. I stood before them, defiantly pointing my finger at each of them in turn; making sure that I would be able to identify each of them later for the police. They were so thick and stupid that they didn't realise that I had won. I had stopped their brutality!

I turned and walked back to Tony, who by now had put the young woman onto our patient carry chair, ready for evacuation to hospital. As we were leaving the premises, the club manager arrived on the scene. Happy, cheerful and smiling he greeted us in a jovial manner. He soon changed his tune when I launched into a vitriolic tirade, about the scum that he employed as doormen. 'My own daughters come to this club' (which was true) I complained bitterly to him. 'You entice young people into these places, sell them drinks, and then have a bit of 'sport' by beating the living daylights out of them'. He looked shocked at my accusation.

'You don't know what he did' (meaning the young man) he replied pathetically. 'I don't give a damn what he has done, if he had been pushing drugs, or knocking one of the girls about, it is not your job to beat hell out of him. You should arrest him and hand him over to the police'. He looked at me and shrugged his shoulders in indifference.

We made our way back out through the crowd of club-goers, and climbed into the ambulance with our casualty. There was no sign of the young man anywhere but someone nearby informed me that he had been taken away by taxi. I presumed that he would be going to hospital.

I helped Tony to settle the young lady onto our stretcher, before we set off. I then set off to hospital with our patient. On our arrival at the hospital, I was surprised *not* to find the young man there; but I did alert the casualty staff to watch out for him.

A few days later I heard that the young man had been brought in by his parents. His injuries included a fractured jaw, damaged eye socket as well as bruising around his body.

Occasionally, when dealing with victims of alleged 'patron abuse' by bouncers, the paramedic can find themselves in fear of either becoming entangled in a fresh attack, or of being drawn into confrontation with the alleged attackers who may still be present. Upon our arrival at the scene, the victim along with their companion may feel that they are measurably safer and secure by our presence. However, this feeling of security can sometimes give them new found confidence whereupon they will then inflame the situation by loudly remonstrating and making retaliatory threats to the alleged attackers. Consequently, in the heat of the moment when tempers are, understandably frayed I have known bouncers to be provoked into a secondary attack upon the victim, necessitating me, the paramedic, to physically intervene to prevent further injury to my patient.

I recall one such case that I dealt with, one cold wet and windy Saturday night. On this particular night we were also carrying an authorised observer who was about to enter the ambulance service.

My crewmate, Jack (a trainee paramedic), and I, along with Stan, observing were making our way back to base, for a meal-break. We had so far that evening, been very busy with one job after another since the starting our duty at 19:00. We were about to make a call at Mr Fry's residence (the chip shop) when ambulance control called us on the radio, diverting us to a local 'fun pub' (now there's a misnomer if ever there was one!).

It was just before midnight as I drove the ambulance into the pub's car park. Unusually, I had to leave my flashing blue lights on with klaxon blaring, in order to clear a way through a very large noisy crowd. Judging by the body language of some in the crowd, I suspected that this may be a bad job.

By the time I had brought the ambulance to a standstill and opened the rear doors, Jack had disappeared into the crowd. Following closely behind, along with a nervous observer, I had to push and shove a way through the crowd of women screaming and men shouting; the hullabaloo was not enhanced at all by the blaring music emanating from the disco just inside the pub. As I reached Jack I could see he was under pressure and feeling intimidated by the crowd, some of whom seemed in danger of falling onto us and the patient. 'Okay Jack...keep calm... just remember your ABCs' I spoke to him above the din of the crowd.

I turned my attention to the baying crowd surrounding us; 'For God's sake, get back! Give us some room'.

We were just outside of the entrance to the pub so there was very little light in the area, but by torch light I could see that the person on the ground was a man aged approximately in his mid-fifties. He was in the throes of a seizure, and had a very serious 'open' head injury.

His two companions, aged about the same, were extremely shocked and distressed, screaming and crying. Their behaviour was also hampering Jack as he attempted to assess and deal with the victims' injuries.

Very quickly, I realised that this was a volatile situation which could escalate, what is more the injured casualty was 'likely to prove' (police jargon for likely to die) from his injury.

Pointing to two brutish looking doormen nearby, one of the men told me, 'those two f****** b******* have kicked and beaten him', (referring to our casualty), 'kicking him over the body and head'.

I turned to our observer and asked him to get back to our ambulance and call ambulance control to request immediate police attendance. Report 'serious assault...query fractured skull...likely to prove', and told him to return to us with our stretcher.

Our priority was to get the casualty inside our warm well-lit ambulance and out of the bedlam so that we could start treating his injuries and be prepared to resuscitate.

Stan arrived back with the stretcher and informed me that police were on the way.

Quickly but, carefully, we lifted the casualty onto our stretcher and into the relative safety of our ambulance. Once inside I made a quick but thorough examination of his chief complaint (main injury). He had stopped fitting but was unconscious I suspected that he had a fractured skull, and a possible brain injury, he needed life-saving intervention and there was also a very real possibility that he had a broken neck!

On occasions like this, it is essential that the ambulance staff, in the back of the ambulance, are allowed to concentrate without interruption dealing quickly and efficiently with the casualty; more so with someone who has such serious injury as this.

There was a large amount of equipment to be employed, needles inserted, drips set up, cardiac monitor set up and monitored, oxy-meter attached and as well as intubating (passing a tube through the vocal cords into the airway) giving life-saving resuscitation to the patient. Plus we had to stem the haemorrhage from the head wound.

With three of us already in the back of the ambulance with the casualty, it was crowded, but at least Jack and I knew what we were doing. Each of us was dealing with different life-saving tasks. Fortunately, our observer Stan was well into his studies, and under my strict guidance he was able to ventilate our patient, using a bag and mask connected to a supply of 100% Oxygen.

We had been on scene for only a few minutes but all the activity made it seem much longer as we worked on the casualty. Time was of the essence, interruptions cost valuable 'life saving' time.

The victims' companions kept interrupting our efforts by opening the doors of the ambulance and trying to climb in, pleading to be stay with their injured friend. They would not accept that there was no room in the ambulance for anyone else. I assured them that I would let them in before we set off for the hospital. This explanation did not suit them; they tried to barge their way in and were in danger of dislodging equipment already attached to their injured friend.

In the end I stepped forward, and grabbed one of the men by the scruff of the neck and absolutely firmly told him, 'get out of the ambulance', (well something like that) and 'to wait outside'.

A few minutes later the door opened again but this time by a policeman. I gave him a quick SITREP (situation report) before we set off to the hospital (the injured man's companions had to follow on by taxi.

The story was tragically simple, the victim a man in his early fifties and married with a family, had been visiting and staying with friends in this area. This was to be his last night before returning home, and so the group had decided to go for a last night out. During the evening, the victim had made some innocent joke (after all...it was supposed to be a 'fun pub') with one of the doormen who apparently took exception to what the older man had said to him.

Consequently, as all three were later leaving the pub, the doorman and his mates set about the gentleman who had made the joke. They almost killed him!

I am glad to say that he did survive, and I am glad that we had something to do with his survival. I have since been back to that same club on another matter and I have seen at least one of those bouncers still working on the door.

In the past, doormen were respected members of society, offering their service to only the most exclusive establishments. For the most part, they were ex members of HMF (Her Majesty's Forces) and were part of a respectable organisation, namely, 'The Corp 'Commissionaires'. Always smartly dressed in a military type uniform, they were courteous and knowledgeable upstanding people commanding respect. They knew what real action was, as many had served in some theatre of war.

These days many of the doormen that I see, all seem to wear the same outfit of black 'bomber ' jackets with matching trousers, black boots (known aptly as Kickers). And they all seem to lack the one thing that I crave.....hair!

Unlike my early years in the ambulance service, it seems that every pub or club has to have someone on the door who looks 'handy', and who is not afraid to join in a gang to beat someone up.

Over the years I have been to too many incidents, where people have allegedly been beaten up by club bouncers; so many, in fact, that I began to keep a mental note of the type of people that became the victims of this 'silent' crime. My opinion is based upon my actual findings at 'grass roots' level, and is not part of a scientific study.

My findings are:

- The majority, of victims were *not* drunk (contrary to what the bouncers had told me at the time).
- The majority were male, aged between 18n and 25 years of age.

- The majority had no history of crime and were decent people.
- The majority were too frightened to make a formal complaint to the police or thought that no-one would believe them.
- The majority claimed that they had been beaten and kicked by more than one bouncer.
- Amazingly some of the victims were young women, who also claimed that they had been verbally abused.

How nice it would be, to be able to go into a club and NOT feel under threat from the staff or doormen; to feel secure in the knowledge that if anyone should try to spoil your evening, the situation would be dealt with calmly, professionally and with the minimum of fuss...without violence!!

◆ ◆ ◆

10 WEAPONS

Sticks and stones may break my bones, but guns and knives are bloody dangerous. You may be quite surprised to learn that ambulance crews do, indeed, have to deal with such weaponry from time to time. I have dealt with at least five incidents involving knives or guns; on two such occasions with direct threat to the safety of myself and my crewmate.

Knives and similar implements have often been an integral part of many emergency calls that I dealt with. Knowing the potential for horrific injury from such weapon's, caused me to harbour a morbid fear of being attacked whilst I was dealing with incidents where there was a suspicion of any kind of weaponry. I learned never to turn my back (even to run away) on anyone I suspected, or known to be armed with such weapons.

The only weapon that I was allowed in my armoury, was my own diligence and alertness; ever watchful of the body language that may signal a person's intention to make an attack; always with the back-up of a crewmate of equal diligence. It may seem absurd, to most decent people, to learn that anyone would wish to harm or threaten ambulance staff, let alone doctors and nurses. Yet every day someone somewhere will be making such an attack on one or the other of the emergency medical staff.

Violent attacks can come at any time of the day or night and can also come from any quarter, be it down at the bottom of the social scale or near the top. There can be any variety of reasons (excuses) offered for this phenomenon; in my view there can be few good reasons for such violent or confrontational behaviour towards any emergency practitioner, whose only aim in life, is to offer help to the sick and injured.

Of all the violent confrontations that a paramedic can face, none can be worse than facing someone who has a weapon of some sort and is displaying a potential for using it, particularly against your-self.

More often than not, knowledge of the presence of a weapon comes out of the blue. An unpleasant surprise and, therefore, there will be little, if any, time to plan for the event. In fact, the only plan a paramedic should have, if knowing of the potential existence of a weapon and its likelihood of being used, is to ask the police to attend the incident too.

Many of my experiences, dealing with people armed with a weapon, came about as a result of me and a crewmate innocently attending an emergency call; the involvement or possession of a weapon only presenting itself to me 'out of the blue', On some of those occasions there was little opportunity for me to call for police assistance and it was unlikely that the police would have arrived in time to prevent any attack anyway. It would be down to my crewmate and me to deal, as tactfully and sometimes physically, with the situation, until we were able to render the weapon safe and out of harm's way.

There were also a couple of occasions where I did (some may say unwisely) actually enter a situation, knowing full well, that there was a real possibility of a weapon (knives) being involved.

We deal with each situation as we find it, flying by the seat of our pants, so to speak. I have on a number of occasions, forcibly disarmed people. I know too that some of my other colleagues have had similar experiences.

The weapon that I fear most is the knife. It is plentiful in its supply, particularly when one is dealing with a domestic dispute within the home, be it a bread knife or a humble potato peeler. Knives are also very easy to conceal. The person wielding a knife does not appreciate the actual damage that the knife can inflict, nor do they have any knowledge as to what vital organs may be underlying the point of penetration. Very often a knife may be brandished only as a threat, but suddenly becomes used in an almost accidental manner and not with the actual intention of killing the victim.

I have attended incidents where women have attacked men with knives; the injury usually being less serious than if a man had used the knife as a weapon. The reason for this phenomenon is that men tend to wield a knife underhand, thrusting upwards into the abdomen, thus causing horrendous injury as the knife penetrates and thrusts upwards into the abdomen. Women on the other hand, tend to use the knife in an overhand way, with a downward thrust, which is often less damaging. However, either event can cause serious damage to the body, due to the penetrating knife severing or even just nicking an internal artery or some other organ.

Finding a knife or indeed any sharp object sticking out of someone is a most unsettling experience, instinct tells you to remove it, but caution prevails and you may leave it in place until you reach the hospital. There, after careful examination, it can be removed, by surgery if necessary.

Unfortunately of late, due to a change in social circumstances, there seems to have been an increase in the willingness of young people, particularly males, to carry knives. Many of these young people are decent kids and are no more than very naive and immature. Almost certainly they would never really attempt to actually stab another person. However, there is a real possibility that given the right circumstances (as they see it) they may threaten to use the knife for 'defensive' purpose. Sadly a paradox of using a knife to threaten someone in this way is that the person initially wielding the knife, all too often becomes the victim of his own weapon, sometimes receiving fatal injury.

Whether or not someone is really intent on using a knife in a deliberate attack, or just using it as a threat was incidental to me. I was always scared and if you forgive the pun, I was on a 'knife edge' until the situation was rendered safe.

Although I have been involved in the pre-hospital care of people who have suffered a deliberate knife injury, none were sufficiently injured enough to die. They were all, however, extremely shocked at seeing a gaping and bloody hole in their body and this focused their imagination on what they could not see, namely their internal being. The victim of a stabbing is usually concerned that something horrible may be going on inside them. Penetrating injuries are often much more serious than they appear from the outside; beneath the hole may lie a disaster area of ruptured blood vessels and damaged organs.

Of all the potentially dangerous knife incidents that I dealt with over the years, *three* in particular stand out. One because I actually felt a perverse satisfaction when telling the victim that he had been stabbed (more in later in chapter). Another involved me walking into an attempt to murder. And the third involved a violent confrontation whereupon a violent man was trying to stab me and my crewmate.

Responding to an emergency call, 'domestic incident' late one bitterly cold and windy evening, found my crewmate (Ray) and I arriving outside a large detached house in a very select part of Wirral. Not the sort of place that we would, normally expect to attend for a domestic incident.

The street was deserted and the house, up a long driveway, was in total darkness. Ringing the front door bell, several times, without a reply, seemed to indicate that the place may be empty. We suspected that this call may be a false alarm, or a wrong address, so we checked back with ambulance control who confirmed that we *were* at the correct location. Our controller went onto to say, that the emergency call had come from a telephone at that address and had been made by a 'distressed gentleman'.

Returning to the house, Ray tried the front door again. Whilst I quickly climbed over the side gate, and dropped down into the back garden; I unlocked the gate for him to follow after me. I only had a small hand-torch, which was in urgent need of new batteries. It was even darker at the back of the house, than it was at the front, due to the lack of any street lighting.

Moving about in the darkness of the garden, I stumbled and

fell over some form of rockery, putting my foot into an icy cold fish pond. Now my shoe was full of icy cold water and one trouser leg was soaking wet, up to the knee. It was most uncomfortable.

Regaining my feet, I stood quietly listening and looking around at the darkened house and garden. Somewhere nearby I heard a woman crying softly. As my eyes were becoming accustomed to the darkness, I could just make out the shape of small shed nearby. Making my way toward sounds of crying I came to the back of the shed and shone my torch. There on the ground, with the failing light of my torch, I could just pick out the small frame of a woman, huddled in a corner. She was very distressed and showed a great reluctance to come out from her hiding place.

Despite the late hour and the very cold night, she was only lightly dressed and she felt extremely cold when I touched her. Probably hypothermic, I thought to myself. I spoke softly, to reassure her.

'Hello, what's the problem, is you hurt?' I enquired, 'Can you tell me what your name is?'. She stood up and came toward me.

'I've had a row with my husband', she cried sadly, 'he's hit me once too many times, this time'.

I took hold of her arm and helped her back towards the house.

Just then Ray came through the gate into the back garden to join us. With the guidance of the woman, all three of us made our way into the darkened house through an unlocked kitchen door.

Once inside the warmth the house and with lights turned on, we were able to see that the woman in her thirties had bruising to her head and face; as well as a number of abrasions about her arms and legs.

I considered that her injuries were consistent with having

been beaten; in this case the beating had, she alleged, been at the hands of her husband.

She told me that there had earlier, been a bitter 'regular' argument with her husband. The argument had escalated into a physical brawl, after which she ran out into the back garden to get away to safety, leaving him alone in the house. I explained to her that there had been no sign of lights when we had arrived, nor could we get an answer at the front door when I had rung the bell. 'I presume that your husband left the house at the same time as you did 'I commented, 'but who called the ambulance?'

With the woman's permission I went on to search the house, leaving Ray to deal with her injuries.

As I made my way around from room to room, I had to turn lights on as I went. In one room I found signs of a struggle having taken place; furniture was upturned, along with some broken dishes and ornaments. Eventually I went upstairs into a front bedroom and switching on the light, I was surprised to find a gentleman sitting on the edge of a bed, bent over with his head in his hands. 'Hello sir, can I help you, are you all right?' I asked. But he didn't reply.

'Can you hear me, what's the problem?' I asked again; placing a hand on his shoulder.

Suddenly he sat upright and pushed my hand away violently. 'P*** off, leave me alone, I don't need your help, get out of my house.' he retorted angrily. He stood up confronting me, aggressively and shouting. He was a thick set man in his late thirties, and well dressed in a smart suit.

I stood my ground and speaking calmly I told him that we had found his, injured wife outside in the back garden and that all I needed was his help to establish what the current situation was.

'Just f*** off out of my house', he shouted, waving his arms at me although he made no move nearer toward me. Despite his instruction to me, to leave, I stayed where I was and closed the bedroom door and stood with my back to it. Now there was only him and I together. First,' I said raising my own voice a bit, 'you stop your shouting and swearing at me, or I will call the police!'. I walked toward him and spoke calmly again, 'come on sit down, let's talk things over, tell me what the problem is. Remember, I'm not your enemy'.

He took a lot of persuading, but eventually he sat down and talked about the recent dispute with his wife, which had started in the kitchen whilst she was preparing supper. Listening to him and the things that he was saying and the manner in which he was saying it, led me to the opinion that this man was arrogant and had an unreasonable streak in his personality. He was quite scathing of his wife in particular, but also of women in general. He saw himself as a 'mans, man' who liked his pint and football etc. He worked hard and played hard. He admitted that it was he who had telephoned the ambulance rather than the police, but only to get someone to help sort out their domestic dispute.

There was a knock on the bedroom door. I turned to see Ray come into the room, he beckoned me to one side and spoke quietly out of 'earshot' of the man to inform me that the man's wife did not wish to go to hospital, nor would she be pressing charges against her husband. I turned to the irate man and told him that his wife was willing to drop the matter.

All I needed now was for him to reciprocate; give me an assurance that there would be no more trouble tonight and I could be on my way. 'No way matey!' he shouted, 'I want that bitch out of here.'

Once again he began his ranting and shouting at me, 'you can get out too....... you bastards'. He moved toward me, but I stood my ground. Speaking quietly and calmly I managed to persuade him to sit down once again, and to listen and talk to me about the problem.

Many domestic jobs are like this; most of our time being taken up counselling the people involved, of whom, all were strangers to us before we arrived. We very soon need to establish a rapport with the stranger, hopefully bringing them around to a more reasonable approach to their particular dilemma. At last I seemed to have reached that rapport with this gentleman. His unreasonable attitude toward me abated and he was now talking more freely to me about many of his problems and how they affected his relationship with his wife.

He confessed to hitting her occasionally, although later he would feel remorse. She never usually retaliated, but tonight she did, she had punched him hard in the back as he was leaving the room, before she herself ran out into the garden. Punched in the back!

That was a phrase that triggered my instinct, as I sat listening to him. 'Turn around, let me have a look at your back' I said as I moved to look. There, high in the back of his jacket was a small hole about an inch wide. I helped him off with the jacket, and I could now see blood on the back of his shirt, which also had a hole in it. By now his arrogance had disappeared and he was suddenly very meek and mild and extremely worried as I removed his shirt to confirm my suspicions. 'Yes', I said to him, 'just as I thought, I think your wife may have stabbed you in the back'.

With that he collapsed back onto the bed absolutely horrified.

'My God, how could she do this to me?' he said audaciously. Fortunately for him (and his wife) the wound had been made with a potato peeler and had not damaged any major organs.

Eventually, after we had wasted another valuable half an hour at the house, the couple agreed to both, attend the hospital without further arguments.

Another emergency call that I can recall involved me and a crewmate, Fred, inadvertently, interrupting a murder attempt! It happened at about 18:00 on a cold wet and miserable evening as we were making our way back to station for a meal-break. We were instructed to divert to attend to an 'unknown incident' at a block of flats. Ambulance control had received only a brief, 999 call from the police control room, reporting that there was some sort of injury incident at this address. As it happened the location of the emergency was only two minutes away from where we were, and so we soon arrived 'on scene'.

Not knowing what exactly to expect, I grabbed my paramedic case and set off quickly in the direction of the entrance to the flats; leaving Fred, to park the ambulance ready for evacuation, before following on after me.

Making my way along a short path, of about fifty metres, leading to the door of the flats I was met by a middle aged woman running, frantically, out of the door. She didn't stop but called out as she passed by, that someone had been stabbed. As I reached to the door a second person, a young man, ran out in panic and said to me, 'Someone is being stabbed in there' before he too ran off.

By now I was already walking through the door and into the entrance hallway. Immediately I heard a man's voice shouting and cursing, and I saw a heavy thick set man of middle age, raining blows down upon a figure lying at the foot of the nearby staircase. I was also aware of a mass of blood on the floor. Instinctively I knew I could not stand by and wait for help. I felt committed to do something to stop the attack. Holding my paramedic case (which was of a large, orange coloured, hard case type) in front of me; using it as a form of shield, I ran at the assailant shouting loudly.

'Paramedic! Get back...get back', I yelled loudly and threateningly.

The assailant looked up and I briefly saw that he looked wild and manic. 'Get back! I'm a paramedic. Get back', I shouted at him again.

Stepping back and without a word, the assailant turned and fled into a nearby flat. As I approached the victim, I was aware of my feet slipping precariously; there was so much blood on the tiled floor that it was difficult to avoid slipping over. Placing my case away from the bloodied area, I bent down to make some assessment of the victims' injuries.

At this point I was grateful to be joined Fred, who informed me that he had spoken, very briefly, to both the people who had run passed me. As priority dictated, before joining me, he had then asked ambulance control to update the police of the urgent situation.

Whilst continuing with assessing the victim's injuries, I quickly outlined to Fred what I had witnessed and warned him about the assailant who was now hiding in a nearby flat behind us. Ever fearful that the assailant may return, we quickly set about assessing the injured man. He too was middle aged and appeared unkempt with several days' growth of beard. Although he was dressed in several layers of shabby clothing we were still able to establish that he had several deep stab wounds to his upper body as well as one through his neck. Although was still conscious he was very aggressive, telling us to, 'F... off', pushing me away trying to stop me and Fred attending to his injuries. There was also a strong smell of alcohol about his person, but we could not count that as the reason his aggression. There was so much blood loss that his brain could be being starved of Oxygen (Hypoxia) which can also lead to aggressive behaviour.

A few minutes later, several police officers rushed through the door, suddenly filling the small corridor. Upon seeing the police, our patient became even more aggressive, yelling obscenities, and lashing out.

With a very quick SITREP, I pointed out the door of the flat to which the knifeman had fled. Within seconds they had kicked the door in and amid a load of commotion, arrested the man that I had seen stabbing the victim.

Eventually, with the aid of a couple of the police officers we managed to get our, struggling, patient onto the stretcher and into the warmth and light of the ambulance. Now hopefully

I could get a couple of intravenous lines (one in each arm) and start to replace some of the fluids that he had lost. The police officers accompanied me in the ambulance to the hospital assisting me with the still aggressive patient.

I learned later, that the stabbing victim had received seven stab wounds, none of which were life threatening on its own, but the accumulative effect of all the bleeding injuries had been such a threat. Moreover, even in the hospital, the doctors and nurses had required the police to restrain the patient whilst treatment was administered.

Our patient survived his injuries. I found out later that the two men were, in fact, friends, who could be seen most days sitting on a park bench drinking cans of strong lager. On this particular day, they had disagreed over something which resulted in the violence.

Later, I was able to reflect on the risks I had unexpectedly encountered and how lucky I had been not to have been a secondary victim of the knifeman; who incidentally was later charged and found guilty of attempted murder!

Another near miss I had with a stabbing incident came about when my crewmate and I responded to a so called 'overdose' emergency. That particular incident took place in the long hot summer of 1981. At that time, under a Conservative government, unemployment had surpassed the two million mark; bringing a wave of public resentment, from many of those effected towards the Government. Eventually, civil disorder broke out and many local authorities the length and breadth of Britain experienced widespread disorder in the form of street rioting.

The rioting started in the Liverpool inner city area of Toxteth. The Toxteth Riots (as they became known) seemed by many, to be a pre-cursor to riots that were breaking out in other cities across the UK.

As you would expect, Merseyside Ambulance Service was

heavily involved, but the riots were not restricted just to the Toxteth area of Merseyside. Rioting took place in many parts of the county and there were several incidents of'copy-cat' rioting on the Wirral peninsula, which is only a couple miles, through the Mersey Tunnel, from Toxteth,

The riots placed an acute and tremendous strain on the resources of all three emergency services, by far the biggest strain being felt by the police. The local core police contingent was insufficient to deal with either the number or size of incidents taking place throughout the area; whilst still trying to maintain 'normal' policing requirements. In order to enhance the local riot policing of response, reinforcements' were brought in, from neighbouring regions, and were deployed to flash-point areas. Many such police reinforcements were brought in from North Wales, which is only an hour's drive away from Wirral. For all emergency services it was a very tense period.

The worst of the rioting took place in the evening and throughout the night. During the rioting our night duty brought with it the risk that we could be caught up in the action; it had soon been realised that many rioters would allow ambulances into areas where the police were, otherwise, being restricted from entering. These areas became known as 'no go areas' although the senior police authority denied that such existed.

It had been another very hot day and the evening was still very humid as I arrived on station, to join my crewmate Ray, for the 18:00 start of our nightshift. It seemed that all the talk on station was about the riots and the involvement of our service. Already one of our two emergency ambulances had been sent out to deal with some general admissions into hospital. This meant that we would be 'next out'. Ray and I carried out our regular routine vehicle and equipment checks, then sat and watched the local television news which was carrying the latest from the Liverpool riot, whilst waiting for our first call.

Our first call was of non-emergency patient admission into hospital, followed by a couple of similar jobs; it was a couple of hours later before we got back for a break, only to find that the other ambulance had been sent across to Liverpool. Again we would be next out. Now late into the evening, the red phone in the station rang out, signalling an emergency call. We were instructed to rendezvous with the police 'incident officer' at a major road junction just outside of a local housing estate. There were reports of a large scale disturbance on the estate, with fires burning and police engaged to protect firemen.

It was just going on 23:00 as Ray and I climbed into our ambulance; switching to a dedicated radio emergency channel, we headed out of the station toward our rendezvous point. I have to confess that I felt a certain amount of excitement, as well as apprehension, at the prospect of being involved (once again) in an event surrounding the riot. I had previously had a similar experience in Toxteth, the previous week.

Tonight, en route to our rendezvous point, we listened into the dedicated emergency channel; to reports of ambulances responding to rioting on another housing estate in Birkenhead, on the other side of the Wirral. It seemed that everyone on duty in the emergency services was in for another busy night.

We had only travelled about a mile from station when ambulance control called us up on the radio. They ordered us to stand down from this call and to redirect to deal with an emergency call involving someone who had, allegedly, taken an overdose of tablets. Ray was driving and knew the area well, so we were soon turning into the street where the incident had been reported. We soon located the address and pulled up outside of a small, but neat, two-up and two-down terraced house.

Alighting from the ambulance, I could hear the muffled sound of heavy beat music coming from the house. I banged loudly on the front door and it quickly swung open wide, releasing a crescendo of blaring music into the quiet night. Even before I could enter the premises, a rather effeminate young man barred my way, and grabbing hold of my arm he stepped out into the street to speak to me.

'Oh, hiya', he said in a soft voice, 'it's my friend', he told me, indicating toward the open front door. 'He's taken an overdose of tablets, I don't know why, but he's doing my head in', he went on, with a shrug of his shoulders.

Without waiting for Ray to join me I went up the front and made my way inside, followed closely, by the young man. The small front room was furnished with expensive modern furniture, as well as a monster of a music centre from which the ear-splitting music was drumming out. To my right stood another two young men; I indicated to one of them to turn the volume down so that I could at least hear myself think.

Directly opposite to me, there were two open doors adjacent to each other. The one on the right leading into a back kitchen and the other, opened onto a set of narrow stairs leading up to bedrooms.

As the volume of music was turned off, a man in his late twenties or early thirties appeared at the door, from the kitchen, looking very angry. He stopped briefly in the doorway of the kitchen and faced me directly. He had long blonde hair, reaching down his back and was dressed in a white towelling bathrobe which was wide open; displaying the fact that he was completely naked underneath. Upon seeing me, with his young friend standing nearby, he began yelling and screaming at me to leave. 'You can just f*** off out of my house' he ranted and raved furiously at me.

Before I could even say 'Hello, can I help you'? my attention was drawn away from him, by the sight and sound of a rather large fearsome Alsatian dog, which was coming down the stairs opposite. The dog clearly had me in its sights, and it was snarling; it's aggression matching that of the owner. I had little time to make any decision. Instinctively self-preservation took over and I dived to my left toward the door, just in time to slam it shut, imprisoning the snarling dog safely on the stairs.

Suddenly, before I could regain my spatial awareness, I felt a hefty shove in the middle of my back, which sent me sprawling onto my hands and knees. In a split second I was up again and turning around to see what had happened to me. I could see that Ray was grappling with the blonde man from the kitchen. The man screaming hysterically and swearing obscenities was armed with a dangerous looking stainless steel meat carving fork and was attempting to stab at Ray and me. He seemed beside himself with rage, but for what reason I did not know. Clearly we could not walk away from this. I shouted at the other men in the room to 'Keep out of it or else,' there was no time for subtlety.

Hanging onto the back of the blonde man, who was going absolutely berserk, I managed to get a firm arm lock around his neck pulling him backwards onto the floor, with Ray falling on top of him. The room was only small and all three of us were bouncing off the furniture and rolling around the small floor area. Now with the man on the floor and on his back, we would need to get him turned over face down to better restrict his movements and gain a degree of control.

Arms and legs seemed to be everywhere; it was a job in the violence of the struggle to know which arm belonged to whom. I grabbed one arm and held onto it tightly, twisting it hard, only to find that the arm I was twisting, belonged to Ray. I quickly let go of it again, but by now our would-be attacker had drawn the carving fork up and brought it down in my direction. I was too slow to get out of the way and it caught my left arm, a glancing blow, causing a nasty abrasion and taking a fine layer of skin off the length of my arm. I remember yelling out as I felt the implement strike me; Ray heard me too and assumed that the blonde man had actually scored a direct hit and stabbed me.

Now with added vigour Ray set about kneeling on the attackers' chest whilst I held onto the hand still holding the carving fork, whereupon, with determination, eventually managed to twist the weapon from his grasp, almost breaking his fingers in the process.

By now the three men who had been in the room were becoming more agitated at the escalating level of violence. The young man who had greeted me at the front door was imploring us not to hurt his friend. 'Don't hurt him will you,' he pleaded with us. 'My God,' I thought, 'are you bloody stupid!'.

Your friend is trying to stab one of us and you're concerned with his safety. What about Ray and me? We have family; we don't expect to have to fight for our lives like this. We'd only come to assist someone in need.

Between us, Ray and I managed eventually to subdue the attacker by holding him face down on the floor. He was still very angry, threatening and unnecessarily aggressive, there was the real danger that he would flare up again when he had regained his breath; we were going to need more assistance, namely the police.

Taking a calculated gamble, I told the three men in the room that they should not move or allow my colleague to get hurt, whilst I was away. I dashed outside to the ambulance, leaving Ray alone briefly. Opening the door of the ambulance, I could hear the radio traffic was very busy with riot information. Grabbing the radio hand-set, I called ambulance control. 'Zulu one.... priority message over', I was still breathless as I spoke. Ambulance control responded immediately. 'Go ahead Zulu one pass your message'.

'Request immediate assistance, to deal with violent patient who has tried to stab a crew member. Over'. 'Roger Zulu one.' Their reply was brief but I knew they would respond with urgency.

I waited for their reply then returned to the house, to find that the man had taken advantage of my absence and Ray was again engaged in a struggle with him. The blonde man had now lost his dressing gown in the renewed struggle; now completely naked, he had managed to get to his feet and was kicking out.

Despite the seriousness of the situation, I couldn't help but feel some amusement at our bizarre predicament.

Once again we became embroiled in a vicious fight, but at least this time the man was not armed, Although he was still exercising his perceived right to get us to leave his home by continuing to kick and punch us. We, on the other hand, could only try to restrain him. We could not mete out any reciprocal violence.

The other side of this situation is that it is somewhat disconcerting to be fighting with someone who is completely naked. I did, in fact consider grabbing his balls, but I considered that this may go against me, should we later recount this tale to our other colleagues. I would not want them questioning my sexuality.

Unknown to Ray and me at this time; the riot which we had initially been responding to, was well and truly brewing and considerably robust, with the police well engaged. Fortunately for Ray and I, a team of Welsh policemen (all big fellows) dressed in full riot gear, had been, sat for an hour, in a mini-bus, less than a mile from our current position and waiting to be sent into the riot. When I had requested police assistance they were ordered to respond to our call for assistance; by the time they arrived at our location a few minutes later they were ready and eager to deal with anything and anyone.

Ray and I were so busy struggling with our violent and swearing blonde friend and trying to keep his companions out of our way, that we didn't hear the police arrive. I can just recall a lot of banging, swearing and shouting, as a crowd of well-built bobbies poured into the small front room, swamping us all. Seeing the obvious situation, the first policemen into the house, pushed Ray and I to one side, whilst at the same time grabbing our would-be attacker and taking over the fight with him, on our behalf.

Within seconds the room was full to bursting with police and the rest of us. Incredibly our blonde friend was unperturbed by the presence of so many policemen in his house and merely turned his aggression (vainly) to them. Punching, swearing and kicking at them, he never stood a chance. He was quickly arrested and being dragged outside into the street. Unfortunately at this time, I was already stepping backward out of the house, as the policemen began to frog-march their still struggling prisoner outside. I stumbled on a doormat and fell backward onto the front step. Inertia seemed to carry the fighting policemen and their struggling prisoner forward, and tripping over me they all fell on top. Now I suddenly found myself flat on my back, with the naked man on top of me, who in turn had several burly policemen on top of him, all of us wedged into the narrow doorway. By the time we had all regained our feet, I was a mass of bruises, plus I still had the injury to my arm to be looked at, at the hospital.

The end of the story is that the man was charged by the police, taken to hospital where it was confirmed by a doctor that he had not taken an overdose of tablets. He later told police that he had merely told his boyfriend, during a quarrel, that he had taken an overdose.

He was never charged with any assault upon either me or Ray. Also, this was not the only violent struggle that Ray and I had with a naked man, but that's another story.

GUNS: Given the right circumstances, the very mention of a gun being held in the wrong hands is enough to evoke fear and can lead to panic. The paramedic's priority may be necessarily changed, by the threat of someone using a gun. The priority will be to remove the patient first, if possible and deal with the injuries later.

A Monday morning at 08:30 found us responding to an emergency call, at a large block of flats near the seafront. The woman caller had claimed a serious assault had been made on her boyfriend. The weather was awful, with high winds and freezing rain, as my crewmate, Graham, and I made our way through the morning rush-hour traffic.

As we pulled up outside of the large tower block, the wind was creating a tremendous vortex which almost knocked us over as we made our way to the entrance of the flats. Once inside, we located the lift and pressed the button and waited. It seemed a long time before the lift eventually arrived to take us up to the fourteenth floor. The lift was typical of many of these places, and, of course, it was Monday morning; it was full of litter and it seemed that over the weekend it had been used as a toilet, for the floor was soaking wet and smelling strongly of urine. I made a note to keep my ambulance case off the floor.

As the lift doors opened onto the fourteenth floor, I could feel a terrific draught and hear the whistling of a tremendous gale howling through the corridors of the building. Somewhere, a woman was screaming, a man was shouting and swearing and a dog barking. 'Would you believe all this?' I commented to my crewmate, 'and it's not yet nine-o-clock in the morning.'

We made our way along a narrow corridor to an open (I use the word open, loosely, for it was actually hanging off its hinges) door, which lead into one of the flats, and from where all the shouting and dog barking was coming from. Given all the commotion, it was noticeable that there were no curious neighbours around.

Entering the flat was like stepping into a hurricane, with paper and all manner of debris, including shards of glass, being blown about the place. We had to manoeuvre around the shattered front door, in order to climb over another (internal) door which was also off its hinges. Inside the flat, every window had recently been smashed. The curtains (what was left of them) were billowing and flapping wildly across the rooms. Most of the internal doors were ripped off the hinges. In every room there was utter destruction. Every piece of furniture was overturned and had been smashed. The floor was covered in heaps of broken furniture, shattered mirrors, broken glass and soft furnishings. It seemed immediately obvious that we were going to have great difficulty getting any patient out of this place, unless they were able to climb out over the debris themselves.

With some difficulty, Graham and I reached a small bedroom, where we found a young man who had been attacked about the head with something like a machete. He was lying on a broken bed and was swearing and cursing at a young woman who was using a piece of torn curtain, trying to stem the bleeding from his head wound. He had a number of deep lacerations on his hands and arms too, some of which were right down to the bone. He was covered in blood, much of which was already beginning to congeal. He was reluctant to tell us what had happened and offered no clue as to who or why his flat had been so disrupted, although I had my own idea as to the reason.

The young woman although uninjured, was undoubtedly severely shocked. She told us, she had witnessed a gang attack upon her boyfriend, here in his flat a short time ago. The attack on her boyfriend was vicious, but she had managed to escape and took the lift down to the street, to telephone 999 calling for help, but *NOT* from the police but from the ambulance service!

Working quickly me and Graham began to dress the young man's injuries, before evacuating him from the mess of his flat; as we did so another young man appeared on the scene. Looking through the shattered front door, he shouted a warning. 'You'd better get out quick, they are coming back now.....up the stairs...with a gun!'

Our patient began to panic and jumped up from the bed barging passed me and Graham almost knocking us over amongst the debris. His girlfriend was screaming, 'What about the f****** dog, look, it's hurt'. Looking into a small kitchen (which was also wrecked), I could see an Alsatian dog, standing forlornly and whimpering. It didn't seem too much of a threat to anyone. The poor animal had two or three large open wounds across its back which also looked as though they had been caused with a machete.

There was no more we could do here, for it was obvious that there was an imminent danger (according to the young man who had shouted the warning) if we remained in the flat. Making our way back down the corridor I was praying that we would not have to wait for the lift, and that none of the returning gang would be in it.

Luckily, the lift was on our floor, and, with relief, we all climbed to take us down and hopefully to safety. As the lift doors began to close, we could hear more shouting and yelling from a group of men, who had obviously used the stairs, and were making their way back to the fat. Thankfully the doors closed and we began to make a welcome descent.

Once outside and into our ambulance, Graham wasted no time in driving off to a safe distance, before calling the police, with the added warning that there may be an armed man in the vicinity of the wrecked flat.

It later transpired that the incident was provoked by a dispute over drugs. The victim had his injuries attended to by the hospital staff; then promptly signed himself out. That was the last I heard or seen of them. As for the poor injured dog. I heard later, that it had been taken in by the RSPCA, hopefully, it made a good recovery.

Very often, people who take an overdose of tablets or some other form of drug can present a danger to the medical staff charged with the responsibility of treating them. Many such patients have psychiatric problems, such as depression. Sometimes they may (wrongly) see the medical practitioner be they paramedic, nurse or doctor, as someone who is aloof and looks down on them disrespectfully. This can have the effect of lowering their self-esteem and may even provoke them to respond in an aggressive manner either with physical or verbal abuse, against the person offering medical assistance.

For this reason, I always advised trainee ambulance staff, 'never turn your back or allow your concentration to stray from any patient who has, or may have taken an overdose.'

The following incident happened when, fortunately, I was

working on an older type of ambulance; one where you could walk through, from the rear saloon and into the driver cab. This is a much preferred design to the latest ambulances, where once in the back of the ambulance the paramedic is isolated from his crewmate, and alone in the back (not nice if the patient becomes violent).

In the early part of my career, violent incidents involving the use of guns or knives was not as common as it has since become. Armed police were a rarity as, indeed were actual firearm offences. As a result of 'gun crime rarity' it is my opinion that the police had a *far different* approach, to an incident in which I genuinely feared for my life, than would otherwise be the case today...

The incident started innocuously enough when we (Ralph, my crewmate, and I) responded to a 999 call made from a public phone booth.

Ambulance control had described the call as 'a strange in manner', a description that could mean anything ranging from the caller being incomprehensible through drink, drugs or some psychiatric reason or even an elderly person with dementia. Basically we had no idea of what we faced until we arrived on scene.

It was just coming up to midnight on a cold miserable night as I stepped out of the ambulance to approach the phone booth from where the call had been made. The phone booth was situated close to the Mersey Ferry Terminal, which, at that time of night, was closed and deserted. The wind and rain blowing in from the river had made the phone booth seem like a welcome refuge for the caller, a man in his mid-twenties as I opened the door to speak to him. He was wearing a khaki Parka, similar what soldiers wear.

Trying to find out what was wrong with him was a problem for he was rambling about something but seemed so confused that I couldn't understand fully what he was saying. There is a technique to interviewing someone who may have taken an overdose; always with tact, discretion and respect. There are many important details that we need to know; the questions need to be asked in order that we and the receiving hospital, can give the most beneficial treatment to the patient. Questions, such as, what was taken? How much or how many? When? Where? Why? To name but just a few.

This young man mumbled something about an overdose but was evasive and even refused to give me his name. Initially he seemed reluctant to leave the phone booth. Eventually I managed to coax him out of the phone booth and into the warm interior of our ambulance where, hopefully, I could establish what his medical needs were.

I felt a blast of warm air as Ralph opened the rear doors of the ambulance as I ushered our anonymous patient inside.

'Just sit down the far end please', I said, trying to sound friendly and directing him to a suitable seat in the ambulance.

'No...I'm OK here', he replied as he took a seat the nearest to the rear doors. I tried to encourage him to move to a different seat but he obstinately refused, so rather than antagonise him I allowed him to remain in that seat. It is not unusual for some patients with some form of depression or suicidal tendencies to try to open the back doors of a moving ambulance and to make an attempt to jump out.

My crewmate closed the doors and with me sitting a few feet away and opposite to the patient, we set of to hospital. In the back of my mind I had a feeling of unease, like a 'sixth sense'.

Being friendly and casual I tried my best to talk to the young man, hoping to gain his confidence and to learn more details about what, if any, overdose he may have taken. His attitude was immediately belligerent and antagonistic and he was unnecessarily abrasive towards me, telling me that he didn't want my help. Despite me continuing to speak nicely to him, he reciprocated by being rude and vitriolic, to the point that I actually asked him why.

'If you did not want my help', I asked. 'why did you call an ambulance?'. Even as I asked the question, I felt that I may have triggered a negative response from him. His answer stunned and alarmed me in equal measure. 'Because, I didn't just want to shoot myself', he replied. 'Are you trying to tell me that you are carrying a gun?' I asked, at the same time not believing that I am asking such a bizarre question.

Everything that happened next took less than a couple of terrifying minutes, and takes longer to narrate than the actual event.

In reply to my question about the gun; the young man did not speak another word but instead reached into the top inside of his coat as if to produce a gun. I reasoned that if he had a gun, or even if he pulled out a water pistol, I would be justified in going for him. Which was exactly, what I did! Jumping up from my seat, at the same time shouting a warning to Ralph, I dived at the man in an attempt to grab him. As I did so, he did in fact pull a gun from his coat and pointed it in my direction. I recall that I had hold of his hand holding the gun and remember twisting it in his fingers in an attempt to make him let go. Meanwhile, Ralph, upon hearing my initial shouted warning, had hit the brakes causing us both to fall forward where we ended up on the floor of the moving ambulance, lying between the stretcher and the row of seats, but with me on top.

In the ensuing struggle I did manage to get the gun from him and I threw it into the driving cab. Unfortunately it hit a seat and immediately bounced back into the reach of young man. There followed a second violent struggle before I regained the gun making sure that this time it was thrown clear.

Ralph had informed ambulance control of the situation and was now speeding down the motorway to the hospital; whilst I forcibly detained the young man, face down on the floor. He continued his belligerence and struggling with Ralph and me all the way into the casualty department, before turning his vile attention upon the nursing staff.

Fortunately, the police, whom we had requested to attend, arrived shortly after our arrival at the hospital. I spoke briefly to them, outside the A&E department to confirm that the man was now unarmed but still potentially violent. With that, they charged into the hospital and secured a very quick arrest of the young man. He was given a quick check-up by the doctor, who confirmed that he was fit for arrest.

It was only when I got back to the ambulance, I realised that my hands were shaking. I could hardly fill out the emergency report form (ERF) I suddenly felt a whole range of emotions. I felt shocked, sick, angry and humiliated, I felt emotionally drained by the past event.

A police officer retrieved the gun from where I had thrown it, in the ambulance. It looked like a 'Smith and Wesson' revolver and was loaded. What I was not to know, is that the gun was only a 'blank' firing replica.

Sadly, the police did not see this incident, in the same serious light as, either myself or my employers did. Therefore, they chose only to charge him with being drunk and disorderly. In my view he was NOT drunk!

As if all that wasn't bad enough, our duty officer arrived and insisted that Ralph and I write out a long and detailed report of the event...before we booked off duty in the morning! This report, along with the report of the duty officer formed the basis of a complaint about the police assessment and subsequent charges made against the man.

Postscript to this event; had this event taken place today, the likelihood is that the man may well have been shot dead or at least, if apprehended, charged with a more serious offence.

As well as the above incidents, I have attended scenes of murders and suicides, where guns had been the weapon used. The illegal use of guns it seems is currently on the increase. What is particularly alarming is that they are being used quite openly and appear to be freely available to anyone who wishes to buy one. In certain quarters they are becoming commonplace items, despite the Government restriction on gun ownership.

It seems the only qualification that you need, in order be able to acquire a gun, is that you must be a criminal. Law abiding citizens, need not apply!

Even today as I write, there are reports of another 'gangland' killing, in Liverpool, by a so called hitman using a gun. I owe it to the good people of Liverpool, to remind you, dear reader, that such incidents are taking place in other towns and cities throughout the UK.

There is often talk of the police being armed, but, to me, what is more worrying is the fact that already some ambulance services have seen the need to issue body protection to some front line ambulance staff.

Even in a war zone, the medic is given due regard for his position, and is usually exempt from attack, thus allowing him or her to administer such medical aid as may be required. But not here it seems, not on our streets

◆ ◆ ◆

11 THE THIN BLUE LINE

Not unsurprisingly, my paramedic career involved a very close working relationship with the police service; not just with individual officers but with the organisation as a whole.

It is the police service that has primary responsibility for the overall management of any 'major incident' which involves either, the fire and rescue or paramedical services. They have the authority to restrict or allow our deployment at a major incident and will do so based on their judgement at the time. For instance, at bomb incidents it is up to the police, as to whether or not, a paramedic may enter the incident field (not always a popular decision with the paramedic whose sole aim is to save the lives of any victim involved). Again with equal frustration the fire and rescue service can be restricted from entering a major incident area.

These police restrictions are based on safety considerations aimed at preventing dangers to other emergency personnel which, could further complicate matters should any become secondary victims.

I recall being first on the scene a bomb blast (fortunately there were no injured victims). Even though my crewmate and I were the first of the emergency services to arrive, and that we had identified the strong smell of cordite (a powerful explosive compound- used for ammunition)and spoken to the first witnesses we were still ushered from the area when the police arrived on the scene.

All my ambulance colleagues got on well with our local police officers and it was not unusual to find a bobby on our station, enjoying a cup of tea or coffee as they passed by on their regular beat. Sadly, these days, the bobby 'on the beat' is not such a regular sight; most of them now deployed permanently in patrol cars.

I recall, late one very windy, winter evening, when our local bobby, PC Jack, we'll call him, called into the station for a warm drink. It had just started to rain so he thought he would just call in to our station to shelter from the weather and of course enjoy a warm drink and a chat with the duty ambulance crew. With his coat undone, helmet off, his personal radio still switched on so that he was still able to listen for calls he settled down.

For about twenty minutes he sat enjoying a mug of hot tea joking and chatting with me and my crewmate. By now the rain outside, driven by high wind, was lashing down making patrolling the streets seem a most unattractive prospect.

Suddenly a radio message came through for him, asking for his current location, because the duty sergeant wanted to rendezvous with him. PC Jack suddenly looked anxious as he replied that he was at the top of Mayfield road (about two hundred metres from our station).

Jumping up and about to dash out to meet his sergeant he realised that his coat was dry which would give away the fact that he had not been patrolling in the rain.

My crewmate had a brainwave; PC Jack hurriedly put his dry coat and helmet on and we took him into the shower room where we sprayed him with cold water from head to toe. We laughed as we watched him dash out to meet the sergeant up the road, soaked as though he'd been patrolling in the rain.

A short time later, Jack told us that he had only just reached the top of Mayfield road when the sergeant pulled up in a car.

'My God lad, you're soaked through' the sergeant had said to him. 'Why didn't you shelter from the rain? I'm sure the lads at the ambulance station would have let you in; maybe even give you a cuppa'.

I, and my ambulance colleagues, shared many social activities with our local police and fire service. Indeed there was a dedicated social club for the three services known as The 27 Club made up, obviously from that well now emergency number 999.

Every year, we would all meet up at the annual Mersey River 'Police Swim'. The River Mersey is a dangerous river to swim in and only the very best swimmer may dare to swim across to Liverpool.

Hosted by Merseyside Police, the swim was held on a summer evening, with police officers swimming the mile across from Wallasey to Liverpool. The Mersey ferry boat, 'The Royal Iris' which had bars, restaurant and a dance floor, was chartered for the event. With all tickets sold to raise money for charity, those of us not swimming remained on board to watch the swimmers dive off the boat and race against the Mersey; race over and everyone back on board, we would all dance the night away and generally have a good time.

I remember organising a charity climb up Ben Nevis; the first in the queue to join-up were some of my ambulance colleagues' followed closely by a team of Wallasey Police men and women. On that trip we also had firemen, doctors and nurses, so that trip was well covered for all eventualities. This type of social event demonstrates the close bond between *your* emergency services. To me, this bond adds a dimension that is rarely found in normal civilian working life, namely camaraderie that excels in crisis and when we need to watch out for each other.

During violent incidents that I, unexpectedly, encountered I knew I could rely on a very quick response from the police. I knew they would not tolerate assault or abuse of me or my colleagues and for that I have a profound admiration.

From time to time I have physically fought a violent patient and have been helped by a police officer to restrain those who would do me harm.

Sometimes, what may appear as a serious incident may later prove to have a funny side.

Late one night I responded to a call, with my crewmate, Billy, to a report that someone had fallen and sustained a head injury. On our way to incident we passed a man who was staggering along the pavement in the opposite direction. The streets were deserted as we pulled up at the location; no sign of a casualty nor the person who had made the emergency call. Acting on a hunch we turned around and headed back along the road and caught up with the man we had seen, staggering, a few minutes earlier.

At first glance, we could see that he had a slight cut and abrasions to his head. He was clearly quite drunk and became abusive as we tried to assist him. He kept shoving us out of the way and fell over in doing so. I helped him to his feet, only for him to stagger and fall again. It was obvious that we couldn't really leave him like this but he insisted he would not go to hospital and so it became a bit of a stand-off.

A short time later a police car just happened to be passing by. Seeing us in debate with the man, two police officers got out and joined us in trying to persuade the man to go to hospital. Even with the threat of arrest he continued to refuse hospital treatment and insisted that he could get home without help.

Eventually as a compromise we offered to take the man home and the two police officers would follow us, in their car. A couple of minutes later we arrived down a very quiet street of small terraced houses, and took the man to his front door. Still very abusive and inebriated he struggled with his door key to open the front door. He wouldn't allow us help him and so the police officers came across to intervene. Again the man was obstructive and threatening to them too and began causing a noisy commotion, which could wake the neighbours up. However, one of the policemen managed to get the key off him and opened the door. Now both officers grabbed a hold on him and dragged/marched him into the house, whilst Billy and I waited outside.

It was a good few minutes before they emerged from the house, closing the front door as they did so. They informed me that they had struggled to get him sit down in the armchair because he was still 'acting up', but eventually they had been able to leave him 'sleeping it off'. 'Job done' I said as we prepared to return to station.

However, just as we were all about to leave, a neighbour

from the house next door; having been woken up by the disturbance came out to enquire as to what was going on? One of the police officers apologised for the commotion and explained that everything was now under control because they had put Mr Brook safely in his house. Unfortunately, the neighbour had some startling news for them; he informed them that the man had moved out of that house some weeks ago and there was now an old lady living there and was probably upstairs in bed!

Me, and Billy made a hasty retreat, leaving the police officers trying to gain entry back into the house because the front door had locked behind them.

It must be obvious that police officers do get injured during their work and so it was that quite often I would deal with such injured officers. I recall responding to a fire call to deal with a policeman who had been overcome with smoke inhalation, whilst rescuing a pensioner from a fire in her house prior to the arrival of the fire fighters.

Sadly some police officers pay the ultimate price for doing their job. Some years ago, my colleagues and I were shocked and saddened when we had to attend a road accident in which two of our very popular police officers died after an elderly gentleman lost control of his car and hit them both. We all knew the men and as such it left an air of gloom over the whole station for some time.

A police motorcyclist was another victim I attended. He had been racing to attend to a 'child RTA' when he misjudged his approach at traffic lights which were displaying red against him. He crashed head-on into a stationery car on the opposite side of the junction. Hitting the windscreen and then slamming onto the roof of the car he ended up injured and unconscious several yards away. I was off duty at the time but instinctively went to his aid...but, not before I checked, first, upon my own wife and child for any injuries. For the car that he had collided with was my own, with me in the driving seat!

Another, more common, police officer injury call can be to do with an officer being attacked by someone they simply want to question. For some reason the attacker thinks it is reasonable to abuse or physically attack a police officer, be them male or female. My own view is that anyone who physically attacks any police officer, or other emergency worker, in the course of doing their duty, should be automatically jailed. Unfortunately, many magistrates seem to live in a different world and will pass down, what many reasonable people would consider inappropriate, lenient sentences.

I have known police officers who have risked their own lives when saving victims in danger, and at least one officer who tackled a knifeman who was attempting to stab a young woman. One policeman friend of mine defied his commander's orders in order to save the life of someone drowning in treacherous seas.

It happened on a bitterly cold January night. A gentleman out walking his dog along the promenade at Blackpool was suddenly engulfed in the heavy seas that were crashing over the seawall. Seeing his dog caught by a wave and being washed away, he made the tragic decision to go in the water to save it. Unfortunately, he too was soon overcome by the strong, freezing cold, waves and high tide.

The alarm was raised and within a few minutes several police officers arrived on scene. With typical police concern for the safety of the public, four police officers went into the water in a vain attempt to save the gentleman.

Sadly three of those officers paid for their bravery with their lives when they drowned. Those brave officer's, were PCs Angela Bradley, Gordon Connolly, and Colin Morrison. The fourth, PC Pat Abram was only just saved, when other colleagues managed to throw a rope around his neck, pulling him ashore, and saving his life with mouth-to-mouth resuscitation.

After that incident police officers were instructed *never* attempt any similar rescue in such hazardous condition again. However, it was some time later when, in similar weather conditions, my friend, constable Chris, who was on duty in Blackpool, dived into the fierce storm waters to rescue a member of the public from drowning.

From time to time it was necessary for my ambulance to be escorted, at high speed, by police, as we escorted a seriously ill patient to other specialist hospitals. Often such high speed escorts would involve several police motorcyclist's riding in a leap-frog manner through The Mersey Tunnel and the busy city centre of Liverpool.

The emergency police escort works like clockwork and it is a privilege though stressful, to be part of it. It works by four police riders starting off at a pre-determined speed and route; one riding directly in front of the ambulance, whilst another races ahead to stop the traffic at the upcoming road junction. Meanwhile, behind the ambulance there may be another two motorcyclists completing the convoy.

As we approach the road junction, the first police rider will be there holding back the traffic and waving our convoy through. After we pass, he will then tag on behind, whilst one of back riders will then take over and race alongside to overtake the ambulance. At this point the driver of the ambulance has to drive in such a way as to leave at gap between his vehicle and other traffic so that the police rider can pass safely at high speed through, what can be a very narrow gap and the nearside or outside of the lane.

For the driver of the ambulance these manoeuvres can be

stressful. Not only do they have to drive with the safety of their passengers, patient, doctors and nurses, in the back of the ambulance, they also have to be acutely alert for the escorting police rider coming alongside at high speed often in the drivers 'blind spot'. The ambulance driver may have to move over to one side, driving perilously close to other slower moving vehicles, so as to allow *just* enough space for the police rider to pass alongside. Not an easy thing to do in heavy traffic and at high speed because the police bikes are only inches away from the speeding ambulance. One wrong move and you could knock the police rider off his bike.

The whole event is noisy, with all vehicles using sirens and blue lights as well as headlights. It is difficult to miss; but some do!

On one such occasion whilst I was driving on such a high speed escort, one of the escorting riders came roaring alongside to overtake our ambulance. As he passed me I was horrified to see a small car pull out from the side of the road and into my lane causing me to brake sharply, coming to a complete halt. Unfortunately, the rider already overtaking me was too late to avoid a collision with the car and so ended up being thrown from his motorcycle sustaining some injuries.

This was a complication that I was not prepared for, but the patient in the back of the ambulance was already in a critical condition; so I had no choice but to drive around the accident and continue on our priority journey with a reduced escort. The other officers would deal with their injured colleague whilst I called up ambulance control to report 'officer down' accident.

I learned later that the main injury that the officer suffered was to his pride. The car driver was justly prosecuted for careless driving.

Late one night, me and my crewmate, Billy, were sent across to 'stand-by' in Liverpool city centre where, we were informed, that, there had been a serious accident involving a Liverpool ambulance crew and we would need to fill the gap in emergency cover for the city. It transpired that there had been a 'hit and run' accident in the city, leaving a pedestrian in a critical condition. It was presumed at that time that the accident may have been caused by a stolen car.

The police were soon on scene along with an ambulance. The paramedic crew dealt with the casualty on the road before hastily transferring him to a stretcher. As they wheeled the stretcher across to the ambulance a terrible coincidence occurred. They too were hit by a car, which also failed to stop.

Both crewmembers were injured; one with life changing injuries and the casualty on the stretcher had a secondary serious injury.

Because the police were already on scene and having witnessed the incident unfold, they immediately gave chase. The chase went on for some miles before the culprits were apprehended.

The next day on BBC Radio Merseyside I was amazed to hear people complaining about police chasing cars, for any reason. Those complaining clearly didn't know the full facts (as is usually the case) and had never found themselves injured by 'hit and run' criminals. Those complaining would only see the police chase some distance from the incident scene and didn't think it was right for the police to engage in a chase. Paradoxically, those members of the public who were actually *at the scene* would *expect* the police to pursue the offenders. It seems the police can't win!

Here on the Wirral Peninsula we have experienced the huge and devastating cost placed on the family of a police officer who was just doing his job. It happened whilst most law abiding people were tucked up, sleeping peacefully in their beds. safe in the knowledge that people like PC Dave Philips and his colleagues were patrolling somewhere in our community ready to do what it takes to apprehend the scum (criminals) who threaten our safety and or steal our property.

On the night shift in October 2015 Dave was engaged with other police officers in a high speed chase around the roads of Wirral. Dave was deployed tactically ahead of the stolen pickup truck and had deployed the 'stinger mechanism' designed to deflate a vehicles tyres.

Unfortunately for Dave, the scum driving the stolen pickup tried avoid the stinger; instead he drove into Dave killing him. The devastating impact was not only felt by all decent people of Wirral but also by every police officer in the country but more profoundly on Dave's lovely family.

The vehicle thief they were chasing had already served time in prison for vehicle theft and had also been involved in previous police chases.

PC Dave Philips was typical, in so many ways, of the police officers that serve to protect the public. Making decisions, within a split second, that may later profoundly impact upon them and their family lives and well-being.

My own opinion is that if you drive in such a way as to engage police in a car chase, then the minimum sentence should be a full life driving ban.

I have worked alongside police officers at road accidents, murders, assaults, suicides and much more. I have shared their emotions. They are not hard unfeeling people but are ordinary family members doing an extraordinary job.

I have been grateful, on many occasions, over the years for the police help and support given to me, particularly when I have been caught up in some unforeseen violent incident some of which are mentioned in this book. Their protection of other emergency workers is a 'given'

◆ ◆ ◆

12 FIRE AND RESCUE

The day that I started my training in the ambulance service happened to be the first day, of the first ever fire service strike... My journey to the ambulance training school in Quarry Street Liverpool took me past the fire station in Penny Lane (of Beatles fame). There outside, stood a group of proud firefighter's, standing around a large oil-drum, which was serving as a brazier with wood burning to offer warmth and maybe a morale boost to these reluctant strikers.

As a child I had been brought up with close links to Birkenhead Fire Station; at that time (seven years since the end of world war two) my uncle was a serving fireman. In those days many of the firemen lived, with their families, on the station.

Birkenhead Fire Station was a large quadrangular shape with three storey flats built around three sides. There was a veranda running along the frontage of all floors and facing into a big yard; each veranda had a wooden gate that opened *outwards* giving access to a brass pole that ran from the top floor to the ground and was positioned for the purpose of firemen, responding to a fire call, sliding in seconds, to the ground instead of them taking the stairs.

The station was positioned in the centre of town at the intersection of two major roads. There were five engine bays facing out onto one road, Whetstone Lane, with a further two bays around the other side and also facing onto another main road. There were seven fire engines in all. Above the engine bays were the offices and below the surrounding flats there were training rooms and stores.

I lived about a quarter of a mile from the station, and used every opportunity to go there to play and hang around the station with my three cousins. I got to know most of the other station kids and their families; both my parents socialised with the fire service community too. Which is why my inherent opinion was that I was fully behind the strike action and felt sorry that they had been drawn into, what was for them, unfamiliar territory.

As an ex-soldier, I was also acutely aware that servicemen and women, along with the antiquated equipment that they would be expected to use, would be no substitute for real firefighters. Initially 'Green Goddess' fire engines left over from the war twenty two years earlier had been de-mothballed and brought back into service. These machines were very basic, slow and cumbersome by modern standards. However, they were the only vehicles available because quite simply the modern fire engine was too complex for soldiers to handle without first undergoing long and complex training.

It never occurred to me that, somehow, I would become involved in a fire service strike or anything related to it. I never considered that I would ever be involved in actual fire incidents, other than to attend to injured casualties. I knew that probably I may, occasionally, work alongside the men and women of the fire service when attending serious road accidents. However, my experience over the years involved a close relationship, professionally as well as socially with the men and women of the fire service of Merseyside.

With several friends in the fire service, I did from time to time work alongside them on fire calls, industrial and road accidents. Although there was always much rivalry and good natured banter when off duty: on emergencies everyone worked together and in harmony towards a common goal of saving victims of some accidental misfortune.

Occasionally there were hiccups in the emergency procedures when dealing with emergencies of joint enterprise. For instance, over the years there were a number of occasions when the ambulance would not be summoned by the fire service, until the emergency was almost over or had been on-going for a considerable time. This was not the fault of the fire-crew (now known as firefighters) but more a fault of emergency administration.

For instance; I can recall one such occasion when two fire engines sped past our ambulance station, on their way to some emergency, blue lights and sirens used to heed their way through the busy town traffic. They stopped further down the road, about a quarter of a mile away from our station. Although I could see their blue flashing lights in the distance, I couldn't see what was going on.

About *ten minutes* later, our station red phone rang out. I took the call. It was a call to attend an RTA, just down the road from our station and at the location where I could see the fire engines.

Less than a minute later we were on the scene of a two car smash. The two fire engines were blocking the road and a specialist incident vehicle from Birkenhead (the next town) was on scene. A considerable amount of extrication equipment was now being packed away, after having been used to extricate a driver and passenger from the vehicles.

Immediately, upon our arrival, we faced a barrage of complaint and criticism from one of the car drivers, as well as from some bystanders', all demanding to know why we had taken so long to get to the accident. Although it was none of their business, I was drawn to say out loudly (so those in the vicinity could hear me) that we had only received the emergency call a couple of minutes ago. And loud enough for others to hear, I spoke to the leading fire fighter and asked why we had only just been called but he declined to explain, merely directing me to a man nearby (the accident witness) who had called the fire service.

I spoke briefly to the witness, who admitted that he lived nearby and knew perfectly well where the ambulance station was, I asked why he had not called an ambulance but instead called the fire service. 'Because I'm a fireman' was his claim. It was a stupid decision based on some trivial local politics; he wanted his mates to get there first! How immature.

Had the casualties had life-threatening injuries, such an unnecessary delay could have had catastrophic consequence.

It never looks good to the public, if the victim of a fire or accident, having been rescued by the fire and rescue service, is then left waiting for a paramedic to arrive on scene and deal with what may be life-threatening injuries.

On another occasion, just a few minutes after I had come off night duty and whilst making a quick call to a friend before going home: I encountered two fire engines outside a house that had suffered fire damage and was still being damped down. As I drove slowly passed I could see firemen attempting to resuscitate someone lying in the front garden of the house. I had all my paramedic gear along with drugs and some fluids in the boot of my car, and so naturally I stopped and went to assist with the casualty.

Whilst introducing myself to the scene and making a quick observation of the scene and assessment of any medical requirements, I enquired if an ambulance had been summoned. I recognised faces of firemen as being from our local fire station. They looked around questioning each other seeking to answer my question. I realised also that they must have responded to this fire and been here whilst I was still on duty.

There were two casualties, one of whom was being resuscitated by some firemen and another casualty lying on the grass showing signs of serious breathing difficulty.

Obviously the ambulance had *not* been requested so I asked one of the firemen to make the call; I then took over the casualty care. I asked them to treat the other patient (who clearly to me had Carbon monoxide poisoning) with Oxygen, whilst I assisted with the resuscitation of the primary casualty.

I intubated a male casualty and continued with CPR until the duty paramedic crew, who had taken over from me a short while ago, arrived to take over.

It is worth noting for the above stories, that the fire station was just around the corner (about three hundred metres) from our station and in my opinion there was no tangible reason why there should have been a delay in requesting an ambulance attendance to this incident.

My view, I think is reasonable, if there is a fire call to a place where there are likely to be people at risk, then the ambulance should be requested automatically. There should not be a delay because of some misguided political ideology of the fire service bosses. After all, if the ambulance turns up at a fire in such circumstances, and it is not needed, it is a simple matter to report vehicle not required (VNR). The practice of not calling ambulances simultaneously, for house fires, had been going on since the separation of the services in 1974. Prior to that time, ambulances shared stations with the fire service and routinely went out together on such calls.

Whenever I received such calls as 'persons reported' I was immediately in a state of high alert, as too would be my colleague; such calls had the potential to test one's nerve, and the effectiveness of your skills to the full.

Although the fire service may be on scene and in significant numbers and dealing with rescue and firefighting, the paramedic may initially arrive with just his crewmate. Arriving at the scene in a crescendo of noise with blue lights flashing, adrenaline, pumping around your body, your pulse racing, you will still need to step out of the ambulance in a calm and well-disciplined manner.

When attending such calls, as protocol dictates, I would firstly make contact with the senior fire officer at the scene. I would then receive his report about any casualties as well as any instructions as to when or where it was safe for us to operate. At big fires there may be a need for several ambulances to attend and be located at various positions around the fire field. For that reason there is a primary need for the fire team and paramedics to know where each other is placed.

Some domestic fires are so horrifying and dramatic to see

that there can be a lot of panic and confusion with members of the public. I can recall attending such scenes where my crewmate and I have been surrounded and even grabbed physically, by anxious people, shouting, crying, and screaming for us to help some victim or other; thus interrupting normal protocol of rendezvousing with the fire officer first.

On such occasions all our senses were employed. Not only did we have to observe the dynamic fire scene, but we would need to remember all details of what or who we saw, what we heard or did. The paramedic may be listening to very distressed people (sometimes several at a time) who may be screaming or shouting, trying in their panic to give him vital information about a victim. At the same time he may be gathering essential equipment from the ambulance; whilst his crewmate will be giving a 'first report' to ambulance control. Add to all this; there may actually be a badly burned victim, literally being handed to him. It's difficult to apprehend everything that is going on but he really does have to keep calm but absolutely alert and instantly, correctly decisive!

At the Bradford Football Stadium fire, the first emergency vehicle on scene was a lone ambulance, which was immediately swamped by panic-stricken people with terrified victims jumping into the back of the vehicle. The poor ambulance crew would have been overwhelmed.

The protocol in serious incidents like that is the first ambulance crew on scene is, *not to engage in treating casualties* but, to make an essential assessment of the situation then pass on a 'first report' to the ambulance control; this allows a more efficient response from all services.

Panic at a fire scene is common, and can be endemic amongst the surrounding people, to such an extent that sometimes you have to be quite firm in your manner with them in order to gain vital information. For instance, if the mother of an injured child is screaming, shouting and pulling you about physically, due to her understandable panic and anxiety, it can stop you dealing effectively with her injured child. You don't have all day; time may be of the essence, the child's life may be in danger and, therefore, you need to calm her immediately.

At a 'persons reported' fire this human trait can be multiplied depending upon the seriousness of the fire, and the number of casualties. I have been involved with a large group of panicking, people all pulling and shouting for my attention to be drawn in different directions. People become aggressive and angry, and are likely to add to the problem of incident control.

On such occasions, when the fire incident is serious, with the number of casualties likely to be high or, injury likely to be very serious, then it is essential that accurate reports are passed as quickly as possible back to ambulance control, so that they in turn can send other ambulances, if necessary, and alert the receiving hospital. Therefore the ambulance crew have to make a very quick reconnaissance, of the incident before they can actually attend to any injured people.

After twenty years working on front line emergency ambulances, I have had many serious fire incidents to deal with; without exception all of them presented the conditions of a 'nightmare' to those directly involved, hence the title of this book.

Since 1974, when the fire and ambulance services were split into separate operational entities, there has been a robust rivalry between the two services. This also brought about a friendly reluctance to offer either praise or tribute to each-others service. We prefer instead to point to each-others inadequacies, but in reality I think it is fair to say that there is a genuine respect for each of the people in the other's service, and an appreciation of each-others' contribution to the saving of life.

For my own part, I have a great admiration for the firemen and women with whom I have worked over the years and I enjoyed working with them as and when the need arose. Should there be a need for their expertise and muscle power, in order to secure the release of an injured patient, be it from a mangled car wreck, or from the bowels of a dirty smelly tank of an oil tanker, then it was with them that I preferred to work. I could trust them with my own safety, relying on them to look after me and my patient. I respect them, and appreciate the respect that they too show to me and the ambulance service.

I have often been amazed at the bravery, and determination with firemen, when they are faced with a 'persons reported' situation. I have seen firemen go where no other man could go, only to reappear a few minutes later carrying a badly charred and still smouldering body, which they then passed onto me and my colleagues so that we may carry out our own task.

Always they work as a disciplined team, and work when necessary in tandem with the paramedic on scene. During our time together there is no animosity only mutual respect, in my mind we have the best fire service in the world. My colleagues and I refer to them affectionately as 'F troop', the 'F' being for fire!

My first ever 'persons reported' came one lovely sunny afternoon, whilst we were travelling back to base; we received the call on our ambulance radio just as we were passing the fire station. Three fire engines were pulling out of the gates, lights glaring, and horns blaring loudly. We waited for the last one to pull out before tagging on behind the convoy. My excitement at that time was profound, the adrenaline pumped around my body, so that I was alert and responsive to everything going on around me.

I was the attendant on this occasion, and I was unsure as to what we may find at the scene, but fortunately for me, I was with a more experienced colleague, and it was to him that I would l rely on for guidance.

Weaving our way through the dense town traffic, we soon arrived at the road where the fire was reported to be; immediately as we turned in I could see at the far end of the road there was a horrible dark mass of smoke billowing up into the sunny sky. Seconds later, I was climbing out of our vehicle and retrieving the oxygen and burns kit from the ambulance locker, before joining my mate, Phil, at the door of a large Victorian house.

Already the firemen were hastily laying out hosepipes, one fireman standing at the door, taking the tallies of those firemen going into the burning building. They were the B.A. (breathing apparatus) men going in to search for the reported occupant.

Within a few minutes, the dense smoke had dispersed, and the fire was almost extinguished. Now Phil and I were called into the building by the fire officer in charge who informed us that there was only one casualty, 'possible DOA'. We were led through a flooded and burned hallway and down steps into a basement bedroom, which had been the source of the fire. Everywhere was burned black and was sodden; water was still seeping down from the wrecked ceiling. The furniture was upturned and still smouldering. The room was still very hot and humid; smoke pervaded the air mixing with the steam from the water of the hose pipes. My eyes were stinging.

Phil explained to the fire officer, that this was my 'first one' (fire death).

I was directed toward the fireplace at the far side of the blackened room. The scene was one of horror, a real nightmare. Lying on the floor, in a foetal position, was the body of someone who was not immediately recognisable as being either male or female and there was a distinctly unpleasant smell of burned flesh. I had only ever seen one dead body before, and that had been a gentleman who had just looked as though he was asleep. This was different; furthermore, it was my job at this point to determine as to whether this person was alive.

My mate, Phil, helped me turn the body over. I remember being surprised the body was still very hot and looked in parts like charred meat with the skin burned away and bones exposed.

Moving the body carefully and gently turning the small frame over onto their back, we established (what seemed obvious to me) that the patient was indeed deceased. It was only just determinable that the body was that of a female, and she had fallen and been lying across an electric fire.

At this point there was no more that we could do other than cover her pitiful body with a blanket, and await the coroner's officer to arrive. Protocol determined that we should stay until we were released from scene by the coroner's officer.

Since that first time, I have attended many such incidents, but no two are alike, and all are unique, although there are, unfortunately some common factors to some house fires.

One such common factor is 'the chip pan fire', which can always be a potentially serious situation. Every year the fire service spend vast amounts of time and energy, not to mention money, trying to teach you (Joe public) how to deal with such incidents in your home. Yet every year hundreds of people are killed or injured, because they take the wrong action when a chip pan catches fire.

The correct action is first do not panic! It's not easy, but you must remain calm. Leave the burning chip pan where it is, turn off the cooker if you can, then place a damp (*not wet*) towel over the top of the pan then leave it alone. The flames should go out, if they do not, then call the fire service, and stay out of the house.

All of the following chip pan fire incidents happened because the people involved did the wrong thing, so readers... please, be warned!

One cold winter evening, just after 18:45, I was returning from the hospital, back to base, hoping as usual that we didn't get a late job, for we were off duty at seven. Unfortunately, just as we pulled into the station yard, our radio crackled out an unwelcome message from control. 'Zulu one, emergency call, please respond to persons reported fire call at number two 'Overly Grange'. Message timed 18.47'.

I grabbed my pen and emergency report form, flicked on the in-cab reading lamp, and wrote down the details, whilst my mate did a quick 'U turn' and drove back out of the station yard, leaving our night relief crew standing at the gate waving to us in an amused fashion. For them, there would be no work, until we got back with their ambulance; we would not have wasted even one minute changing crews, for all emergencies get an immediate response.

Soon we were passing the local fire station; I noticed that all three engines were out, and on the roadway I could make out by the light from the street lights the familiar trail of water, that fire engines seem to leave as they pass around corners or obstacles.

Three minutes after leaving station, I was climbing out of our ambulance, leaving my mate to book us 'on scene' before he would follow and join me.

The fire was in a lovely detached house, on the corner of a street in one of the better areas of the town and as far as I could see in the evening darkness, there seemed to be a substantial amount of damage to the property.

The fire service had been in attendance for some time; long enough to actually extinguish the main fire which apparently had started in the kitchen. There were hose pipes all over the place, some of which were supplying water from hydrants to the fire tender, which in turn relayed it down other hoses and into the house.

Stepping over the hoses and wading through water, which was several inches deep, I made my way (as directed by the officer in charge of the 'fire field') through the blackened and still smoking hallway. Treading carefully I turned left into a large blackened and burned room, lit up by the mobile arc lighting system of the fire service. Everywhere in the house was still incredibly hot and humid. All the furnishing, walls and ceilings blackened, burned and now soaking wet and the carpets were afloat until you trod on them.

One of the firemen shrugged his shoulders when he spoke to me, 'All this from a bloody chip pan' he sounded understandably exasperated. We both looked around, and he directed my attention to a man whom I could see down a narrow passageway.

'He's the owner of the house'. He went on, 'He says he is all right, but obviously you will need to check him over'. What an under-statement that turned out to be.

My mate and I made our way down the short passageway to the house owner. It was immediately obvious to us that he was, in fact, very seriously injured; so much so, that with the amount and severity of burns to his body, he was not feeling any pain and as is so often the case, he was totally unaware of how serious his injuries were.

What had looked, in the poor lighting conditions, like burned clothing hanging from his body was in fact large sections of his own skin, burned and blistered, hanging in oily looking layers over the waistband of his trousers. What looked like oversized plastic gloves hanging from both of his hands was also his skin. They actually looked like rubber gloves full of fluid (plasma). His head and face were badly burned, and I could smell his burned flesh, along with his burned hair.

He was wandering around the kitchen as we approached. He seemed very impatient and irritated by our appearance; waving us away with impatience demanding that he did not wish to go to hospital because as he could see it (due to the lack of pain) there was nothing wrong with him. His voice sounded very hoarse and breathless, indicating to me that he had some airway trauma as well. He was definitely in a serious state.

Understandably, he was in severe mental and physiological shock. It took all our skills in diplomacy, just to get him to sit down whilst we began to quickly apply wet sterile dressing to his injuries. Eventually we persuaded him to allow us to administer a high rate of oxygen; and this we did whilst I quickly finished off his dressings. Meanwhile my mate had returned to the ambulance to ask our control to relay information, to the hospital, regarding our patient's serious condition. This would give them vital time to be ready to receive us when we arrived.

Whilst attending to patients it is vital that we have a thorough picture, as to what the exact events were, surrounding the incident. We also need to know a great deal of personal information about the patient's previous medical background; collectively this information is referred to as 'the history'.

The history in this case, was that the elderly gentleman had been cooking the tea, whilst his wife was out on an errand. Unfortunately, he had let the oil in the chip pan overheat, and it had caught fire. Meanwhile he had sat in the lounge and only became aware of the fire when smoke began to drift into the room. Whereupon, he dashed into the kitchen, and grabbing a bowl of water from the kitchen sink, he threw it over the blazing chip pan. This resulted in an immediate explosion of hot blazing oil, which spewed up into the air and covered him completely from head to toe, whilst at the same time setting fire to the kitchen.

Despite the best efforts of the hospital staff, and us the gentleman died from his injuries before the night was out.

Another similar incident happened one lunch hour. I was on station, just having my own lunch, when I heard the emergency phone ring out, followed instantly by a message on the station tannoy. 'Emergency call for Zulu one, 'Please attend a 'persons reported' at seventeen Brighton Crescent'.

We knew the address and within a few seconds my mate and I were climbing into the ambulance and leaving the station with all lights and klaxons blaring. We made our way through the busy lunch time town centre, and arrived a few minutes later at the scene, just behind the fire station.

Leaving the service to deal with the fire, we concentrated on two casualties of the fire, namely two schoolgirls.

On this occasion, a young girl of about eleven years of age had come home from school with a school friend during the lunch time. One of the girls decided to cook herself some chips. Whilst waiting for the chips to cook, they both decided to watch 'Neighbours', that well known Australian soap opera on

TV. Eventually, well into the programme, one of the girls noticed a 'funny smell' only it was not so funny! On investigating the smell, and now a good degree of smoke, they found that the chip pan was ablaze.

Unfortunately, one of the girls picked up the burning pan; whilst her friend opened the kitchen door, leading out into the garden, so that the burning chip pan could be thrown outside.

That of course was a major mistake, because the draught from the open door caused the flames in the blazing pan to flare up dangerously. The girl carrying the pan threw it away but in doing so caused blazing oil to spill out covering her legs, as well as onto her friend's arm. On top of that it also set the curtains and part of the kitchen units alight.

A neighbour was alerted by their screams and called the fire service and ambulance, before attempting to put out the fire which was now blazing up the kitchen door and back into the house. There was considerable damage to the kitchen, and of course the young girl needed skin grafts to her leg injuries whilst her friend got away with minor burns.

One winter evening at about 18:30, I was on base enjoying a welcome tea-break with my crewmate, Frank, when the emergency call came in. The message was simple 'Emergency call at 47 Seaview Street. Someone has been burned with a chip pan'.

A few seconds later, Frank and I were jumping onto our ambulance and heading out of the station. The address was not far from the station, and I knew that the people at the incident scene would be able to hear our sirens as we left. I commented to Frank that I thought this may well be a bit more than just a chip pan injury. Past experience had taught me that chip pans rarely presented minor incidents.

A few minute later, we were pulling into the dimly lit street and driving down looking for the correct house number. Further down the street a man stood in the middle of the road waving to attract our attention. Pulling up near to the man

Frank got out and followed him into a nearby house. 'Presumably', I said to myself that the casualty must be inside. I opened the back doors of the ambulance, grabbed the burns kit and followed Frank into the house. Passing by the kitchen I looked in briefly and noted mentally that there was no sign of any chip pan. In a back room, Frank was already busy dealing with a man who had burns to both his arms. I opened the burns kit and set about assisting Frank with the casualty. 'What happened?' Frank asked the man

'Chip pan caught fire and I threw water on it', he replied with a little embarrassment. I quickly cast another glance into the kitchen, but still saw no sign of a chip pan. 'Where is the pan now?' I interjected on Franks questioning of the casualty...

'I left it in the kitchen sink, at my house *up the street*, number thirty five'.

Without more ado I left Frank with the injured man and made my way quickly on foot back up the street to number thirty five.

On leaving his house, in a panic, the casualty had left his front door open; now upon entering his property my original suspicion was confirmed. The kitchen was well ablaze with fire spreading rapidly to other parts of the house.

Running back to our ambulance and grabbing the radio handset, I called up ambulance control, to request fire service attendance at this address, for a kitchen fire. Having passed the message, I re-joined Frank and his patient to give them the bad news about the house.

The injured man, who lived alone, was burned by the blazing chip pan oil about his arms. His initial response was to run out of the house seeking help from his friend a few doors away. The friend called the ambulance before attempting first aid on the burns. Little did either of them realise that there was now a fire in number thirty five, which was now in danger of consuming the whole house.

Within a few minutes, the fire service arrived, and after a quick 'SITREP' with the leading fire officer, we took our casualty to hospital.

Fire calls can present all sorts of dangers and hazards, not just to victims and fire fighters but also to other emergency responders such as police and ambulance. In the past, I have had to deal with police officers overcome by smoke and fumes, who had attempted some rescue whilst waiting for the fire service to arrive.

However, one incident which I was involved in could have proved tragic to me and my crewmate, George. The incident was caused by a misunderstanding between me and a fireman on the scene of a tower block fire.

Answering a fire call to a ‘persons reported’ at a twelve story tower block in Wallasey, found us arriving, one summer evening, at the scene of a serious flat fire high up the building. With flames and smoke shooting from all the windows of the flat and the reports of ‘persons reported’ I immediately asked ambulance control to send another ‘back up’ ambulance.

Several fire engines were already taking up the space in the small car park as well as on the surrounding roads as we arrived. We couldn’t risk our ambulance being hemmed in by other emergency vehicles so we needed to park in such a way that we would be free to make an emergency evacuation from the scene.

George drove our vehicle up onto the pavement, and together we gathered what essential equipment we may need and headed across the car-park to find the leading fireman, who would then give us more information.

Stepping over a maze of hosepipes, and trying to make myself heard over the cacophony of noise (which these occasions present) I spoke with the leading fireman who had to shout to make himself heard above the noise. He confirmed that this was a ‘persons reported’ fire call, and directed us to another fireman who was stationed inside the foyer of the tower block.

Carrying all our equipment, plus a cumbersome carry chair; me and George made our way inside and rendezvoused with a fireman who was standing by two lift doors. One for the even numbers and one for odd number floors and it was his job to monitor BA crews in and out of the area of fire. 'The fire is on the ninth floor', he told us and went on to say, 'I don't have any news of casualties yet but I've got a BA crew going in now.' He advised us that we could go up in the lift, to the floor *below* the fire; where any casualties could be brought to us for treatment.

George and I, laden down with all the equipment, crowded into a somewhat small passenger lift that would take us to the eighth floor. With all our equipment, it was a tight fit. I hit the eighth floor button ascending to what we thought would be a safe area for treating casualties. Reaching our destination the doors opened and, before either of us could reach for the button again to close the door, the lift suddenly filled with thick, black toxic smoke; instinctively we both fell to the floor, our equipment falling across the door and stopping it from closing. Within seconds, our lift was full of acrid smoke and it would have been dangerous for us to stand up and attempt to descend.

Now lying almost flat, there was at least some breathable air at floor level. It seemed obvious that this was, in fact, the floor that the fire was on. The lift door tried kept trying to close, but could not because we and our equipment was preventing it from doing so.

Opposite, across the floor a couple of metres away, I could see daylight showing under the bottom of a door. Realising, that it probably lead out onto a balcony and to relative safety we decided to make a dash for it. Crouching low and with all equipment except the carry chair, we scurried across the short distance and barged through the door, out onto a balcony and into fresh air, shutting the door behind us.

Out on the balcony we were surprised to find a middle-aged couple lying on the floor and unseen from the ground below. They looked shocked, but also relieved to see George and me.

The woman quickly explained that it was their flat that was on fire which had started *after a chip pan* caught fire. They had tried to put the fire out, but caused a flashover when they threw water on the burning pan. Because the smoke had been so bad, and they couldn't get the lift to come up to their floor quickly enough they had sought refuge in the fresh air outside on this balcony.

Unfortunately for them, (and now us) the flames were shooting out of the nearby windows just a few metres away from the balcony. Thick, choking smoke was swirling all around us. The woman's husband had a chronic asthma condition and was showing real signs of respiratory distress. As well as his asthma condition, his wife too had been out on this smoke-logged balcony long enough to be suffering from smoke inhalation so we set about giving Oxygen to them both

However, George and I were both feeling the effects of

smoke and fumes and so we too took turns on the Oxygen.

Looking over the balcony, I could see the crowds below all looking up at the fire; we had no way of knowing if they could see us. In the distance I could see another ambulance had arrived and the crew were waiting at the bottom of the flats, obviously wondering where we were. We had no hand held radios in those days, and it was useless to try shouting, I knew that the noise of all the fire engines and pumps at ground level would make it impossible for anyone down there to hear us.

After being out on the balcony for about ten minutes, there was a commotion at the door. Suddenly the door opened and a fireman, still wearing his BA equipment, stepped through. As he took his face-mask off his face was a picture as he looked at us all lying there on the floor of the balcony. He looked amazed as he surveyed us huddled there in the corner. He couldn't quite make out how we had got there; and didn't seem to like it when I said 'We were here before you mate'.

We had been lucky not to be injured or suffering too badly

from smoke inhalation. There had been a mix-up, regarding the floor level of the fire, in our conversation with the fireman at the entrance to the flats.

In 1995 there was another firefighters' strike which lasted some time. Again it was the military forces that were brought in to cover for the striking fire crews. This time, however, the ambulance service played a more significant role in emergency fire calls, in so far that ambulances were simultaneously deployed, from the police control room, to all fire calls.

Because modern ambulances are quicker than the 'Green Goddess' fire engines used by the Army, and also the fact that local ambulance crews knew their local area meant that we could be 'on scene' quicker than the Army fire crews. It, therefore, became our job to respond and give 'first reports'.

On a couple of occasions my first report was one of 'persons reported'. This would implement a secondary response from an RAF or Navy crew, who were already military service trained in breathing apparatus (BA), and travelled to the fire in a minibus separate to the Green Goddess'. They did not carry any fire fighting equipment save for a couple of hand-held fire extinguishers.

On one occasion my crewmate, George, and I responded to a fire call in block of flats several miles away from the Army fire base. We were first on scene and upon our arrival could see thick black acrid smoke pouring from the windows of a flat several floors up. At the entrance we were met by a resident who told us that a man lived alone in the flat that was on fire. Although there was no solid evidence at this point that he was actually at home I felt it prudent to send out a 'possible persons reported' before making our way up to the flat.

Carrying Oxygen and other essential equipment we made our way to the floor below the fire (as is the safest procedure) before climbing the final flight to the floor concerned.

Smoke was immediately the problem, the corridors had ventilation ducts which took away most of it but there was enough smoke and fumes to make our eyes stream. We got close to the actual flat and could see that the front door was open, but such was the density of the smoke that, it would have been impossible for anyone to venture inside without breathing equipment.

There were several flats to each floor so George and I set off knocking on the doors urging people to evacuate until the fire had been put out.

Looking out of the window, I could see our ambulance standing alone in the street below with a small crowd of people looking up at the fire but with no sign yet of the Army fire engines. A few minutes later I was relieved to see the arrival of the minibus carrying an RAF BA crew. A few minutes later they joined up with us and, after a quick SITREP, they set off through the thick smoke and into the burning flat carrying only an axe, torches and a couple of fire extinguishers

I looked out of the window...still no fire crew.

Minutes passed before the RAF BA crew emerged from the smoke. They reported that they had investigated only part of the flat; the other part was burning too severely for them to enter without water.

Eventually the Army fire crew arrived, about twenty minutes after the original call. Now all they had to do was put the fire out. I went down to meet them and give them a SITREP. By now a janitor had arrived on the scene and with his help the Army crew set up water to the 'Dry Riser'[i] which would get water to the affected flat.

The flat had been free of occupation but had been burgled and presumably set on fire deliberately.

A group of soldiers carried reels of hose up to the effected floor and connected to the dry-riser water outlet. 'Water on' one shouted. I heard the message being relayed down to the ground floor. Two of the soldiers and a sergeant stood ready at the door of the burning flat awaiting water to come through the hose. 'Water on' the sergeant screamed louder this time.

Someone below shouted back. 'The water is on Sergeant', but still no water came through the hose. It soon became quite farcical when it was found that all the dry-riser outlets, *below the fire*, had been deliberately opened by vandals.

Worse still, on the floor where the outlet was open, water was cascading out at a phenomenal rate and flooding many flats. Naturally residents were complaining; not about the vandals but about the inexperienced soldiers not having checked the dry-riser system first.

When the fire was eventually extinguished the soldiers would be tasked with mopping up the flooded flats and no doubt many damage claims would go into the local council.

During the strike I attended one particular fire call that all paramedics were dreading. It was early on a November evening when we received a call over the ambulance radio, to attend a 'persons reported' house fire in the Birkenhead town centre. I was working alongside trainee paramedic, Jack, who was driving. Even from half a mile away we could see flames lighting up the dark evening sky. Traffic ahead of us, was slowing up and impeding our approach as drivers slowed down to view the fire. Jack was forced to drive the last half mile down the wrong side of the road before pulling up at the front of a terraced house.

The house was in the middle of a block of pre-war houses that had been recently been emptied to allow the council to refurbish them. Now the top floor of one of them was well ablaze with flames shooting up through the roof and out of the upstairs windows. There were lots of people milling around but one, who approached me as I stepped out of the ambulance, was a woman from a nearby occupied house She informed me that she had made the emergency call and went on to say, 'there was a group of kids playing around in there', before adding, 'I am sure they didn't come out'.

Jack called up to our control room to verify a 'person's reported' fire whilst I went to the front door of the house to see if there was anything I could do. I felt that the bystanders may be expecting something from me and Jack; but what?

The front door opened easily as I pushed on it; I was surprised to see that the lower ground floors were sufficiently illuminated, by the flames from the fire upstairs and that there was surprisingly little smoke downstairs. Initially I could see that the lower rooms of the house were free of furniture (obstacles). I made a quick calculated risk-assessment and reckoned that I could quickly run across the empty downstairs rooms to reach the stairs.

I waited a moment for Jack to join me at the open door and told him of my plan then I asked him to watch out for any dangers to himself or me and to shout a warning to me if necessary.

With that I ran into the house calling out as I did so, to anyone who may be inside. A quick glance into the back kitchen showed it clear. I reached the foot of the stairs, which were not yet ablaze and looked secure and sturdy. I could see flames in a bedroom at the top of the stairs. Now, still calling out to anyone who may be inside, I approached more cautiously up the stairs to a point where my eyes drew level with the upper floor. Beside the bedroom, opposite, there was a narrow landing to my left, leading to other bedrooms which were all on fire. I could see the floor and all doorframes were burning too

There were loud bangs and crackling from the fire. The window and roof had gone so that there was a draught blowing up from downstairs which was, obviously clearing the smoke and fumes upwards and out of building. However, I had gone as far as I could, the flames were too much and I was unsure as to the security of the actual floor so I made a hasty retreat. I was confident that any kids that had been in the house before the fire were not in there now.

Several minutes later, the Army arrived, followed a short time later, by the RAF BA crew.

I attended many fires during the strike, some of the fires re-ignited hours later because the inexperienced Army firefighters had not damped down the fire sufficiently enough. I went to one factory fire three times in one day, due to poor damping down.

We also had to deal with soldiers who were injured during some fire calls although none too serious.

Whatever the skills and enthusiasm of the Army firefighters they were, and never will be, a suitable 'stand in' for professional firefighters.

◆ ◆ ◆

13 FIRE SERVICE STRIKE 1995

In the winter of 1977 (the, so called, Winter of Discontent) the fire service held its first ever national strike; coincidentally, starting on the day that I joined the ambulance service.

Firemen throughout UK manned picket lines outside their stations; the public showing their support for the firemen's actions by donating money into collection boxes (buckets) to help the men and their families over the coming weeks of hardship which eventually went beyond Christmas.

We, the ambulance staff, (like most of the population) had a great sympathy for the firemen; knowing as we did of the poor pay and working conditions that their job offered along with the risks that their job entailed.

It had only been three years earlier that the fire service and ambulance services had (under government instructions) split into two separate organisations; the ambulance service was placed under the direct control of the NHS, becoming the emergency response wing of the National Health Service.

Previously housed together in one big complex within the town centre, we shared many facilities such as catering, workshops, garages and dormitories (yes we could sleep on nights - we even had a blanket issue!). Despite the services being separated, the staff of the both fire service and ambulance service still maintained many of the social links and friendships that had developed over time. For a time the ambulance staff also maintained certain working conditions such as our working patterns (in those days - twelve hour working) as well as similar pension rights.

When the first fire service strike took place, there was very little impact on the ambulance service; we continued to respond to fire calls as and when we were requested to so.

The 1977 National Strike lasted for ten weeks and, fortunately, there were no significant fires or incidents in our area during that time.

The Government ordered the armed forces to step in and provide a basic fire and accident cover during the strike and so the Army was called upon to provide soldiers, who manned the old 'Green Goddess' fire engines, most of which had not been used since the war. The soldiers' fire training was rapid and basic, as was the machinery that they would be using. Although it had been suggested that soldiers should be allowed to use the modern fire engines, it was considered that training soldiers to use modern fire engines and the accompanying array of equipment would take too long. Furthermore the union representing the firemen had threatened not to use any fire engines (when the strike was over) that soldiers had used to 'break the strike'.

The RAF and the Royal Navy also provided some personnel who were already trained (for their own regular military requirements) in using BA (breathing apparatus).

The military personnel were not necessarily deployed to their own home town; they were more likely to be strangers both to the job of firefighting and to their particular area of deployment and so, it fell to police officers traveling with them to act as guides directing them to the fires.

The fire service strike in1995 (18 years later) took on a different format insofar that the strike was not a single national event, but a series of random strikes taking place in several different counties throughout The UK and at varying times. It was more fragmented and some may say more disruptive for the authorities, but less costly to the firefighters and their union. Most of the strikes were based around local issues but fundamentally they were about pay and conditions, cuts to annual leave and reductions in manpower.

In 1995 Merseyside firefighters engaged in this strike campaign with the dispute lasting almost nine months in which time the firemen took a series of short strikes as opposed to one continuous one. There were many serious fires as well as lives lost and people injured. Although it was never officially accepted, that those who perished may have lived had there not been a firefighters' strike.

To cover the strikes, a fleet of twenty four Green Goddesses fire engines and ten RAF fire rescue units were deployed, on standby at various locations (mostly Territorial Army centres) throughout Merseyside. The soldiers and RAF responded well, throughout the strike period, within the limitations of their training and equipment.

Again, as in 1977, it was the Army, who formed the bulk of the fire cover duties and on the Wirral Peninsula it was soldiers from the Welsh Guards who came and manned the wholly unsuitable antiquated Green Goddess vehicles, guided to fires by police escort. Teams of RAF firefighters who were experienced with using breathing apparatus (BA) would follow, separately, in a minibus fitted with blue lights and sirens. The RAF minibus was a much faster vehicle which tended to arrive at fires well before the Army firefighters which meant that they then had to wait around for the soldiers to arrive before they could work together as a proper firefighting unit.

Because soldiers were not used to fighting fires, nor was their training in that particular field adequate it was considered, advisable that the ambulance service should play a more significant role in supporting them and acting in a first response capacity. By doing so, it was anticipated that ambulance crews responding to any fire calls would be able to reach the scene of the fire more rapidly than the Army or RAF teams and, therefore, would give a vital 'first report in regard to confirming the type of fire and whether or not it may be 'persons reported'.

The ambulance service also deployed extra ambulance cover, so that we could still maintain our normal day-to-day emergency response capability, whilst at the same time offering vital support to military fire teams.

Other than being informed that we would be acting as

first responders, there was not much more discussion or advice given to ambulance staff with regard to any of the wider issues or risks that we may face. We were merely told do a rapid recce and communicate a 'first report' to ambulance control who, in turn, had a direct line to the fire control centre. What else were we expected to do? It didn't seem a very pleasant prospect to just sit around at what might be a very dramatic incident, doing nothing while waiting for the Army and RAF to arrive.

As part of the emergency services, members of the public may expect us to do more. I think, it was *just assumed*, that because ambulance crews were used to dealing with any and all emergencies, we would just 'play it by ear' and cope with each fire call as it happened.

Consequently me and many of my colleagues did find ourselves involved on the front line of some dangerous fire calls; it would have been nice (if not advisable) to have received some expert advice *before* the strike began, knowing that we would likely to be placing ourselves in more danger than was usual for us.

As well as the first response by ambulance crews, our service (to their credit) re-deployed some of the officers from their office jobs, along with hastily trained volunteers from our ambulance garage mechanics group. Together they set up a few very efficient 'fast response rescue units' using Range Rover Discovery vehicles equipped with all necessary arc lights, generators etc., as well as a substantial range of cutting gear.

During the strike, these units were called upon, almost daily, to respond to victims trapped in vehicle crashes as well as a range of other entrapment emergencies. To their credit, working outside of their 'comfort zone' they presented a formidable team and did effect many rescues. As an aside to the setting up of these teams of mechanics, many of them gained first-hand experience of emergency work and as such when the strike was over, several later applied to train as paramedics.

All 999 fire calls were made as usual, but the telephone

company directed such calls to the police, who then re-directed the information to the ambulance service, whereupon an ambulance 'first response' crew was immediately deployed.

Because the Green Goddess fire tenders are a much slower vehicle, (travelling as slow as twenty miles an hour up hills, and around town) we, in our much faster ambulances, and with our comprehensive topographical knowledge were much faster and we tended to reach most fire locations first.

Upon arriving at a fire, and being first 'in attendance' we would do a quick reconnaissance, and then radio through a 'first report' to ambulance control confirming the nature of the fire along with any relevant information, such as 'persons reported'. This information was then passed onto the fire crews heading to the scene.

Often the ambulance crews arriving first on scene would be faced with the embarrassing situation of having to stand, idly by, whilst waiting for the soldiers to arrive

Fires are organic, in that they grow and spread, creating rapidly changing hazards with potential danger to people within the vicinity; it was often the case that ambulance crews 'first on scene' were occupied keeping members of the public away from the danger of the fire. Occasionally we would need to intervene to stop people from putting themselves in danger with some ad-hoc firefighting attempt. Many such types were keen to test their ladder skills or try out there new garden hose.

During the 1995 firefighters strike I was deployed to many fire calls, some of which were serious and others less so.

The soldiers and their antiquated vehicles were based at a Territorial Army base in the town of Birkenhead which was regarded as being, roughly, the centre of the strike area. From there the Army were expected to give fire cover to most areas of the Wirral Peninsula. This meant that the Green Goddesses were travelling to emergency fire calls over much greater distances, than would the regular fire service and could take up to twenty minutes or more to reach locations that the regular fire service could reach in less than half the time. In my view these fire tenders should have been more strategically placed around the region, but I also realise that this would pose problems of security for the military crews.

Having been in the Army myself some years ago, I had been looking forward to working alongside the soldiers but my enthusiasm was occasionally troubled by their unbridled use of profanity within the public domain.

Whilst the soldiers will present a well-disciplined unit within the regiment, I am afraid that I cannot say the same about them when they were working within the civilian environment. At times they seemed like a fish out of water, and even looked ill-disciplined. Regardless of what time of day or night, and regardless of who was in the vicinity, be it adult or child, the young soldiers never seemed to moderate their bad language. They cursed each-other's mistakes with the maximum of profanity; screaming loudly to convey their message to all within shouting distance.

As so often in the fire field, due to the noise levels caused by the commotion of firefighters and fire engine high pressure pumps, it is usually shouted instructions that form simplest method of communication particularly, to someone a distance away. However, such communication methods can lead to mistaken messages being passed on, thus allowing for confusion and some-times dangerous mistakes to be made.

For instance, at one serious house fire that I attended, a soldier was high up a ladder with a hose, from which the water was only a pathetic dribble. 'More pressure' he shouted. Another soldier standing at the bottom of the ladder responded instantly, relaying the message and also shouting, 'More pressure'. The message was meant to be heard by a soldier who was operating the powerful pump on the fire engine about one hundred metres away; the noise from the pump made it virtually impossible for the pump operator to hear instructions shouted to him over that distance and so he was blissfully unaware for the need to increase the water pressure.

Meanwhile, the soldier at the top of the ladder was becoming increasingly anxious because by now flames from the fire had broken through the roof of the building and were fanning towards him.

Again, but louder this time, he shouted for '*More pressure*' with the message again being relayed by the man at the foot of the ladder, 'More pressure!' Still the water only dribbled out from the hose and the situation was becoming dangerous and ludicrous to the point that even members of the pubic began to shout for more pressure too.

Now in exasperation a voice from the top of the ladder screamed

'YOU F...... STUPID C ... MORE F...... PRESSURE'.

The message was dutifully and accurately repeated, but seemingly louder by the man at the foot of the ladder, who screamed at the top of his voice with all the expletives included. It seemed that everyone in the streets around would have heard this incredibly obscene shouting match. All, except, the man standing next to the pump!

Eventually I watched as another soldier was told, 'Go and wake that dozy C . . . up, and tell him more pressure'. They did, and eventually the man at the top of the ladders got more pressure!

Although this incident raised a few laughs when I recalled it to my colleagues back at base it did, in fact, dent the image of 'our lads', particularly as this seemed to be the norm rather than the exception.

I understand all too well what goes on inside an army camp, but their commanding officers ought to give due consideration to this point, should they ever be called upon again to help in some civilian capacity. It's because I hold the Army in such high regard, that I make these points, for in my view they let themselves down.

The soldiers were often like a fish out of water; that said they also did a great job taking considerable personal risks at times, in their efforts to contain and extinguish a fire. Considering that they were not seasoned firemen, and that their only real experience of firefighting was 'fire stag' duty back in their respective camps, I take my hat off to them.

Paradoxically, the RAF teams were well rehearsed, and well-disciplined. They always presented a professional image; but then they were trained firemen serving with The RAF. They would arrive separately in a minibus, usually before the Green Goddess fire tenders and could enter a smoke logged building, because they were equipped with BA and suitable attire. In fact their uniform and equipment was almost identical to that worn by civilian firemen.

During the strike, many of my colleagues across the region, found themselves 'first on scene' at serious fires; consequently they did not stand by as mere spectators but felt drawn to attempt rescue of victims, some successful...some not! Like some of those other paramedics, I found myself and crewmate, on a few occasions, entering a burning building to look for someone who had been reported as being inside.

One such case happened around 19:00 one November evening when me and Julian responded to a 'persons reported' house fire.

As we negotiated our ambulance through the heavy evening traffic we could see in the distance, the glow of the fire lighting up the early evening sky. We were still about a mile away but I could feel my adrenaline 'kick in', mentally preparing me for whatever we may be faced with. Safety of ourselves and others would be my priority. I ran over, in my mind, what my approach should be in preparation for any and all eventuality; all the time hoping that the military fire crews would already be in attendance, although I doubted it.

A few minutes later we arrived at a row of empty houses alongside a busy main road. The houses had been, boarded up awaiting demolition; one of which was well ablaze with angry flames shooting out of the upper windows and breaking through roof. Moreover there was no sign yet of the Green Goddess fire engines.

As we alighted from our ambulance, a middle aged woman ran across to us in a panic. 'There are two young lads still in that place' she said excitedly, pointing to the blazing building and went on to explain that although the houses were boarded up at the front, there was access around the back of the property.

Julian grabbed our radio hand-set and called a priority message to our ambulance control, informing them of possible 'persons reported'.

Meanwhile I made my way around to the back of the house in search of a safe access for me to try to ascertain if there was anyone in the building. I knew that Julian and I would be limited in our ability to make rescue attempt; I was acutely aware of the paramedic's code of self-preservation. Rule number one, watch for dangers to yourself and to bystanders.

As I pushed through the backyard gate with Julian close behind me, I could see the back kitchen door was partly open, furthermore the fire, though serious, was confined to the upper floors of the house. Quickly making our way across a small yard we reached the open door and peered inside. To our surprise, we could see that the lower rooms, illuminated by the glow from the fire upstairs, were virtually smoke free. It was obvious that the heat from the fire upstairs was causing a strong upward draught drawing air in through this open door which in turn pushed the smoke and fumes up and out of the upstairs windows, thus was keeping the ground floor clear.

Julian waited at the back door, watching after me and keeping an eye on the progress of the fire whilst I made a quick dash inside. I was able to check quickly and safely that the lower rooms were free of casualties. I was aware of the loud sound of the fire above, crackling and the roar of flames. Still shouting out to anyone who may be inside, I ventured up the stairs but as I neared the top it became apparent that no one could survive up there. Flames were licking up from the carpeted floor and all the bedroom doors were ablaze, so turning quickly I ran back out of the building into fresh air. The whole thing had taken less than one minute.

It was a couple more minutes before the RAF BA fire team arrived who, in turn, were soon joined by the Army. Only then could a concerted effort be made to extinguish the fire before searching for victims. I am glad to report that before the fire was fully extinguished all persons were accounted for....no casualties!

One Saturday afternoon, my crewmate and I attended a fire in a high rise block of flats. Upon our arrival outside the building, we could clearly see flames and smoke pouring from one of the flats on the sixth floor. We were first on scene so we sent an early report back to ambulance control, who in turn would confirm the fire, to the Army and RAF fire crews.

Having passed our message, my crewmate and I made our way to the affected floor, carrying Oxygen, a burns dressing kit and my cumbersome paramedic case; with so much equipment we would need to use the lift on the opposite side of the building. As we left the lift and made our way toward the fire we were met by smoke curling along the ceiling indicating that the fire had broken out of the flat and was compromising residents escape route.

Getting as close as we could to the actual flat that was on fire we could see a huge amount of thick, black toxic smoke coming from an open front door and presenting a potential for the fire to spread to other flats. Realising that people may still be in some of the flats on this floor; we banged on doors and shouted for them to leave this floor.

Once again, the RAF crew arrived before the Army, but they

were unable to enter the burning flat without a water hose, and so we waited several more minutes until at last we saw the Green Goddess fire engine was arriving and the soldiers setting the task of pumping water up through the dry riser, to the fire.

On high rise buildings such as this, there is a large pipe running up the building, known as the 'dry riser'. From ground level the fire service can connect a high power hose to the dry riser, and pump water into it and up to the appropriate floor level. As this pipe passes each floor level, there is a valve onto which a hose can be connected, thus taking water to the fire on any particular floor. For instance: if the fire is on the third floor so the water passes the closed valves on the first and second floors and will come out at the open valve of the third floor...simple!

Unfortunately, on this occasion some idiot vandals had already opened the valves on each floor, thus allowing water to escape through the open valve on the first floor and flooding that level in a few inches of water before it could be closed. This debacle was repeated for each floor until each valve in turn was closed; incredibly all floors below the fire had been flooded with several inches of water before water reached the actual fire. Water damage ran into many thousands of pounds.

Of the fire, there were no injuries; the flat was empty at the time.

On another occasion when working during the strike period, I witnessed a most bizarre situation whereupon regular firefighters were refusing to get out of their fire engines to relieve soldiers at an on-going house fire.

It happened one Saturday evening as Julian and I were just at the beginning of a nightshift. It was just after 18.15 when we were dispatched to a house fire. We knew that the regular fire service had been on a twelve hour strike that day but were now back to work the same nightshift that we were on.

Arriving at the fire scene we were met by an incredible site. The house on fire was about quarter of a mile down a very narrow lane, barely wide enough for one car. The lane was blocked completely by three Green Goddess fire engines, with seemingly miles of hose-pipes running to water hydrants in all directions.

At the top of the lane were three regular fire engines with experienced fire crews still sitting inside. Meanwhile, a heated debate was going on between a senior fire officer and a senior Army officer. The argument was based upon the regular fire-fighter taking over the duties of the soldiers (mid-fire) and dealing with the house fire.

It would soon transpire that the fire had begun a couple of hours before the firemen were due back off strike and on duty. As a result the Army had been engaged for some time in trying to extinguish the blaze (in a listed building) and were now hoping to be relieved by the regular fire crews. The problem was that the lane was completely blocked by Army personnel and equipment and to add further complication, one of the Green Goddess fire engines had broken down with a serious oil leak and would need to be towed out from the lane. The task of changing over was too immense to be contemplated and so the regular firefighters returned to their station, leaving the Army to finish the job which they had started.

I felt sorry for the house-owner, for he felt like 'the piggy in the middle' distraught and trying to make sense out of nonsense. He may have reflected on the fact that, had the firemen not been on strike, then *their* expertise may have prevented the total destruction of his lovely home.

Another problem with the inexpert firefighting skills of the Army firefighters was the recurring flare up of fires previously extinguished by the soldiers. Several times I returned to fires which were thought to have been thoroughly extinguished and damped down only to suddenly re-ignite.

One thing is for sure, firemen going on strike should be an unacceptable practise in a civilised society, I may say the same applies to paramedics and nurses etc. *But* employers of such personnel should afford more respect and decent working conditions than they sometimes do. It takes a strong, fair management to create a genuine team-spirited approach between the workforce and those who govern them. I know what it is like to feel undervalued and disregarded by an employer.

We were all glad when the firemen settled their dispute and returned to normal working. May we never see the Green Goddess on our streets again.

◆ ◆ ◆

14 DOCTORS

Paramedics represent just one piece in the long chain of emergency care services. As part of that chain paramedics enjoy a professional empathy with other practitioners of emergency medical aid and rescue. Being part of such a large and varied team brings with it a sort of unwritten bond of loyalty and confidentiality; an allegiance to your fellow professionals; allegiances that sometimes test your own personal integrity and the validity of your reluctance to report something that you know is wrong.

Before paramedics could be introduced into the public domain, many complex political factors had to be explored and challenged. There were many voices of opposition that had to be won over by sensible and logical argument, as to the virtues of training ambulance men and women to perform advanced life-saving support. The perceived need for paramedics was the subject of much debate and contention. The most vociferous argument, both for and against the introduction of a paramedic service came from within the medical profession, with many doctors taking opposing views. Some for support – but under very strict medical control!

Others were totally against the idea of Advanced Life Support (ALS) being bestowed upon ambulance staff, 'after all weren't they only like taxi drivers?' I heard it said. Those medical opponents preferring instead to 'scoop and run'. In other words – just pick the patient up quickly and run to the nearest casualty department.

Eventually the argument for the introduction of a paramedic service was won, thanks mainly to a few eminent members of the medical profession.

Because of the initial reluctance of some doctors to acknowledge the value of a trained paramedic service, there was now feeling of gratitude, from the ambulancemen and women towards those who had changed their opinion and now deemed it safe to recognise our advanced life-saving contribution.

Gratitude, confidentiality, and allegiance all feelings of loyalty toward fellow professionals which, at times, caused me to question the integrity of such strongly held views. On several occasions during my career, I had occasion to question my own stance of looking the other way; say nothing, don't rock the boat, keep quiet and don't complain. No room for 'whistle blowers'.

Many years ago, (before paramedics were born) when ambulancemen/women were not looked upon in very high esteem by many doctors, I had occasion to seriously question the unwritten code of allegiance and loyalty that I held toward these fellow professionals who seemed to regard us as little more than taxi drivers (no offence to taxi drivers).

One afternoon, when attending to a woman (in her early thirties) who had collapsed, unconscious, in the street my crewmate, John, and I were so surprised by her rapidly deteriorating condition that we informed the hospital to be 'standing by'.

On our initial observations she was looking grey, cyanosed and her breathing was extremely poor, she was, by all accounts, critically ill. Wasting no time at the scene, we quickly put her onto our stretcher and into the ambulance ready for a rapid journey to hospital. Suddenly, as we were about to leave the scene she suffered a cardiac arrest. By reflex we began to resuscitate her using the only equipment available to us, in those days, namely Oxygen, oral airways and bag and mask resuscitator as well as carrying out chest compressions.

Locking the stretcher in position John left me in the back whilst he would radio ahead to the hospital to give them an update. Now as we raced towards the hospital I managed to do good CPR (Cardio Pulmonary Resuscitation) on the woman (quite a difficult task in the back of a speeding ambulance). With no ECG monitor it was impossible to know what was happening with her heart but her skin colour had improved to the point where she was looking better; and her eyes, previously dilated, were now looking a more normal size, proving that I was at least preventing her from dying *at this point*. I considered that the receiving emergency team would have a good chance of resuscitating this patient successfully.

We raced towards the hospital arriving just five minutes later. 'Plenty of time for a resus team to assemble' I thought to myself as John and I unloaded our patient.

Surprisingly, there was no reception team waiting to meet us. Pushing through the hospital doors of A&E, we hurried down the corridor toward the resuscitation room, all the time we were still carrying out CPR. It was only as we reached the doors of the resus room that a nurse appeared in front of us.

Barring our way. 'Hang on boy's...what have you got there?' she queried – ignoring the evidence of her own eyes.

Ignoring her presence and her question we negotiated around her and into the deserted resus room. John and I exchanged glances of disgust as we unceremoniously lifted our patient up on to the empty hospital trolley. 'This patient is in cardiac arrest' I replied sarcastically, wondering why she could not see the obvious.

Our patient was now on the resuscitation trolley but there was still no sign of any emergency team arriving. Indeed, it was only now that I noticed how quiet the casualty department was. John and I continued to carry out CPR whilst the nurse stood questioning us; obviously trying to determine whether or not she should call for a cardiac arrest team.

Eventually, after a brief spell of inactivity she did call the team by way of a special hospital emergency telephone number. Within minutes doctors and nurses were assembling around our patient, making valiant efforts at resuscitation; sadly too late for the patient. She could not be resuscitated after so long without proper attention. It may be that she would have died anyway, but we will never know because the team where never given the opportunity to respond to this dire emergency – until it was too late.

It later transpired that the hospital had received our request to be standing by to receive a patient in cardiac arrest – but due to some new hospital ruling – they would not assemble a cardiac arrest team before a nurse had seen the patient to make an independent assessment.

This, effectively, meant that any patient suffering a severe heart attack or cardiac arrest had to first make the journey to hospital; so that a nurse could check that the ambulance crew were indeed correct in their diagnosis.

Looking back on it; it seems crazy that such a rule could have been implemented at all. But that was an example of how little faith they had (at that time) in ambulance crews ability to make any accurate diagnosis.

Later that day, I was told by one of the nurses that the young husband and children of the dead woman had come to the hospital in a very distressed state. The grief of the woman's family, it seemed, had rubbed off on the nursing staff and they too were upset, she told me.

I was more than upset! I was bloody annoyed and bitter that the hospital staff had wasted so many vital minutes by the refusal to respond to our initial standby request. 'It's a pity you didn't bother to do your best then isn't it?' I said sarcastically to the nurse, before storming out of the department.

I made a written complaint to my CAO (Chief Ambulance Officer) about the hospital not accepting the word of ambulance staff, particularly in such serious cases as a coronary emergency. The rule was immediately changed and since then all such requests are responded to admirably.

As a postscript; this one event made me realise that ambulance staff needed to upgrade their emergency medical knowledge and skills so that in future we could do more for the patient and maybe as a second thought, gain some respect from those 'above us'. For it seemed to me, at that time, that even the most junior of nurses did indeed regard us as little more than taxi drivers.

Many times in the past, I had delivered patients to hospital in a state of cardiac arrest. Having placed the patient on the resuscitation trolley, my crewmate and I would be expected to stand back out of the way, so that the resus team could work, unhindered. I watched many successful resuscitations; patients being shocked and given life-saving drugs along with perfect CPR. A good resuscitation team, in action, is a splendid sight to behold as each team member plays his/her own part in the complex emergency.

Many years later the situation changed, for it was widely accepted that paramedics CPR skills are as good as – if not greater than that of some doctors. Nowadays, paramedics work alongside the resuscitation team and are on a more equal footing.

My colleagues and I often traded stories of 'turning a blind eye' to things that we had seen to be wrong or negligent; be it in a hospital, nursing home or a GP administering treatment within our presence. Always our complaint was the same. If it was an ambulance crew doing things wrong or being negligent, they (the medical profession) would not ignore the matter, they would have no hesitation in reporting any perceived wrongdoing.

Over the years I heard of complaints made against an ambulance crew by hospital staff, doctors, GPs and midwives. There seemed to be a simple procedure for them to follow if they wished to complain about ambulance staff; nor did they display any reluctance to do so. On the other hand there was no procedure where we could make complaint or even air our views of genuine concern.

Answering a 999 to deal with a man suffering sudden chest pains, I arrived at the address to find a middle-aged gentleman who, as well as severe chest pain, was also cyanosed and having severe breathing difficulties. He was very distressed, agitated and frightened, fearing he was about die and was barely able to speak due to his breathlessness.

Reassurance and calmness would be the key to getting him safely to hospital; with haste but not rushing him, we calmly carried him out of his house and placed him comfortably on the stretcher in the ambulance. Soon with an initial high rate of Oxygen he began to settle.

He was 'So frightened' he told me, he thought he 'was going to die.' I had a job getting him to settle down, but eventually after a few minutes of careful and calm reassurance from me he began to relax. His wife came along too and her presence offered another level of reassurance to him. We didn't race to hospital; no lights and horns just a nice steady journey.

By the time we reached the hospital he had responded well to my limited treatment (pre-paramedic days) and he was now able to speak coherently, and his colour had regained some normality.

Whilst my crewmate and I wheeled him into the resuscitation room, his wife went to the reception area to 'book' him in.

Making our way into the emergency room were met by a woman doctor who immediately began to question the man as to his reason for being here (the hospital) at the same time ignoring my attempts to give the usual verbal handover and speak on his behalf.

She spoke quickly with a strong foreign accent (which even to me was difficult to understand) and, as such, my patient had equal difficulty too. She seemed oblivious to the fact that he could not understand her questioning and quickly became impatient with his slow response and kept firing questions at him. I did my best to intervene and give her a proper brief as to his condition. It seemed that she was determined to ignore me and with her hand raised to me, waved away my attempts to give my report.

My crewmate and I carried on working, and gently lifted the gentleman onto the hospital trolley and placed an Oxygen mask over his face.

Still she continued her questioning, but now her manner was antagonistic. Suddenly the gentleman became very agitated with her; his demeanour changed for the worse and he became very breathless and now experienced difficulty in speaking at all. She on the other hand became insistent upon his answering her incomprehensible questions.

My mate and I watched the poor man become more and more distressed to the point where he suddenly sat bolt upright clutching his chest, pulling off the Oxygen mask and told her to 'Shut up and F**** off!'

Clearly incensed at this very sick man's reaction to her unnecessary questioning; her response was immediate. She slapped him hard across the face! His response was equally immediate. He fell back on the stretcher in cardiac arrest!

I never forget the look of horror on her face as she looked up towards me and my mate. I just looked right back at her with utter contempt and shook my head in disgust. My mate and I started immediate CPR and carried on with resuscitation until the resus team gathered to take over, from us.

As always happens in these events, the most senior doctor took charge of the resus team and acted as team leader in order to orchestrate the attempt to save the patient's life. My mate and I stood back, observing the action, meanwhile the doctor who had slapped the man prior to his arrest, was herself drawn into the team; as would be expected, the team leader wanted to know more detail in relation to the mans' condition prior to his emergency arrival at the hospital.

Now she looked around at my mate and I (like a cat caught in the glare of headlights). I could detect the plea in her eyes hoping for some interjection from us and so save her the embarrassment of being unable to furnish the team leader with the important information that could help determine the outcome of the resuscitation. Without concern for her embarrassment and *only* with concern for the patient, I stepped forward and gave a full detailed verbal report which was accepted with thanks.

Neither my mate nor I ever made any report about the woman doctor and, thankfully, the patient did survive. Neither my mate, nor me made any mention of what had precipitated the gentleman's cardiac arrest.

Fortunately for that doctor, the gentleman's wife did not witness her slapping her husband. My crewmate and I (reluctantly) turned a blind eye.

Thanks to her, I was left with a feeling of disgust with myself. Had she (the doctor) taken the trouble to let me speak (which is the normal procedure) then I could have explained what was wrong with the gentleman and his wife could have filled in any 'gaps'.

Thankfully that was a long time ago and it was a 'one off'.

Very early on in my ambulance career, our training instructor had related a true story about a young woman who had been found dead on the shores of the River Mersey.

Her body was recovered from the shoreline and taken to the hospital where it was certified by a doctor as life extinct before her body was transferred to the mortuary and placed in the refrigerator to await the coroner's examination. A short time later, prior to post mortem, a mortuary assistant noticed that she had tears running down her face. There was an immediate dash to the resuscitation room where an emergency team worked on her, eventually saving her life. She was discharged from hospital a short time later, having originally suffered very severe hypothermia.

Upon hearing that story, I was surprised that a doctor could certify someone as being dead when, in fact, they were not. However, over the years I have read, in newspapers, from time to time of such cases happening in other parts of the country. I wondered just how widespread is the mis-certifying of death?

My own experience only serves to amplify the question. I was carrying out an assessment of a newly qualified ambulance technician, when the ambulance radio crackled into life. Ambulance control instructed us to respond to an emergency call at an address some miles away. It was late afternoon on a very cold winter's day as we pulled up outside the house on the sea-front. Stepping out of the ambulance, I was acutely aware of the cold biting wind blowing in from the Irish Sea and stinging my face.

As I headed up the path to the house a policeman came out of the front door and hurried to meet me. 'Look' he said, sheepishly 'I hope you don't mind me calling you out on a day like this but I really need some advice.

He explained how he had been called to this house by neighbours who were concerned for the elderly man who lived there. After making a forced entry he and his colleague had discovered the body of an old man lying behind the front door. As police protocol demanded, they had requested the attendance of a doctor to certify death before any further formalities could be taken.

A short time later, a doctor had attended and did, indeed, certify that the old man was deceased, and duly signed a certificate to that effect before leaving the police officers to await the arrival of funeral directors to remove the body.

'Now,' the officer went on to explain 'my colleague *thinks* he saw the old man's eyes move, although I haven't seen anything myself. Can you check it out for us?'

Following the officer through the front door, I was aware just how cold the house seemed to be. Inside a narrow hallway I was shown the figure of a frail old man, only partially clothed and lying on a tiled floor; his body was totally white. Kneeling down in the confined space, I reached to feel for a pulse in his neck and was immediately struck by the extreme icy coldness of the old man's body. Now, joined by my crewmate, Jane, I began a more thorough examination of the old man. Both police officers reiterated that the doctor had certified death, and even showed me the certificate.

Already I was having doubts with the doctor's diagnosis; unsure as to whether the old man was dead or not. 'It's a brave man who has said that this person is dead' I voiced my opinion openly to Jane and the police officers as I began to respond to my own instincts about the condition of the body. In my mind he did not look dead. Jane ran back to the ambulance to fetch our cardiac and pulse Oxygen monitors; these would help to establish life extinct or not.

Meanwhile, opening up my paramedic case, I made preparations to intubate and ventilate the man should I consider it necessary or a viable option. Moments later Jane returned and, together, we set about attaching him to the cardiac monitor and oximeter. Almost immediately we had a dramatic result.

The old man's heart *was* beating! Albeit very slowly (profound bradycardia) but nevertheless it was beating, but there were no visible signs of breathing. I realised that I could not walk away from a beating heart, particularly in cases of hypothermia; there is a 'fail safe' rule for such occasions namely; a *freezing* body is not dead – until it is *warm* and dead.

'Right Jane' I said 'we will treat him (the man) as a cardiac arrest with full resuscitation for profound hypothermia'. Even as I inserted the intubation tube into his trachea the ECG monitor showed, visually on the screen, that his heart was reacting to my intervention – displaying signs of VF (Ventricular Fibrillation – a condition that could, *normally*, be shocked in a warm patient- *but not in hypothermia*).

With cardiac compressions and artificially ventilating him with a high Oxygen rate we continued resuscitation for a few minutes before making a run for the hospital.

Whilst we were both working on our patient and planning our evacuation of the man, I was aware of one of the police officers having a conversation, over his radio, with police control. I heard him say something to the effect that 'the paramedics are resuscitating the old man'.

A few minutes later as we were placing the old man onto our stretcher there was knock on the front door and two men entered the hallway. They looked somewhat perplexed as they saw what was happening and told us that they were from the funeral directors, 'come to collect a body'. 'I'm sorry mate ...there's no way I am handing this patient over to you just yet....we're off to the hospital', with that we pushed passed them with our patient on the stretcher.

Minutes later we were speeding towards the hospital, with me in the back still carrying out CPR, administering Oxygen and checking the monitors. Jane alerted the hospital A&E to arrange for a team to be waiting to take over from us.

Sadly all our efforts were in vain for the old man, despite being warmed up, died some hours later in hospital.

As a postscript to this story; unknown to Jane and I, A 'Breaking News' story about 'paramedics resuscitating a person presumed dead' had been broadcast on local radio (actually as we were engaged in our efforts to save the man). Just who alerted the radio station, we did not know, but our management ordered an immediate enquiry to establish that Jane and I had carried out our duties to the letter. Which we had; and which was later confirmed, by us both receiving a commendation for our decisions and subsequent treatment in difficult circumstances.

Another somewhat similar story was recalled to me by another paramedic. He explained to me, how when responding to an emergency call designated as 'a collapse' both he and his crewmate had approached the house carrying their equipment when they were met by a doctor who was coming out of the front door; 'going to fetch something from his car'. Quietly greeting them he spoke briefly to explain how he had been in the vicinity when someone, from the house had asked him to attend to the collapsed patient until an ambulance, which had been called, arrived at the house.

Upon entering the house he had found a woman, in her late thirties, lying collapsed on the floor. He quickly established that she was deceased and had informed the family members who were present; now distressed and gathered in a back room.

'Sorry lads nothing for you to do' he commented as he continued to his car. The ambulance crew entered the house to see if they could assist the distressed relatives who were inside. Automatically the paramedic went to the 'dead body' whilst his mate went to meet the woman's family in a back room. In the front room the paramedic found the body of the young woman – as described by the doctor – lying collapsed on the floor. Instinctively he knelt down beside the body, and ran through the basic protocols of assessment - running through the ABCs, checking for any signs of life. 'Bloody hell' he exclaimed. 'She's still got a pulse!' he shouted to his mate in the other room. By reflex both men leapt into action, treating the situation as a respiratory arrest (patient stopped breathing...but heart still beating).

Furniture was quickly pushed back out of the way, giving them more room to work on resuscitating the patient on the floor. The paramedic box was opened up displaying an impressive array of life saving equipment and drugs. Within a moment of walking into the room, both crew were well into their resuscitation attempt when the doctor returned, expecting only to issue a death certificate.

He looked flustered when he saw what was going on, for he had declared that life was extinct. Her family had now come from the backroom and were shocked to see these events unfolding. After a short time the woman began to respond to the very high level of Oxygen and drugs being used for her resuscitation. Eventually the crew could cease their efforts for the 'dead' woman *was* no longer!

She sat up and had to be restrained from standing up altogether. The shocked family were overcome with emotion and confused to see her (a daughter) arguing with the ambulance crew, as to whether or not she should still go with them to the hospital.

It later transpired that the woman patient was a regular drug user who had taken heroin which, in turn, had suppressed her breathing to the point that she had collapsed; her heart continued to beat for several minutes thereafter when a family member found her. Had the paramedic just taken the doctor's word and not done his own checks on the body; the woman would almost certainly be dead.

Recently I read in a national newspaper that, somewhere in another part of the country, a doctor making a home visit had certified his patient as dead. On that occasion too, something happened to cause the patient to be successfully resuscitated.

All this makes me think that doctors working outside the hospital or in a surgery environment should carry some basic cardiac monitors so as to avoid making such catastrophic misdiagnosis. Also they should keep up to date with the latest and correct procedures for resuscitation.

I know of a case where a doctor was called upon to carry out emergency resuscitation on a man who had suffered a sudden cardiac arrest. In his efforts to save the patient he actually broke twelve of the patient's ribs (so many broken ribs would be a major injury on its own).

The A&E unit receiving this patient did a remarkable job for they managed to save him despite his severe rib injuries; his resuscitation may have been more complicated by such a significant injury.

Overall, paramedics have a very good working relationship with most doctors most of whom appreciate the difficult circumstances that we often encounter in the 'outside hospital' emergency. Most doctors understand that the fundamental element of our job is the transport of seriously sick or injured patients to a medical aid unit. However, providing transport only, would mean that many patients would not survive the journey to hospital, or at least their chances of recovery would be very much diminished. Which is why most doctors, accept the benefit of paramedic pre-hospital care.

Doctors are not used to the rigours and stress of emergency care on the street, and when they are caught up in some emergency incident they can be like a fish out of water, simply because they do not usually carry a range of equipment with them. On the other hand many paramedics do carry life-saving equipment in their own cars and can, and do stop at incidents that they may come across in their 'off duty' time.

During one of my off duty periods, as I was out driving when I came across a road accident involving a pedestrian, lying in the road with serious head injuries and surrounded by a group of people kneeling beside the casualty.

Retrieving my paramedic case from the boot of my car before pushing through the group, I placed the paramedic case down on the ground for all to see, removing the need for me to explain my intervention. A man kneeling alongside the casualty stretched his hand out to me in greeting. 'Hello' he said, 'I'm a doctor...a surgeon...I'm glad you're here, I am not used to seeing a casualty at the point of injury. What can I do to help?' he enquired from me; not in the least bit aloof.

Together we worked professionally to deal with the seriously injured casualty until the ambulance arrived. Afterwards he thanked me for 'stepping in'. I felt privileged to have enjoyed his respect of my profession.

But in truth I know that we (paramedics) had studied and worked hard, over the years to earn it!

◆ ◆ ◆

15 ACCIDENT AND EMERGENCY

Busy accident and emergency departments are probably the most dynamic and, sometimes, by necessity, chaotic places in which to work within a hospital.

Full of drama and urgency; all manner of human life is played out there. Day or night, people from the lowest rung on the social ladder to the rich and influential arriving in A&E; all will be treated with equal care and treatment. As the saying goes 'life is a rich tapestry' if you want to view that tapestry then this is the place to work; quite often stressful, but rich in drama and excitement.

Occasionally A&E doctors and nursing staff may enjoy a lull in the stream of casualties coming through the door, but this can very quickly (within minutes) dramatically change if a serious accident or major incident occurs. A serious road accident with a couple of badly injured victims can immediately demand a lot of medical resources.

Major incidents are quite rare but when they do happen they place a huge, immediate demand on all hospital services with the A&E department being the primary point for casualty treatment. Major incidents are usually declared when some serious event happens which may involve great loss of life or large numbers of casualties, or a combination of both, bomb incidents, train crashes or motorway pileups for instance.

The hospital then draws upon its Major Incident Plan which will involve calling in, at a moment's notice, all available doctors and nurses as well as some surgeons and ancillary staff. Outpatient departments may need to be cleared of patients with minor complaints, who will be told to return later. Other patients occupying casualty beds may be transferred to other hospitals so that the A&E staff can focus on the victims of the current major injury.

In major incidents or serious accident events the A&E department

might look chaotic but, in fact, it is the hospital working in the most efficient emergency role; to extremely high standards and with everyone moving methodically with haste and well-practiced discipline and professionalism.

In my experience the accident and emergency department seemed to have a dual life of its own. There was the daytime life where everything seemed more relaxed and less stressful but at night there was a different dynamic in A&E departments. By necessity the night staff seemed to be of a different nature than the day staff (not a criticism).

Night staff had to be always on their guard and forever alert, and savvy; watchful for potential trouble from various people coming in for treatment. They seemed to be less inclined to allow bad behaviour from potential trouble makers, stand no nonsense was the order of the night staff. Not only was their concern for their own welfare but also for the other patients, for whom they had a duty of care.

Drunks were often badly behaved, belligerent and threatening, not just toward the hospital staff but sometimes also towards other decent people who were waiting innocently and patiently in the waiting area. As such, a hospital waiting area can be a worrying experience at night.

Even at night some of the people waiting for treatment may be frail and elderly or sick young children, brought in by a worried parent, who had suffered some illness or injury which had brought them to A&E. These innocent people may feel vulnerable, frightened and anxious because some drunken yob is shouting and generally being abusive. Drug addicts were equally worrying, for their behaviour could be bizarre and potentially dangerous.

The place can be noisy and intimidating to many people who are not used to exposure of this level of late night social mix. If waiting times are perceived to be too long then that may add tension to the crowded area. Sometimes it's not a nice place to be.

I recall one Saturday night when a new bride and groom turned up along with a noisy group of friends. The bride's lovely white dress was liberally streaked with the blood from her new husband's bloody face. They were, as you may expect, somewhat inebriated and in their distress were loud and shouting profanities. It would seem that the new husband had been in a fight at his own wedding reception.

Without doubt a hospital waiting area at night can be more raucous and daunting than it otherwise may be during the daytime.

It seemed to me that all A&E night staff that I worked with, were of a different temperament than those of the day staff. Night staff chose to work these difficult shifts and so were less inclined to accept any, profoundly, bad behaviour. To all patients they showed a pleasant and good natured patience and when necessary, made allowance for the effects of drink, drugs, on a person's behaviour but could be firm with any belligerent patient. They *were no less* courteous, caring or sympathetic than their daytime colleagues but night time did bring different challenges for the night staff and they were never inclined to accept too much abuse from drunks.

Generally speaking, me, and my colleagues had a great professional relationship with all hospital nursing staff and doctors; often joining them, along with police and firefighters at social and charity events. I was on first names terms with many of the A&E nursing staff as well as with some of the doctors. All this meant for a good team spirit and we could all work together as and when the need arose; and it also meant that I was never refused a welcome cuppa in the small tearoom at the back of the 'cas'.

It was in that small tearoom in the early hours of one morning when, during a brief quiet period in A&E, my crewmate, Gordon, and I sat enjoying a quick coffee as well as a laugh and a joke with some of the doctors and nurses before booking 'clear' and returning to base. After about ten minutes and having enjoyed some of the A&E staffs' funny anecdotes and general good natured banter my mate and I left with a friendly farewell.

Once back in our ambulance I booked 'clear, returning to base' whilst Gordon drove off out of the deserted hospital grounds; approaching the exit we were suddenly aware of a lot of blue lights approaching and within seconds three fire engines cut across our path making their way down to the maternity unit at the far end of the sixteen acre hospital complex.

Gordon instinctively spun our ambulance around and followed after them arriving seconds later. As I alighted I could see that firefighters, wearing breathing apparatus, were already making their way into the maternity unit, through smoke that was pouring from the main entrance. I quickly located the leading fireman who gave me an initial assessment. His report was of a very serious nature. Although the actual origin of the fire was unclear there was a tremendous amount of smoke billowing out of open windows and the main entrance door. The fire alarms were sounding through the unit.

The senior maternity nursing officer reported to me that there was an immediate need to evacuate the whole unit. This involved evacuating forty mothers with their new born babies as well as about a dozen premature babies from the 'Special Care Baby Unit' (SCBU) all in incubators. Also there was a profound likelihood that patients, as well as staff, would be suffering some degree of smoke inhalation.

I left Gordon to contact ambulance control to report a 'major incident' at the hospital whilst I ran back to the A&E department (about one hundred metres away) to alert them of the developing situation.

Arriving back in the casualty department less than two minutes after having left, I made my way back into the tea-room; interrupting their light-hearted banter and I hurriedly informed the casualty staff of the unfolding serious incident over at the maternity unit and the need for them to prepare for a (very rare) possible major incident.

Given that I had been there a few minutes earlier laughing and joking with them, it took a few seconds for it to sink in that I was not now joking, but serious. One of the nurses jumped, saying 'He's not joking.' Suddenly everyone moved; the brief quiet spell of the night was washed away with the realisation that I was, in fact, reporting a genuine emergency incident and on their doorstep!

I returned to Gordon who, by now, had called ambulance control with a major incident report. Now our combined job would be to act as incident officers until a more senior ambulance officer arrived on scene to take over.

Every major incident is different in every conceivable way and, therefore, despite annual, joint service exercises for such rare events there is no specific format to cover every scenario; it may be said that a major incident has a life of its own. It is uniquely organic and on such occasions, those initially dealing with it will have to 'fly by the seat of their pants'. And so it was this night.

The fire service and maternity nursing staff were evacuating mothers carrying their babies out into a cold night and assembling on the car park some of whom were suffering from smoke inhalation as well as shock and distress. It was several more minutes before other ambulances arrived to assist the many patients needing help.

Some of the nurses from A&E, who had come over bringing wheelchairs and blankets, were now hurriedly ferrying the mums with their babies back to the warm A&E department. Paramedics arriving on scene were immediately occupied with giving treatment to some of those who were suffering from smoke inhalation and transporting them over the short distance to the main part of the hospital.

Whilst some firefighters fought the fire; others helped the

specialist neonatal nursing staff to disconnect the many wires, pipes and tubes from, cumbersome incubators (still with tiny babies inside) and manoeuvre them outside to waiting ambulances.

Meanwhile, the A&E was cleared of all but the most urgent cases from the waiting area with the advice to return later in the morning. Some doctors and anaesthetists were woken up at home and asked to come in to assist with emergency influx of so many babies in incubators.

Meanwhile, our ambulance control was contacting outside ambulance services requesting backup; resulting in ambulances from as far away as Manchester heading for Wirral. And so it was that a quiet spell in A&E unit suddenly escalated to a 'full on' emergency all within a matter of a few minutes.

When delivering a patient to the A&E I was usually met with good natured and jovial staff; often sharing a light hearted comment but a totally professional attitude. Such a warm welcome to the casualty unit could be beneficial in a reassuring way, to patients who may frightened or anxious by their experience and unfamiliar surroundings.

Occasionally I would bring a patient in who, quite simply, was unpleasant, belligerent or even physically aggressive. No amount of pleasantries from nursing staff or doctors could placate them. They had some grievance or issue that they *just had to voice*.

No matter the provocation, the nursing staff would try to cajole or even plead with such patients to be more cooperative but often to no avail. Sometimes swearing and spitting patients were just so unpleasant that it was very difficult for me not to intervene more robustly, however, once such a person became physically aggressive and assaulted nursing staff, then me or my colleagues would intervene.

I recall being in the casualty unit late one night when I witnessed a vile character of a man, swearing shouting and gesticulating at a young nurse who was vainly trying to calm him down. Apparently he was annoyed because he was asked to wait his turn in the queue of other patients waiting to be seen by a doctor.

Seeing the nurse was becoming afraid of him I went forward to see if I could help persuade him to calm down; too late. Before I could interject he cleared his throat and spit directly into her face, following up this vile assault with a venomous comment that he 'had AIDs.' It took me a split second to grab him and throw him, face down, to the floor whereupon I struggled, briefly, to get a good grip of his head and hold his face flat to the floor facing away from me. Fortunately, a man waiting nearby who had been watching events unfold joined me in detaining the violent patient until the arrival of the police who arrested him.

The young nurse was left to clean herself up and then, despite her distress, carried on with her duty.

Some nurses were more, savvy than others. This was clearly demonstrated to me late one evening when I delivered an unconscious woman to the casualty unit one night. The woman was a known 'regular' patient with a drink and drug problem; also known for her belligerence to nursing staff.

I had answered an emergency call from worried members of the public who had found the woman (in her early thirties) lying on the pavement in the street. I recognised the woman as one of our 'regulars' and carried out an 'unconscious patient check' namely, the Glasgow Coma Scale (GCS) – a neurological test to determine a person's level of consciousness.

Because of my previous knowledge of this woman I expected her to jump up and become obstructive and argumentative at my intervention. However, on this occasion she did not respond as I had expected, to any of the tests that I carried out on her. She remained totally unresponsive to me; unconscious even through the test for pain (I usually rub my knuckle into the top of the breastbone, which is painful but harmless).

Arriving at A&E I was met by one of the nurses- I'll call her Sandra, (who also knew our unconscious patient). At Sandra's request we put the patient on a trolley in a side room; Sandra carried out a similar routine of the GCS, as I had done so earlier. She too found no response from our patient. Looking across at me Sandra gave a sly smile and winked; suspicious that our patient may be feigning unconsciousness.

Then leaning close to the unconscious woman's ear she whispered something, which I couldn't hear, into the woman's' ear. 'You F...... Cow,' suddenly our unconscious patient - *was no more!* Swinging her legs off the trolley she glared at Sandra and screamed at her, 'I'm not F...... staying here with you. You cow' and grabbing her handbag, stormed passed me and my mate, and out of the hospital, 'F' ing and blinding as she went.

I couldn't help but laugh and asked Sandra what it was that she had said to bring about such a miraculous recovery. She just smiled, tapped the tip of her nose with her finger, 'Just need to be savvy with her' she said, and without actually telling me what it was that she had said.

Whatever it was it was not something from the Glasgow Coma Scale. *[8]

The A&E day staff is just as professional and caring as their colleagues on night duty. But it is only fair to say that in my time the days didn't seem to hold as much threat as did nights. However with twenty four hour drinking and the surge in drug use it may soon become a similar threatening environment.

Essentially days bring different risks to the public and of course different that has a 'knock on effect' for the hospital and staff.

During the day there are more people out and about, roads are busier, children are out and about (school holidays can be worse than the normal), industry is up and running. Weather can also have a greater impact during the day (for all the above reasons). Snow, ice, rain, fog, early morning sunshine to mention just a few; all can cause disaster all can be a 'nightmare' and cause the A&E to become overstretched. But always, all the staff will be ever cheerful, caring and professional ever willing to put their skills to the test so as to preserve your life.

---

[1] The Chief Ambulance Officer was Mr Albert Guinea who was the youngest person to hold such a post. He held that post for no less than thirty years. He was a fair and firm CAO who cared about the men and women under his command.

[2] The Neil Robinson Stretcher was a strange looking piece of equipment designed to hold a an injured or sick patient securely whilst removing them from engine room spaces or other compartments, down cliffs as in mountain rescue, or indeed any difficult area where a traditional stretcher would not be of use. Some are made of bamboo and lined with canvas. When wrapped around the victim, mummy fashion it gives sufficient support so the victim may be lifted vertically.

[3] I have not included their surnames because I have been unable to trace them for permission to publish. However these were the first Merseyside paramedics a claim that others sometimes erroneously make

[4] In any major emergency event it is established procedure for the senior ambulance person, of the first crew on scene, to act as incident officer (until such time that a more senior officer arrives to take over) so as to rapidly assess and gather and report accurate details of the incident and to request the appropriate emergency personnel and services, from the ambulance control. The incident officer will be primarily responsible for managing the incident and will not always have time to deal with casualties.

[5] Crush Syndrome can occur when a limb is crushed and trapped for longer than ten minutes. When the limb is released it can allow large quantities of toxic substances to re-enter the circulatory system and cause renal failure. The toxic substances are caused by the blood lying stagnant in the trapped limb.

[6] ERF (emergency report form) initially these forms were merely a basic pink slip offering very little information. It was only when Advanced Life Support procedures (paramedical treatment) were introduced, that a more detailed form was brought in so as to gather as much medical history as possible. More importantly, the ERF is designed to record precise details of treatment and drugs etc., given during emergency pre-hospital care.

[7] Likely to Prove, is terminology for probable death from the injury.

[8] The Glasgow Coma Scale (GCS) is a neurological scale which is used by medics to establish the level of a patient's unconsciousness. It is based on a patient's verbal response, eye opening and response to pain.
Each response is on a scale of 1-5 (1 being the lowest.

---

[i] Dry riser is a normally empty pipe that can be externally connected to a pressurised water source by firefighters it is a vertical pipe intended to distribute water at multiple levels of a building. It is part of the fire suppression system.

ABOUT THE AUTHOR

Dale Cropper

I worked with Merseyside Ambulance Service (now known as North West Ambulance) for twenty years before falling victim to a road accident the likes of which I had dealt with throughout my career. A bus rammed into the stationary ambulance that I was sitting in causing significant enough injury to me, to curtail my career.

During my time in the ambulance service, I set up (in 1980) The Wallasey Branch of The Association of Emergency Technicians (AEMT) and drew in ambulance personell from across Merseyside.

I served as Chairman for seventeen years during which time we set up (against the wishes - at that time- of our employer) An ALS course leading to paramedic qaulification.

I also ran a night school for ambulance technicians who wished to progress onto paramedic qulification.

At the time of my accident I was training to become a national ly qualified instructor whilst at the same time working with trainee paramedics as an assessor.

In my off duty time I served as Chairman for a number of charities related to autism, learning disability and our local community centre.

Printed in Great Britain
by Amazon

79650351R00149